Andrew Warren, Managing Director, Condé Nast Johansens

Welcome to the 2003 edition of our Guide to Recommended Hotels, Inns & Resorts North America, Bermuda, Caribbean, Mexico & Pacific.

I am pleased to announce that Johansens is now part of The Condé Nast Publications Ltd., publishers of Vogue, House & Garden, Condé Nast Traveler and other prestigious monthly magazines.

New ownership has resulted in some exciting changes that we hope you agree, make the Guide easier to use and our recommendations easier to locate by country and then alphabetically by state or region.

By opening both cover flaps you can now refer to the contents of the Guide and the amenity symbol definitions whilst the Guide is laid open at the hotel of your choice.

We feel sure that you will enjoy visiting our recommendations for 2003. These can also be found, some offering special rates and featuring their chef's favourite recipes, on our website www.johansens.com

Please remember to mention Condé Nast Johansens when you make a reservation and again when you check in. You will be made to feel very welcome.

THE CONDÉ NAST JOHANSENS PROMISE

Condé Nast Johansens is the most comprehensive illustrated reference to annually inspected, independently owned hotels throughout Great Britain, Europe and North America.

It is our objective to maintain the trust of Guide users by recommending through annual inspection a careful choice of accommodation offering quality, excellence and value for money.

Our team of over 60 dedicated Regional Inspectors visited almost 3000 hotels, country houses, inns and resorts throughout 30 countries to select only the very best for recommendation in the 2003 editions of our Guides.

No hotel can appear in our guides unless they meet our exacting standards.

NORTH AMERICA, BERMUDA, CARIBBEAN, MEXICO, PACIFIC

Turn to the page shown for the start of each region, country or state

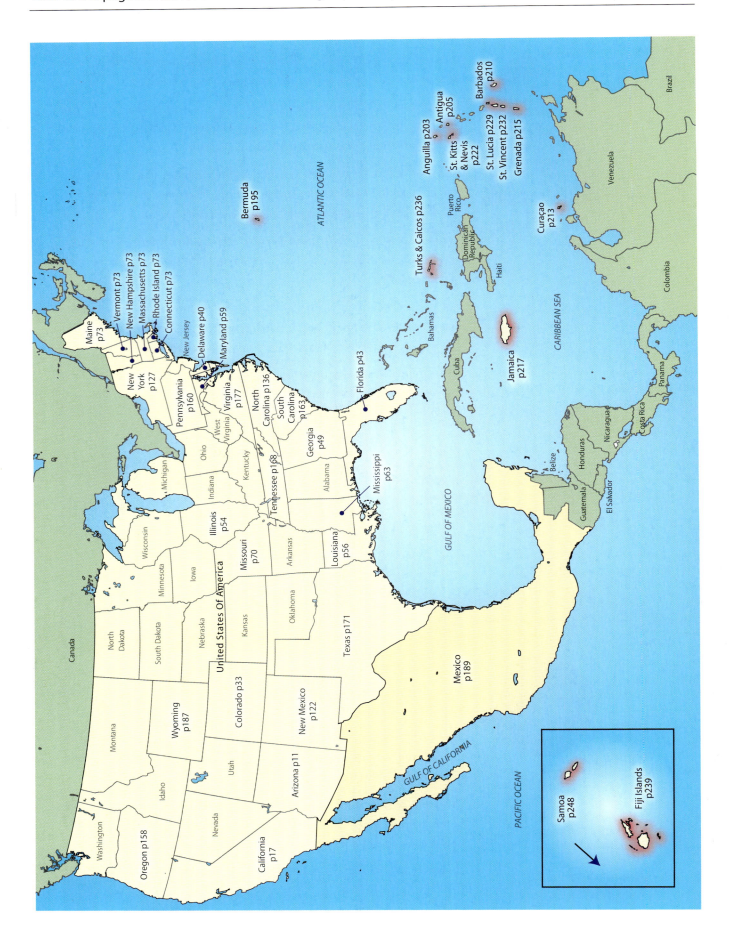

Condé Nast Johansens Guides
Recommending only the finest hotels in the world

As well as this guide Condé Nast Johansens also publishes the following titles:

Recommended Hotels, Great Britain & Ireland

440 unique and luxurious hotels, town houses, castles and manor houses chosen for their superior standards and individual character

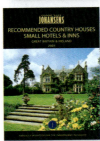

Recommended Country Houses, Small Hotels & Inns, Great Britain & Ireland

280 smaller more rural properties, ideal for short breaks or more intimate stays

Recommended Hotels, Europe & the Mediterranean

320 continental gems featuring châteaux, resorts and Charming countryside hotels

Recommended Venues for Business Meetings, Conferences and Events, Great Britain & Europe

230 venues that cater specifically for a business audience

Worldwide Listings Pocket Guide

Features all recommended hotels and serves as the perfect companion when travelling light

When you purchase two guides or more we will be pleased to offer you a reduction in the cost.

The complete set of Condé Nast Johansens guides may be purchased as 'The Chairman's Collection'.

To order guides please complete the order form on page 285 or call FREEPHONE 1-800-564-7518

CONDÉ NAST JOHANSENS

Condé Nast Johansens Ltd., 6-8 Old Bond Street, London W1S 4PH
Tel: +44 (0)20 7499 9080 Fax: +44 (0)20 7152 3565
Find Johansens on the Internet at: www.johansens.com
E-Mail: info@johansens.com

Publisher North America:	Lesley J. O'Malley-Keyes
Regional Inspectors:	Susanne Andrey
	Laura Bowles
	Christine Calloway-Holt
	Mollie Christensen
	Shirley Dooley
	Suzanne Flanders
	Martin Gistren
	Dana Halliday
	Grant Howlett
	Michael Kelly
	Susannah Mcpherson
	Mary Parker
	Brenna Reardon
	Betsy Welch
Production Director:	Daniel Barnett
Production Manager:	Kevin Bradbrook
Production Controller:	Laura Kerry
Senior Designer:	Michael Tompsett
Copywriters:	Stephanie Cook
	Norman Flack
	Debra Giles
	Rozanne Paragon
	Leonora Sandwell
Sales and Marketing Director:	Tim Sinclair
Promotions & Events Manager:	Adam Crabtree
Client Services Director:	Fiona Patrick
P.A. to Managing Director:	Siobhan Smith
Managing Director:	Andrew Warren

Whilst every care has been taken in the compilation of this Guide, the publishers cannot accept responsibility for any inaccuracies or for changes since going to press, or for consequential loss arising from such changes or other inaccuracies, or for any other loss direct or consequential arising in connection with information describing establishments in this publication.

Recommended establishments, if accepted for inclusion by our inspectors, pay an annual subscription to cover the costs of inspection, the distribution and production of copies placed in hotel bedrooms and other services.

No part of this publication may be copied or reproduced, stored in a retrieval system or transmitted, in any form or by any means, electronic, mechanical, photocopy, recording or otherwise, without the prior permission of the publishers.

The publishers request readers not to cut, tear or otherwise mark this Guide except Guest Reports, Brochure Requests and Order Coupons. No other cuttings may be taken without the written permission of the publishers.

Copyright © 2002 Condé Nast Johansens Ltd.

Condé Nast Johansens Ltd. is part of The Condé Nast Publications Ltd.

ISBN 1-903665-10-8

Printed in England by St Ives plc
Colour origination by Icon Reproduction Ltd

Distributed in the UK and Europe by Portfolio, Greenford (bookstores). In North America by Whitehurst & Clarke, New York (direct sales) and Hunter Publishing, New Jersey (bookstores). In Australia and New Zealand by Bookwise International, Wingfield, South Australia.

WWW.JOHANSENS.COM

Visit the Condé Nast Johansens web site to:

- Print out detailed **road maps**
- See up to date accommodation **Special Offers**
- Access each **recommended hotel's own website**
- Find details of places to visit nearby - **historic houses, castles, gardens, museums and galleries**

Condé Nast Johansens Home Page

Search for hotels and business venues

Access local places to visit

Link to latest Special Offers

Users can log in as an Online Member to receive regular e-mail updates, complete guest survey reports and create their own Personal Portfolio of favourite recommended hotels

Example of Recommended Hotel's Web Entry

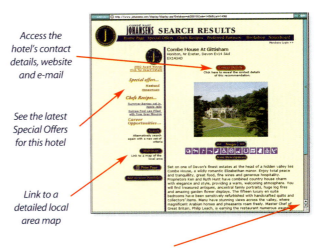

Access the hotel's contact details, website and e-mail

See the latest Special Offers for this hotel

Link to a detailed local area map

Scroll down to find details of places to visit nearby

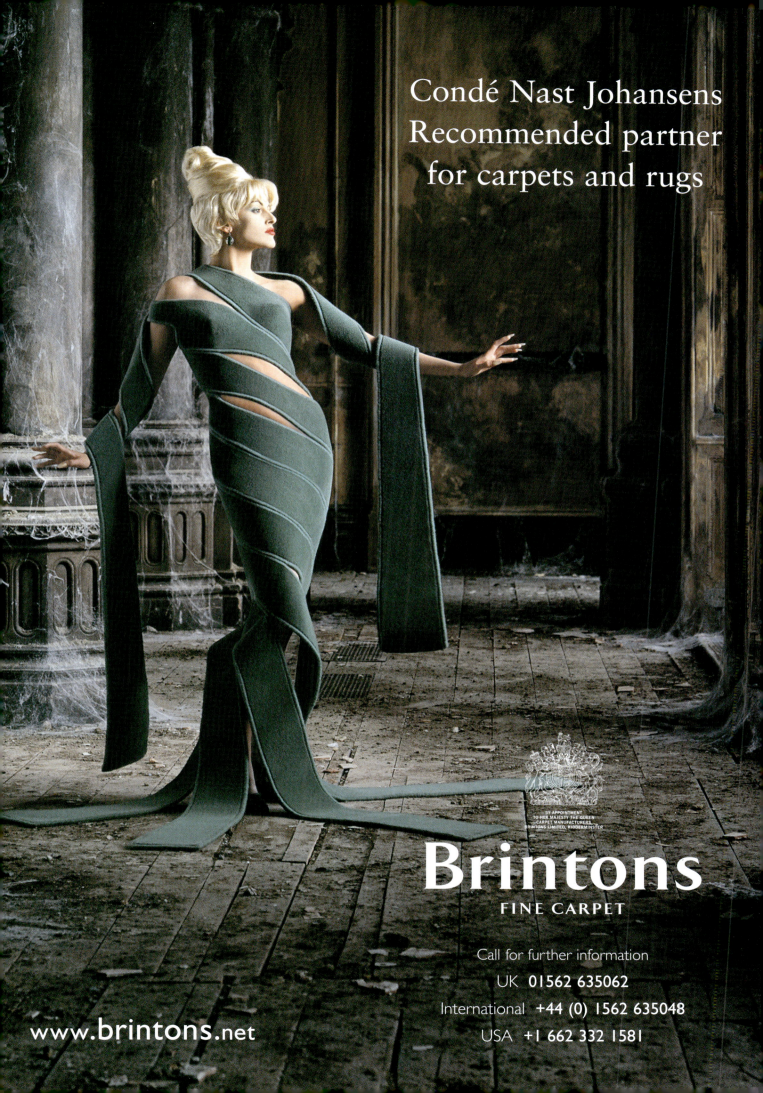

2002 Awards For Excellence

The winners of the Condé Nast Johansens 2002 Awards for Excellence

The Condé Nast Johansens 2002 Awards for Excellence were presented at the Awards Dinner held at The Dorchester hotel London on November 12th, 2001. Awards were made to those properties worldwide that represented the finest standards and best value for money in luxury independent travel. An important source of information for these awards was the feedback provided by guests who completed Johansens Guest Survey reports. Guest Survey forms can be found on page 286.

North America: Most Outstanding Hotel
Wheatleigh – Massachusetts, USA, p95

"Such an elegant hotel - exquisite food and amazing wine cellar."

North America: Most Outstanding Inn
The Willows – California, USA, p26

"Surrounded by Mediterranean style at this luxurious villa, the feeling was of grandeur and elegance."

North America: Most Outstanding Resort
Turtle Island – Yasawa Islands, Fiji, p246

"The warmth of Fijian hospitality and the seclusion of this most romantic island."

Condé Nast Johansens Special Award for Excellence
Henderson Village – Georgia, USA, p50

"Service impeccable. A true display of Southern hospitality."

Rise and Shine

While you're away, get each day off to a flying start.

Because the world doesn't stop when you do. Sudden market shifts and new global business developments can change everything. But if you know you're in touch, you can relax.

Which is why the FT provides you with essential tools and business information to help keep you ahead, wherever you are.

During your stay you can get constant access to the very latest business developments and market news from Europe's leading business resource, making sure you retain your competitive edge even whilst at leisure.

Ask for the FT at your hotel's reception.

PERFECT HOSPITALITY BEGINS WITH PERFECT FORM.

Classic furniture from Selva is the calling card of exclusive establishments.
By creating uniquely stylish surroundings, Selva spoils
not only your guests, but you, as well: with custom solutions,
creative ideas, and the most modern logistics. We would be happy to make
an appointment for you to visit our hotel furnishings showroom in Bolzano.

HOTEL STYLE
A brand of Selva Style International

In UK and Ireland: Lidija Braithwaite - LPB Agencies   16 Lenham Avenue, Saltdean   Brigton, East Sussex BN2 8AE
Tel./Fax 01273 385 255   Mobile: 0771 852 2 746   e-mail: lpbagencies@cwcom.net

Selva AG/SpA, I-39100 Bolzano (Italy), Via Luigi-Negrelli-Straße 4
Tel. 0471 240111   Fax 0471 240211   e-mail: selva@selva.com   www.selva.com

Arizona

Hotel location shown in red with page number

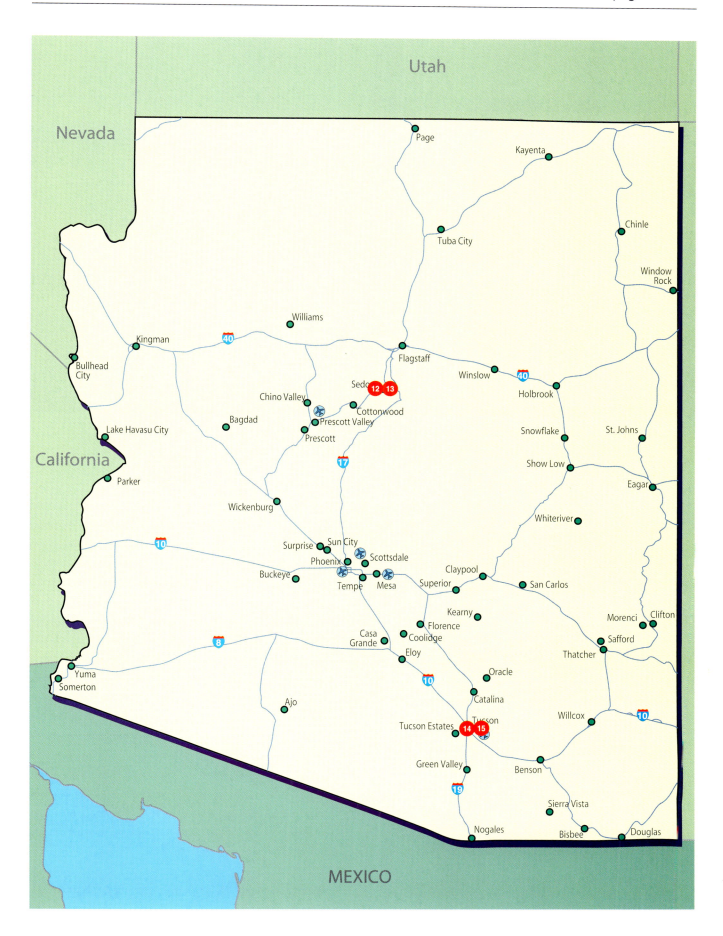

Canyon Villa Inn

125 CANYON CIRCLE DRIVE, SEDONA, ARIZONA 86351

Directions: From Phoenix, Interstate 17 North for 114 miles, exit 298, left onto Highway 179 for 7 miles then left onto Bell Rock Boulevard to Canyon Circle Drive, turning right

Web: www.johansens.com/canyonvillainn
E-mail: canvilla@sedona.net
Tel: 1 520 284 1226
Fax: 1 520 284 2114
US Toll Free: 1 800 453 1166

Price Guide:
rooms $189–$279

New in 1992, this inspirational Spanish mission style inn is set at the foot of the Coconino National Forest, and every inch of its design maximises the green trees, red rocks and azure blue skies of the spectacular countryside of Sedona. All 11 of the guest rooms have balconies or patios, and each is designed with a different theme, with appropriate furnishings including lovely family antiques. All have Jacuzzis, a welcome luxury after clambering over the miles of trails! Owners Les and Peg Belch reside on the premises to maintain impeccable perfection and service to their guests. Mornings begin with a sumptuous breakfast including home-made cinnamon rolls. Afternoon hors d'oeuvres are an opportunity to mingle with the other guests from all over the world. The Villa does not serve alcohol, but there are licenced shops nearby. Peg and Les happily arrange dinner reservations at recommended restaurants, Jeep tours, hot-air balloons, horse-back rides and the Verde River Canyon Train Excursions to explore the area. Grand Canyon is a short two-hour scenic drive. 2 golf courses are nearby and Sedona bustles with galleries and shops. The Villa has a heated pool, sun terrace and library with peaceful reading garden.

Our inspector loved: This peaceful hideaway with it's spectacular view of the mountains.

L'Auberge De Sedona

L'AUBERGE LANE, PO BOX B, SEDONA, ARIZONA 86339

Nestling deep in Sedona's spectacular red rock country, L'Auberge de Sedona offers an unforgettable experience. A French style inn renowned for superbly creative gourmet cuisine, it is idyllically situated along the banks of Oak Creek and surrounded by superb rose gardens, orchards brimming with fruit, towering cliffs of magenta and deep green trees. The magnificent, picturesque countryside is highlighted by the area's famed, huge red rocks and brightened by brilliant azure blue skies. Secluded cottages scattered around a handsome lodge provide all the amenities for a relaxing retreat from the hustle and bustle of the modern world. Here there is peace, tranquillity and privacy. Interiors are delightfully decorated and furnished; there are charming fireplaces, elegant fittings, luxurious drapes and home-from-home comforts to satisfy the most discerning visitor. All guest rooms offer unmatched scenic views from attractive balconies or patios. A large pool and jacuzzi provide a welcome repose and luxury while sipping poolside drinks after exploration tours and hikes over the surrounding countryside. Sedona bustles with shops and galleries. There are 2 golf courses nearby and riding, tennis, hot-air ballooning and Verde River Canyon Train excursions can be arranged. The Grand Canyon is a 2 hour drive away. Special gourmet, golf, adventure and romantic packages are available.

Our inspector loved: A real haven, serene & beautiful with excellent cuisine.

Directions: From Route 179 turn right onto 89A. The Hotel is about 200 feet ahead on the right.

Web: www.johansens.com/laubergedesedona
Tel: 1 928 282 1661
Fax: 1 928 282 2885

Price Guide:
rooms £170–$250
suites $280–$450

ARIZONA - TUCSON

TANQUE VERDE RANCH

14301 EAST SPEEDWAY, TUCSON, ARIZONA 85748

Directions: From I-10, take the Houghton Road exit north. Turn east on Speedway Blvd, to the dead end where Ranch driveway begins.

Web: www.johansens.com/tanqueverde
E-mail: dude@tvgr.com
Tel: 1 520 296 6275
Fax: 1 520 721 9426

Price Guide:
rooms $270–$520 (double)

Established in 1868, Tanque Verde Ranch is a Mobil 4-star ranch resort, recognised as the last luxurious outpost of the Old West. Located on 640 acres in the spectacular, lush desert foothills of the Rincon Mountains, adjacent to the Saguaro National Park and Coronado National Forest, the ranch offers breathtaking mountain and desert views. The scenic, tranquil beauty coupled with an energy of various activities, make this a rejuvenating and unforgettable experience. The 74 authentically decorated rooms and suites are fully air-conditioned, most with fireplaces and patios. Rates include three delicious meals a day and all of the ranch activities, including horseback riding, tennis, hiking, mountain biking, nature programmes, a children's programme and more. Three sparkling pools, two whirlpool spas and two saunas provide the perfect way to relax after a long day in the saddle. Relax on the verandah, watching the fabulous Arizona sunset; enjoy a festive outdoor barbecue, and a scenic breakfast ride to the Old Homestead – the magic of the American West is waiting for you here. Resort quality facilities in the beautiful setting of a historic ranch make Tanque Verde a unique and special experience.

Our inspector loved: One of the most exclusive treasures with acres of beautiful terrain for horse riding, a peaceful and quiet hideaway.

WHITE STALLION RANCH
9251 WEST TWIN PEAKS ROAD, TUCSON, ARIZONA 85743

A welcoming atmosphere envelopes this old Southwestern ranch, surrounded by a 5-mile expanse of desert. The White Stallion Ranch combines the informal ambience of a working cattle ranch with the comforts of a holiday resort. There are 32 bedrooms clustered around the ranch in separate buildings. All are air-conditioned with private bath whilst de luxe suites offer fireplaces, whirlpool tubs and king-size beds. The True family has created a convivial environment throughout the ranch and this is clearly evident in the popular bar. Here, guests relax in casual attire and enjoy the hors d'oeuvres and drinks at 'Happy Hour'. A full selection of breakfast dishes is served in the attractive dining room. Inviting recipes may be savoured at the buffet at lunch or at dinner, which is also served family style. Outdoor pursuits such as hiking, tennis, basketball, horse riding and swimming are available on site. Other pastimes include hay rides, playing with the animals at the petting zoo and enjoying the indoor redwood hot tub. Traditional cowboy entertainment is offered at the ranch including moonlight bonfires, barbecues, weekly rodeos and enjoying the native wildlife. Denim and stetsons are very welcome!

Our inspector loved: An enchanting and beautiful setting for horse riding and so enviably situated on the outskirts of the city, a real gem for privacy and comfort.

Directions: The ranch is adjacent to Saguaro National Park. From I10 take exit 246 Cortaro Rd, go west to Silverbell Rd. Go north to Twin Peaks Rd, 15 mins from freeway.

Web: www.johansens.com/whitestallionranch
E-mail: info@wsranch.com
Tel: 1 520 297 0252
Fax: 1 520 744 2786

Price Guide:
rooms $232–$320
suite $284–$388

JOHANSENS PREFERRED PARTNER FOR HOSPITALITY RECRUITMENT

**CHH EXECUTIVE SEARCH
PO BOX 2429
CHARLOTTESVILLE, VIRGINIA 22902
TEL. 434 977 5029
FAX 434 977 5431
www.chhsearch.com
chhsearch@aol.com**

CALIFORNIA
Hotel location shown in red with page number

# CALIFORNIA
Hotel location shown in red with page number

CALIFORNIA - EUREKA

Carter House

301 L STREET, EUREKA, CALIFORNIA 95501

Directions: Off highway 101, approx. five hours north of San Francisco.

Web: www.johansens.com/carterhouse
E-mail: 301.wines.com/wines
Tel: 1 707 444 8062
Fax: 1 707 444 8067

Price Guide:
rooms $126–$197
suites $195–$500

The architectural charm of the old coastal city of Eureka has earned it the name 'The Williamsburg of the West'. The Carter House consists of four generously appointed Victorian mansions that embellish the edge of Humboldt Bay at the entrance to historic Eureka's Victorian district: The original Carter House, the Hotel Carter, the Carter House Cottage and the Bell Cottage. The attractive interior décor and furnishings are the setting for hospitality of the highest class. Guests are welcomed by an aura of luxury and comfort. Beautiful fabrics, fresh fruit and flowers and a tasteful combination of modern and classical amenities enhance the restful and cheerful atmosphere. Extra services are at hand. Breakfasts and dinners are a gastronomic delight – just-caught seafood and garden-fresh produce are served by Restaurant 301, one of only 81 Wine Spectator Grand Award winners worldwide. The 3000-selection, 25,000-bottle wine cellar is thought to have one of the best collections of American Cabernets in the world. Before and after meals, hors d'oeuvres, cookies and other nourishments are offered. Things to do locally include sailing, rowing, golf, tennis, riding, walking, going to the theatre, the concert, the Avenue of the Giants, the Redwood National Park and the Sequoia Park and Zoo.

Our inspector loved: The menu and wine list on offer at the Restaurant 301, a gastronomic delight.

GINGERBREAD MANSION INN

P.O.BOX 40; 400 BERDING STREET, FERNDALE, CALIFORNIA 95536

Built in 1899, the Gingerbread Mansion Inn retains many of its original features such as exquisite turrets and carvings. A unique combination of Queen Anne and Eastlake styles, the house is elaborately trimmed with ornate gingerbread decorations. The interior has been carefully restored and features plush carpets, rich Victorian wallpaper and cosy fireplaces. The eleven en suite bedrooms are furnished with an individual touch and are enhanced by lace comforters, claw foot bath tubs or tiled fireplaces. The warmth of the hospitality extended at the inn is shown in the small nuances such as the robes and bedside chocolate at turndown. Afternoon tea is served in the four Victorian parlours and comprises freshly baked cakes, biscuits, pastries and other delights. An extensive menu of home-made dishes is served in the elegant Dining Room at breakfast. There are excellent restaurants within easy walking distance. Guests may explore the Pacific coast and the Giant Redwoods; just a 1/2 hour drive away. Ferndale is a State historical landmark, with well-preserved Victorian homes, old-fashioned boutiques and grand English gardens.

Our inspector loved: *Afternoon tea served from 4pm in the Victorian parlour*

Directions: The hotel is 5 hours north of San Francisco. Take the 101 Freeway, take Ferndale exit. Then 5 miles to centre of town, turn left at bank.

Web: www.johansens.com/gingerbreadmansioninn
E-mail: innkeeper@gingerbread-mansion.com
Tel: 1 707 786 4000
Fax: 1 707 786 4381
US Toll Free: 1 800 952 4136

Price Guide:
rooms $150–$200
suite $240–$385

The Bed & Breakfast Inn At La Jolla

7753 DRAPER AVENUE, LA JOLLA, CALIFORNIA 92037

Directions: West of Highway 5 between San Diego and Los Angeles. Exit onto Jolla Village Drive

Web: www.johansens.com/bedandbreakfastinnatlajolla
Tel: 1 858 456 2066
Fax: 1 858 456 1510

Price Guide:
rooms $159
suite $379

This lovely inn stands in the cultural centre of the seaside community of La Jolla in northern San Diego. The beach, with its multitude of watersports, is just a block away, the Museum of Contemporary Art is across the street and close by are the Scripps Institute of Oceanography and U.C San Diego. Built in 1913, the inn is one of the finest examples of Irving Gill's Cubist style architecture and is listed as Historical Site 179 on the San Diego Registry. The original gardens were planned by renowned horticulturist Kate Sessions and enjoyed by John Philip Sousa and his family when they lived here in the 1920s. The gardens are still magnificent and feature a shady patio where guests can enjoy the tranquillity over late afternoon wine and cheese. Many of the bedrooms and suites overlook the gardens and some open onto them. All the rooms are individually and beautifully decorated in elegant cottage style and offer every modern facility. Superb breakfasts are served in the intimate dining room or in the garden. The inn is only a short stroll away from a variety of restaurants and shops and within easy reach of Old Town San Diego.

Our inspector loved: *A charming and favourite place in the heart of a delightful beach resort.*

MILL VALLEY INN
165 THROCKMORTON AVENUE, MILL VALLEY, CALIFORNIA 94941

30 minutes north of San Francisco and set in a unique location at the foot of Mount Tamalpais, surrounded by magnificent redwood trees, this romantic hideaway combines the quaint charm of a historic Californian mill town with the sophisticated air of a modern European hotel. A modern, Tuscany-style ambience prevails throughout, and the 25 distinctive bedrooms, including two cottages built along a creek, offer an eclectic style and King or Queen-sized beds. All reflect a respect for nature and incorporate furnishings handcrafted in Northern California. Breakfast is served on the splendid, flower-filled Sun Terrace and includes fresh fruit and local pastries. Mill Valley with its bustling plaza surrounded by shops, boutiques, cafés and fine restaurants is within easy walking distance. Just outside the town, guests can enjoy the beauty of Northern California, which includes San Francisco Bay, miles of hiking and biking trails, Muir Woods National Park, Muir Beach and Mount Tamalpais. A must is a scenic drive along the coast on the famed Highway One. Conference facilities are available; the Terrace Room offers space for small meetings and presentations.

Our inspector loved: *The historic charm and grove of Redwood Trees hidden away in the heart of this old mill town.*

Directions: From San Francisco airport drive north on 101, west on 380 to 19th Avenue. Take Highway 101 after Golden Gate.

Web: www.johansens.com/millvalleyinn
E-mail: mgr@millvalleyinn.com
Tel: 1 415 389 6608
Fax: 1 415 389 5051

Price Guide:
rooms $165–$220
suites $399

Doryman's Inn

2102 WEST OCEAN FRONT, NEWPORT BEACH, CALIFORNIA 92663

Directions: From Los Angeles South 405 Freeway to 55 South Freeway until it ends and becomes Newport Blvd. travel over the bridge into Newport Beach towards Balboa Peninsula.

Web: www.johansens.com/dorymansinn
E-mail: info@21oceanfront.com
Tel: 1 949 675 7300
Fax: 1 949 675 7300

Price Guide:
suites from $195–$380

Visitors to Doryman's Inn can expect superb ocean views, modern elegance with old world charm, exceptional comfort and a supreme standard of service together with the friendliest of welcomes. The attractive interior décor and furnishings are the setting for hospitality of the highest class. There is an aura of luxury, serenity and contentment. Fine fabrics, easy seating, lots of framed mirrors and oil paintings on the walls and a tasteful combination of modern and classical amenities enhance the cheerful ambience. The guest rooms at this small boutique hotel are particularly attractive; each is furnished with an individual touch and enhanced by tasteful decoration and every home-from-home requirement. There are rooms with authentic Victorian wallpaper in warm peach tones, with King-size and Queen-size brass beds, vintage cast-iron trundle beds, European antiques and bay windows onto a breakfast patio. The Bellagio room will remain in guests' memories for years; old world charm graces this immaculate room which is decorated in shades of gold, green and maroon. There is a dining table for 2 and a luxurious gold-leaf jacuzzi. All guest rooms have fireplaces and superb marble sunken baths. Excellent meals are served in the Hotel's exquisite dining room. A charming breakfast area and terrace overlooks the sea.

Our inspector loved: A very intimate romantic place close to the pier.

CALIFORNIA - PALM DESERT

Shadow Mountain Resort & Club

45750 SAN LUIS REY, PALM DESERT, CALIFORNIA 92260

This excellent golf and tennis resort is situated just 13 miles from bustling Palm Springs and nestles in 20 lush acres at the foot of the majestic San Jacinto Mountains within walking distance of the chic shops, excellent restaurants and art galleries and unsurpassed evening entertainment of upmarket El Paseo. Shadow Mountain is a desert gem, friendly, comfortable and unpretentious. Visitors can choose from guest rooms, luxury one, two and three-bedroom condominiums and villas, some situated around four magnificent heated pool and spa areas. All are decorated in cool shades and furnished to the highest standards with every modern facility. The resort offers unlimited complimentary tennis on 16 championship courts and features the acclaimed Desert Tennis Academy Golf is available at the Gene Sarazen-designed Shadow Mountain Golf Club and at various Coachella Valley courses. There are four pools, five therapy spas, saunas, massage parlour, basketball court and exercise equipment. Four-wheel desert driving, horse riding and hot air ballooning can be arranged. The nearby Joshua Tree National Park, Indian Canyons reservation and desert museum are worth visiting. Breakfast, lunch and refreshing cocktails are served at the Courtside Café dining and bar venue.

Our inspector loved: *The great appeal to the sports enthusiasts, with its tennis and golf facilities, surrounded by majestic mountains.*

Directions: From Los Angeles take Freeway 10 to Highway 111, close by airport.

Web: www.johansens.com/shadowmountain
E-mail: res@shadow-mountain.com
Tel: 1 760 346 6123
Fax: 1 760 346 6518

Price Guide:
rooms $111–$200
suites $268–$572

CALIFORNIA - PALM SPRINGS

Caliente tropics Resort

411 EAST PALM CANYON DRIVE, PALM SPRINGS, CALIFORNIA 92264

Directions: From I-10 take Palm Springs Hwy 111 exit; this becomes Palm Canyon Drive. Or from Palm Springs airport take Tahquitz Canyon Way to Palm Canyon drive and turn left.

Web: www.johansens.com/caliente
E-mail: info@Calientetropics.com
Tel: 1 760 327 1391
Fax: 1 760 318 1883

Price Guide:
rooms $110–$225
suites $130–$295

Opened in 1964, the Resort soon became a playground magnet for many celebrities including Elvis and Frank Sinatra's 'Rat Pack.' Re-opened in May 2001 after an extensive $2.2 million facelift, it is now one of the last and greatest Polynesian-styled hotels of the 1960's. Splendid facilities include the original but completely renovated 65 foot swimming pool and 12 person therapeutic pool. Boutique-style, guestrooms feature custom furnishings and display watercolour prints by a local artist and the exterior has been renovated to celebrate the original mid-century look. The Resort is completely non-smoking and is pet-friendly; canines receive biscuits on arrival. For guests who enjoy garden walks the Resort provides an abundance of mature shady palms and tropical Tiki huts in which to relax. Continental breakfast and in-room beverages are complimentary whilst intimate dining can be enjoyed in the adjacent restaurant or one of the many excellent places within walking distance. There is also a complimentary daily newspaper and nightly turn-down service. The Tahitian Lanai is a picturesque spot for a private outdoor reception and can accommodate from 10 to 250, alternatively, 10 to 40 persons can be accommodated, theatre style, in the traditional Polynesian/South Seas Reef Room.

Our inspector loved: The relaxing Tiki huts.

L'HORIZON

1050 EAST PALM CANYON DRIVE, PALM SPRINGS, CALIFORNIA 92264

L'Horizon was originally built in 1953 by the architect William Cody as a retreat for the actress Bonita Granville and her husband Jack Wrather. Over the years it enjoyed a reputation as a hangout for numerous movie moguls and glamorous guests including Cary Grant and Marilyn Monroe. Today it has been carefully restored in keeping with its mid-century modern style, and still provides a peaceful, secluded haven in the heart of exclusive Old Palm Springs. Within its walls at the foot of the magnificent Mount San Jacinto lies an oasis of beautifully kept gardens and flowers, all set around the pool. The luxurious rooms and suites are decorated in pastels to reflect the soft tones of the desert, and the bathrooms combine up-to-date facilities with original 1950s tiling. Breakfast can be served to your room, on your private patio or poolside, and staff are on hand to assist with restaurant reservations and leisure activities. As well as an impressively stocked library, bicycles and table games on site, there are numerous activities available locally, including an aerial tramway, horse riding, hiking, ballooning, tennis, golf and rock climbing. Visits can also be arranged to galleries, concerts, museums and a nearby Indian village.

Our inspector loved: *A very pleasant environment with its palm-skirted landscape.*

Directions: From LA Freeway 10 to 60 to Palm Springs. Airport is close by in Palm Springs.

Web: www.johansens.com/lhorizon
E-mail: hotelslhorizon@palmsprings.com
Tel: 1 760 323 1858
Fax: 1 760 327 2933

Price Guide:
rooms $135–$650

CALIFORNIA - PALM SPRINGS

The Willows
412 WEST TAHQUITZ CANYON WAY, PALM SPRINGS, CALIFORNIA 92262

Directions: From Los Angeles take Freeway 10 to 111, close by airport

Web: www.johansens.com/willows
E-mail: innkeeper@thewillowspalmsprings.com
Tel: 1 760 320 0771
Fax: 1 760 320 0780
US Toll Free: 1 800 966 9597

Price Guide:
rooms $295–$575
Summer rate $250–$450

The Willows is a delightful ochre stucco and red roofed, very private villa shaded by tall palm trees and overlooked by the heights of Mount San Jacinto from where a waterfall tumbles into a pool just outside the stone-floored dining room. Built in 1924 in the Old Palm Springs Village, The Willows has been meticulously restored to its former Mediterranean-style grandeur, refinement and elegance. The architecture is striking, with beautiful mahogany beams enhancing the great hall and frescoed ceilings on the cool veranda. Honeymooning film stars Clark Gable and Carole Lombard and the scientist Albert Einstein are amongst the many distinguished guests who have enjoyed the villa's luxurious ambience. The eight bedrooms are excellently furnished with antiques and sumptuous linens and have private baths, stone fireplaces, hardwood floors, garden patios and mountain views. Guests enjoy a full gourmet breakfast and afternoon hors d'oeuvres in the restful dining room. Excellent lunches and dinners prepared in a French restaurant opposite can be served in the villa. Energetic guests can walk an original stone path through a hillside garden to secluded lookouts to contemplate and view the sun-blanched surrounds. Others may want to just relax around the shaded swimming pool or take advantage of nearby tennis and golf facilities

Our inspector loved: A very stylish secluded haven in the centre of town.

CALIFORNIA - SAN FRANCISCO

NOB HILL LAMBOURNE
725 PINE STREET, SAN FRANCISCO, CALIFORNIA 94108

Connoisseurs of hotel life call the downtown Nob Hill Lambourne "San Francisco's Healthiest Hotel" because of its collection of rejuvenating spa services and amenities which have left them feeling healthier than when they arrived. Its 20 luxurious and tastefully appointed bedrooms embody an innovative concept for both the leisure and business traveller. Each guest room and suite is designed to function as an office as well as an elegant place to spend the night. Each has a mini-kitchen, fax machine, voice mail, a complete library of San Francisco-based movies – and luxurious fluffy mattresses and down pillows which many guests insist on purchasing when checking out. Exercise equipment is in every suite; there is an Oriental-inspired spa treatment room, a variety of spa packages, aromatherapy bath amenities and a "sprayology" remedy bar for the ailing traveller. A wine reception is held every evening. For all its executive and healthy living trimmings the Lambourne is far from computer driven. It has quiet, efficient service and stylish comfort. There is a relaxing lounge and breakfast room and although there is no restaurant, there are many dining areas close by. Valet car parking service.

Our inspector loved: The peaceful tranquility in the heart of San Francisco.

Directions: The hotel is in downtown San Francisco within easy reach of the Powell Street and California Street cable car route.

Web: www.johansens.com/nobhilllambourne
E-mail: nhl@jdvhospitality.com
Tel: 1 415 433 2287
Fax: 1 415 433 0975
US Toll free: 1 800 274-8466

Price Guide:
rooms $180–$240
suites $260–360

CALIFORNIA - SAN FRANCISCO BAY AREA

GERSTLE PARK INN
34 GROVE STREET, SAN RAFAEL, CALIFORNIA 94901

Directions: From Highway 101, exit at Central San Rafael, go west on 4th Street, left on D Street, right on San Rafael Avenue, left onto Grove Street.

Web: www.johansens.com/gerstlepark
E-mail: innkeeper@gerstleparkinn.com
Tel: 1 415 721 7611
Fax: 1 415 721 7600

Price Guide:
suites $179–$245
cottages $220–$275

Set in the heart of Marin County, just 11 miles north of San Francisco, the Gerstle Park Inn is a breathtaking example of elegance and refinement nestled in a park-like setting amidst giant Redwoods. The historic San Rafael estate, over a hundred years old, continues to provide a beautiful location for those wishing to escape city life. The interior is a testament to exquisite taste, furnished luxuriously throughout with antiques and fine examples of Oriental and Western art. The rooms are no less stunning, both in terms of spacious comfort and the numerous conveniences and amenities offered. Each room is en suite with its own private balcony; King suites have Jacuzzi tubs. Full gourmet breakfast is served in the dining room which overlooks the gardens through the arched windows. Guests may help themselves to various snacks throughout the day and are invited to mingle on the verandah with a glass of wine, served daily at 5.30pm. The croquet court, fruit orchard and superbly manicured gardens invite simple relaxation; other activities include to hiking, biking, a ferry trip on the Bay or Wine Country excursion. Downtown San Rafael is a only a short drive or leisurely stroll to shops, restaurants and theatres.

Our inspector loved: *The perfect combination, sophisticated elegance and home comforts conveniently located in splendid country surroundings.*

WOOLLEY'S PETITE SUITES
2721 HOTEL TERRACE ROAD, SANTA ANA, CALIFORNIA 92705

Known locally as 'Orange County's best-kept secret', Woolley's Petite Suites is a well-situated hotel offering comfortable accommodation and value for money. Ideal for those wishing to explore the delights of California, many major tourist attractions are within the locality of this pleasant hotel. The accommodation comprises 183 junior suites, beautifully appointed with king-size beds, fold-out sofas and a thoughtful range of additional comforts. Cable television, a wet bar and a micro-kitchen all add to the home-away-from-home atmosphere. Children under twelve may stay in their parents room for free. The breakfast service is excellent; a sumptuous buffet caters for every need. The hotel's meeting facilities can accommodate up to 80 people. Guests can spend a day in nearby Disneyland, play golf or take a tour of Newport harbour.

Our inspector loved: This very personable and delightful beach resort hotel.

Directions: Woolley's Petite Suites is conveniently located to the Orange County/John Wayne airport, just off the Newport Freeway 55.

Web: www.johansens.com/woolleyspetitesuites
E-mail: wps@petitesuites.com
Tel: 1 714 540 1111
Fax: 1 714 662 1643

Price Guide: (incl. breakfast)
Suite $89–$109

CALIFORNIA - SANTA BARBARA

UPHAM HOTEL
1404 DE LA VINA STREET, SANTA BARBARA, CALIFORNIA 93101

Directions: From LA take Freeway 101.

Web: www.johansens.com/uphamhotel
E-mail: upham.hotel@verizon.net
Tel: 1 805 962 0058
Fax: 1 805 963 2825

Price Guide:
rooms $175–$275
suites $290–$425

Standing serenely in an acre of beautifully mature, landscaped gardens in the heart of downtown Santa Barbara, this is the oldest continuously operated hotel in Southern California. It is a popular vacation venue not only because of its comfort, quality and high standards of service but because it is close, but not too close, to bustling Los Angeles. Santa Barbara is a red-tile, white-adobe, flower-decked town in the lovely natural setting of the Santa Ynez Mountains. More than a century ago travellers arrived here on horseback, by carriage or steamship to enjoy the surroundings and 'healthful climate' and stayed in a 'New England-style boarding house featuring the best accommodations of the place'. Today, that boarding house is the Upham Hotel, fully refurbished and restored and providing the same traditional hospitality as it did in those days. The hotel combines the bed-and-breakfast comfort of 50 guest rooms and suites with the private luxury of five garden cottages, all tastefully decorated and with every up-to-date amenity and a thoughtful range of extras. The Upham has been awarded the California Grand Hotel Award for the Best Small Hotel in Southern California, and the adjoining restaurant, Louie's, has been nationally recognised by Travel and Leisure. A number of major attractions are within easy driving distance.

Our inspector loved: A charming & quiet hidden treasure with a Victorian flair.

THE GEORGIAN HOTEL
1415 OCEAN AVENUE, SANTA MONICA, CALIFORNIA 90405

This charming 1933 Historic Hotel sits on Ocean Avenue between Santa Monica Boulevard and Broadway Avenue. From the subtle Art Deco lobby one can view the famous Santa Monica Pier and the Pacific Ocean from every window. The third street promenade, a multitude of restaurants and Santa Monica Place Mall are within two blocks. 56 guest rooms and 28 suites are accessed by a manned lift, the only one left in the city. The Speakeasy Restaurant serves breakfast daily and is fabled to be haunted. It was recently featured on the History Channel due to this frequent and spooky activity. The space is available for hire after noon for an event of your choice. In addition the hotel offers three other meeting rooms, all perfect for an intimate meeting. Voice mail Data Port two line telephones, an in-house work out facility and safes in all rooms are some of the modern amenities that bring this historic hotel into the future.

Our inspector loved: *An ace promenade location, charming and a very personable and elegant hotel.*

Directions: Los Angeles International Airport is 8 miles away.

Web: www.johansens.com/georcian
E-mail: sales@georgianhotel.com
Tel: 1 310 395 9945
Fax: 1 310 451 3374

Price Guide: (Special Packages available)
rooms $235–$298
suites $350–$525

CALIFORNIA - TIBURON

WATERS EDGE HOTEL
25 MAIN STREET, TIBURON, CALIFORNIA 94920

Directions: North from San Francisco airport to (101) 380 west to 280 north to 19th Avenue over Golden Gate Bridge east on Tiburon Boulevard.

Web: www.johansens.com/watersedge
E-mail: watersedgehotel@jdvhospitality.com
Tel: 1 415 789 5999
Fax: 1 415 789 5888
US Toll Free: 1 877 789 5999
Price Guide:
rooms $195–$450

As its name would suggest, this two-level hotel rests on a historic dock in the delightful city of Tiburon and boasts spectacular panoramic views of the San Francisco Bay and skyline. Inspired by the exotic merchant trade of the Bay, the contemporary Asian décor combines wooden floors, subtle lighting, original artwork and stunning floral arrangements to create an atmosphere of intimate, simple elegance. In the L-shaped lobby sits a comfortable red sofa, and wine is offered here by the fireside and on the spacious deck in the evenings. All bedrooms feature fireplaces, white feather beds and private balconies, while some benefit from the fabulous views. A deluxe continental breakfast is delivered to each room daily and cable TV, movies, CDs and robes are also provided. Tiburon has much to offer with its marina, old town, galleries, boutiques and fine dining all on the hotel's doorstep. Sailing, fishing and hiking can be enjoyed nearby, and guests can easily catch a ferry from the adjacent landing to San Francisco or Sausalito, visit Muir beach and woods, or even take a trip along the Pacific Coast Highway.

Our inspector loved: The Waters Edge atmosphere and the panoramic views of San Francisco and Alcatraz.

COLORADO
Hotel location shown in red with page number

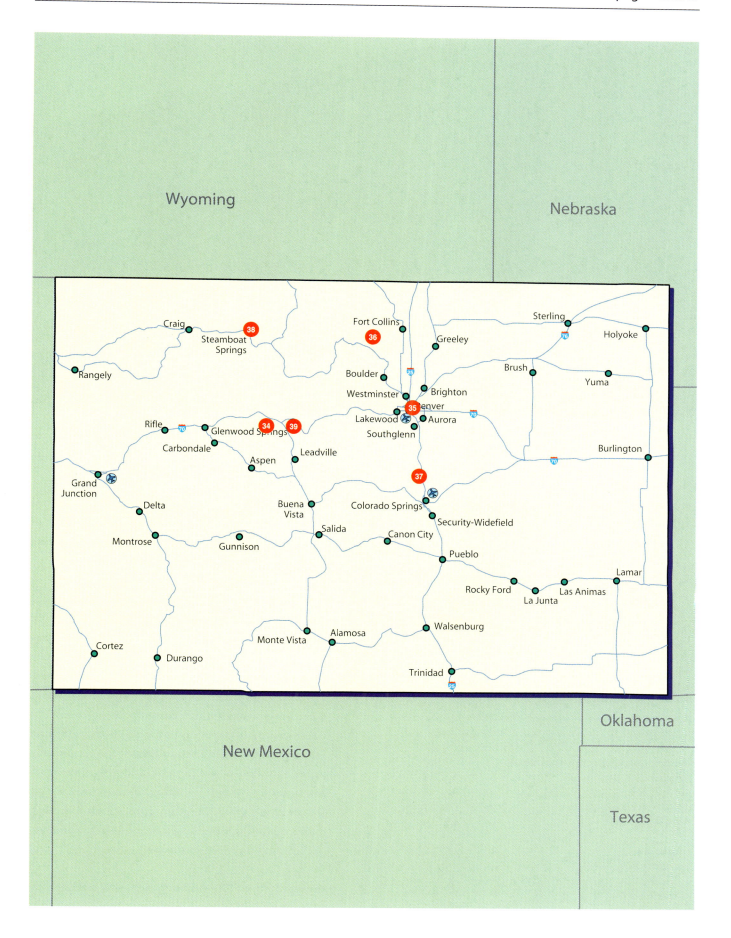

COLORADO - BEAVER CREEK

THE INN AT BEAVER CREEK
10 ELK TRACK LANE, BEAVER CREEK RESORT, COLORADO, 81620

This cosy modern Inn lies deep in the beautiful Rocky Mountains surrounded by lush pine forests. In winter it is a wonderland of snow and sparkling Christmas lights; in summer a peaceful, sunny haven where guests can relax and enjoy the spectacular scenery. Small enough for the attentive and efficient staff to remember everyone by name, The Inn at Beaver Creek is so close to the ski slopes that a chairlift is just steps away from the breakfast room. It is a bed and breakfast style resort designed to provide a little western adventure with more than a little added luxury. There is a choice of 45 stylish guest rooms and one superb suite, each enhanced by an oversized bathroom, delightful décor and every home-from-home comfort. Light meals can be enjoyed in the popular Lobby Bar. The Inn has an outdoor heated pool and hot tub, steam and sauna rooms and heated underground valet parking. A range of tempting activities is available nearby, from rafting, rock climbing and cycling to hiking, fishing, golf and, of course, skiing and snowmobiling. Shopping enthusiasts will find plenty to enjoy in the village, across the street. Excellent conference, meetings and banqueting facilities for gatherings of 10 to 100. Complimentary resort shuttle service.

Directions: From Denver International Airport take I-70 west and leave at exit 167. Or fly direct to Vail and go east on I 70 to Beaver Creek.

Web: www.johansens.com/innatbeavercreek
E-mail: vbcrp@vailresorts.com
Tel: 1 970 845 5990
US Toll Free: 1 800 752 0538
Fax: 1 970 845 6204

Price Guide:
rooms $99–$600

Our inspector loved: *The convenience of the ski-in, ski-out location, not to mention the golf course just down the road.*

Castle Marne
1572 RACE STREET, DENVER, COLORADO 80206

Historic Castle Marne, a Victorian property transformed into a bed and breakfast inn, is both charming and elegant with a unique atmosphere. Many vestiges of the castle's past are scattered throughout the rooms such as hand-rubbed woods, family heirlooms and ornate fireplaces. Following a careful restoration, original features dominate the interior, which is enhanced by rococo gilt mirrors and fine antiques. The individually decorated bedrooms are stylish and display nuances of the period. Guests are made to feel extremely welcome by the friendly and hospitable owners. The comfortable parlour is ideal for reclining and reading a book beside the beautifully carved fireplace. Special private six-course candlelight dinners can be arranged. Guests may indulge in scrumptious breakfasts and afternoon tea. House specialities include stuffed tomato with egg and spinach purée topped with parmesan and Jack cheeses and the home-baked cakes and scones at teatime are a delight to the palate. There are several museums and historic sites clustered around the area. Other attractions include the zoo, botanical gardens or perusing the shops at 'Cherry Creek

Our inspector loved: *The surprise of the tree-top level private decks with hot tubs that adjoin several of the rooms.*

Directions: From DIA, Pena Boulevard head to I-70 west, exit Quebec Street. Travel south (left) to 17th Avenue, turning right to York Street. Turn left into 16th Avenue and then right to Race Street (3 blocks)

Web: www.johansens.com/castlemarne
E-mail: info@castlemarne.com
Tel: 303 331 0621
Fax: 303 331 0623
US Toll Free: 1 800 926 2763

Price Guide:
rooms $105–$255
suite $255

COLORADO - ESTES PARK

THE STANLEY HOTEL

333 WONDERVIEW AVENUE, PO BOX 1767, ESTES PARK, COLORADO. 80517

Directions: From Denver take Highway 36 through Boulder to Estes Park. (About 75 minutes)

Web: www.johansens.com/stanleyhotel
Tel: 1 970 586 3371
Fax: 1 970 586 4964

Price Guide:
rooms $179–$299
suites $299–$1500

The Rocky Mountain National Park attracts thousands of visitors every year and guests arriving at Estes Park will not be disappointed at the spectacular views afforded from The Stanley Hotel. Built in 1909 by F.O. Stanley after a recuperative stay here during the winter months, the Hotel was built in neoclassical style and its vast pilasters, Palladian windows and Georgian cornices and mouldings are all reminiscent of a bygone age that is reflected throughout the Hotel. Much of the interior of the Hotel has been retained to its original form and the staff are discreetly attentive and proud of the Hotel's heritage; learning about its history plays a key part in a stay at The Stanley. The heated outdoor swimming pool and the veranda offer breathtaking views across the valley and entrance to the National Park is less than 6 miles away. The area is extremely evocative; it is from this Hotel that Stephen King wrote "The Shining," returning recently to assist in the television production. Besides hiking, the area has excellent shops and a great number or art galleries that are well worth a visit although the therapeutic powers of a leisurely swim watching the mountains lend themselves to a relaxing getaway.

Our inspector loved: *The breathtaking view of snow capped mountains from the Hotel veranda.*

THE CLIFF HOUSE AT PIKES PEAK
306 CAÑON AVENUE, MANITOU SPRINGS, COLORADO 80829

Built in 1873 as a boarding house, the Cliff House is Colorado's second oldest operating hotel and was originally a key stop on the stagecoach trail. In the last couple of years it has been the subject of a $10 million refurbishment programme and is now a characterful hotel that pays tribute to its heritage, yet offers guests the very latest in modern comforts and luxury. There are 55 rooms and suites, each individually designed, including the wonderful "Celebrity" suites that reflect their previous inhabitants, including Clark Gable, Teddy Roosevelt, Henry Ford and Buffalo Bill Cody. The hotel has gained wide renown for its gourmet dining and outstanding friendly service and is a very romantic getaway within an hours' drive of Denver. The menu is based on Colorado ingredients and traditional French cuisine, enhanced by some modern international twists. The hotel's Colorado Experience Coordinator will tailor a package of fantastic adventures to make this a memorable Rocky Mountain escape. The Pikes Peak Cog railway goes to the 14,100 feet summit and there are numerous trails, hikes, rock climbs and jeep tours. The Garden of the Gods is fascinating, as are the cliff dwellings of the native Americans. Don't miss the world's highest suspension bridge at Royal Gorge Park.

Our inspector loved: The celebrity themed rooms, especially the "Clark Gable suite"

Directions: From Colorado Springs west on US24. 10 minutes to Manitou Springs, exit south through town to Cañon Avenue.

Web: www.johansens.com/thecliffhouse
E-mail: information@thecliffhouse.com
Tel: 1 719 685 3000
Fax: 1 719 685 3913
US Toll Free: 1 888 212 7000

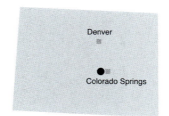

Price Guide:
rooms $129–$189
suites $179–$449

COLORADO - STEAMBOAT SPRINGS

VISTA VERDE GUEST RANCH
PO BOX 770465, STEAMBOAT SPRINGS, COLORADO 80477

Nestled deep in the Rocky Mountains, Vista Verde is a truly unique ranch experience for all seasons. The 500-acre property offers accommodation in secluded, spacious log cabins or deluxe lodge rooms. Each cabin has a private hot tub on the deck to relax in whilst enjoying the panorama of the national forest. In summer the crisp air and clear skies invite you to rise early, enjoy a breakfast of fresh berries, pastries and eggs, and then try your hand at relaxing. Fishing, hot air ballooning, hiking, white water rafting, kayaking, as well as horse riding, with or without instruction, are among the many activities with which to fill each day. In the evening enjoy a drink on the deck or cool off under the water of the fountain deck designed by the owner, Suzanne Munn. As the sun sets, a gourmet dinner is served in the main lodge, or on some evenings there is an informal cookout. In fall, the rivers run lower, the elk move back in and the aspens prepare for a magical colour extravaganza. A winter ranch experience is a must! Guests can hot air balloon, sleigh ride, cross-country and downhill ski, ice climb or horse ride, before they return to après ski at the parlour, dip into their own hot tub, and then enjoy a gourmet dinner.

Directions: Fly into Hayden airport for transfer to ranch or drive from Denver airport (approx. 4 hours).

Web: www.johansens.com/vistaverderanch
E-mail: reservations@vistaverde.com
Tel: 1 970 879 3858
Fax: 1 970 879 1413

Price Guide: (incl. activities and meals excl. tax)
rooms $260–$370

Our inspector loved: TBA

SONNENALP RESORT OF VAIL

20 VAIL ROAD, VAIL, COLORADO 81657

Meaning literally "sun on the alps" the Sonnenalp resort is in a truly spectacular setting at the base of one of the favourite ski mountains in the world, in the heart of Vail, itself a truly international village. Family run for the last four generations the hotel sets the standard by which other resort hotels are judged. The commitment from every member of staff is exemplary and truly complementary to the luxurious facilities and stylish presentation that is found throughout the hotel. The ideal hideaway for both couples and families there really is something for everyone here, from the exhilarating mountains with hiking and skiing to the Sonnenalp's own manicured golf course and fantastic Vail shops and restaurants. The Sonnenalp Spa is a wonderful retreat with hydrotherapy treatments, exercise classes and even personal trainers on hand to ensure every whim is fulfilled. Dinner can also cater to every mood, from Ludwig's elegant sun-filled dining room to the Bully Ranch where blue jeans and tin pans are the order of the day, or even the King's Club for a night cap and some Broadway numbers. The surrounding area is full of interest with Beaver Creek nearby and Vail mountain and village on the doorstep.

Our inspector loved: *The sumptuous breakfast buffet.*

Directions: From Denver west on I-70. After approx 100 miles exit at Vail Village exit 176, head towards ski mountain, the Sonnenalp is on the left.

Web: www.johansens.com/sonnenalp
E-mail: info@sonnenalp.com
Tel: 1 970 476 5656
Fax: 1 970 476 1639

Price Guide:
suites $240–$1660

Delaware

Hotel location shown in red with page number

BOARDWALK PLAZA HOTEL

OLIVE AVENUE & THE BOARDWALK, REHOBOTH BEACH, DELAWARE 19971

Built in 1990 and equipped with every modern amenity, the Boardwalk Plaza transports guests back to Victorian times and the service afforded by the attentive staff is one reminiscent of bygone years. Upon walking through the lobby, guests are welcomed by lively parrots, caged or not! Set in Delaware's premier resort town of Rehoboth Beach, the accommodation comprises a varied selection of rooms and suites, all of which have T1 Internet access and are bedecked with interesting antiques or fine period reproductions. The friendly owners have collected many pieces over the years to enhance the rooms and recreate the elegance and authentic character of the Victorian age. Victoria's Restaurant is situated adjacent to the thriving boardwalk, with a view of the Atlantic from every table, and here, diners may sample an array of tasty dishes made with fresh produce such as local fish, shellfish and Black Angus beef. Rehoboth Beach is a particularly convivial area with special events and festivals throughout the year. Other activities within the area include boating, fishing, kayaking and simply lazing on the beach.

Our inspector loved: *The elegance of this Victorian style hotel whose staff give a service not often experienced in modern times.*

Directions: From route 1 south, turn left off route 1 onto route 1A which becomes Rehoboth Avenue, then left onto 1st street, right onto Olive Avenue to the Boardwalk. Boardwalk Plaza is on the right.

Web: www.johansens.com/boardwalkplaza
E-mail: bph@boardwalkplaza.com
Tel: 1 302 227 7169
Fax: 1 302 227 0561

Price Guide:
rooms $119–$499

THE WHITE COMPANY
LONDON

Elegant Toiletries and Guest Amenities available exclusively from Pacific Direct

Email: sales@pacificdirect.co.uk   www.pacificdirect.co.uk   Worldwide Sales Telephone (+44) 1234 347 140   USA Toll Free 1-877-363-4732

exceed your guest expectations — luxury toiletries and amenities from **pacific direct**

Pacific Direct

www.pacificdirect.co.uk

international telephone:
(+44) 1234 347 140

e-mail sales@pacificdirect.co.uk

USA office:
call toll free 1-8777-363-4732

e-mail pdirectusa@aol.com

Florida

Hotel location shown in red with page number

FLORIDA - DELRAY BEACH

THE SUNDY HOUSE RESORT

106 SOUTH SWINTON AVENUE, DELRAY BEACH, FLORIDA 33444

Directions: Between Boca Raton and West Palm Beach

Web: www.johansens.com/sundyhouse
Tel: 1 561 272 5678
Fax: 1 561 272 1115

Price Guide:
On application.

This resort is a welcome retreat and elegant tropical getaway in an unspoiled South Florida beach town situated between Boca Raton and West Palm Beach in an oasis of peace and calm. Guests have a choice of luxury accommodation. There are four one and two-bedroom apartments with fully equipped kitchens and laundry facilities, private patio or balcony and state-of-the-art audio-visual equipment. For the height of luxury, there is a 'honeymoon' cottage with every facility from Jacuzzi and fireplace to flat screen plasma television. In addition there are six new, equestrian-themed guest rooms in the stables. All offer classic hotel amenities and overlook a natural tropical swimming pool. Three elegant dining rooms offer superb New Florida cuisine with talented chef Johnny Vinczencz using the finest and freshest exotic fruits, herbs and spices from the resort's gardens to prepare sumptuous and innovative dishes. The house itself, Delray's oldest, is the lovingly restored former home of a local mayor. It was built in 1902 and is listed in the National Register of Historic Places. Renovated estate grounds feature a tapas bar and the Taru Gardens, an area of spectacular exotic flora with waterfalls, tranquil fish pond, gazebos and glimpses of native wildlife.

Our inspector loved: *The De La Tierra Restaurant.*

SIMONTON COURT HISTORIC INN & COTTAGES

320 SIMONTON STREET, KEY WEST, FLORIDA 33040

Located in 2 acres of lush tropical gardens this elegant collection of cottages, manor house and townhouse is positively idylic for rest and relaxation at the very most southern point of the USA. Formerly a cigar factory, this collection of elegant buildings has gradually become the benchmark for attentive service in the most picturesque of settings. Vast tropical palms shade the 4 swimming pools and hot-tub and gentle sea-breezes caress the verandas, whilst a series of pretty brick paths connect the various buildings by twinkling night-lights. Guests may choose to stay in one of the 6 enchanting and beautifully restored factory workers' cottages that boast the very latest in luxurious amenities yet still retain the period charm of their 1880 origins. These make the most wonderful hideaway for privacy-seekers although the suites and guest bedrooms in the main house are breathtakingly appointed and many have private sun-decks or porches, king-size beds and jacuzzis. The sunset over Key West is a well-fabled sight and Simonton Court is just 3 blocks walk away from the top spot from which to view. Similarly Duval Street is just a stone's throw away; the home of many wonderful boutiques and fashionable pubs.

Our inspector loved: *A unique gem nestled on 2 acres of tropical gardens.*

Directions: Take US Highway 1 to Key West and then follow Roosevelt Boulevard to Truman Avenue. Turn right on Simonton Street and continue to Eaton Street. Turn left just past the Eaton Street intersection.

Web: www.johansens.com/simontoncourt
E-mail: simontoncourt@aol.com
Tel: 1 305 294 6386
Fax: 1 305 293 8446
US Toll Free: 1 800 944 2687

Price Guide:
rooms $129–$309
cottages $259–$690

FLORIDA - MIAMI BEACH

THE INN AT FISHER ISLAND

ONE FISHER ISLAND DRIVE, MIAMI BEACH, FLORIDA 33109

Directions: Ferry leaves from McArtur causeway (I 395).

Web: www.johansens.com/fisherisland
E-mail: hotel@fisherisland.com
Tel: 1 305 535 6080
Fax: 1 305 535 6003

Price Guide:
rooms $325–$1680
suites $540–$2170

Accessed only by private ferry from Miami and Miami Beach, Fisher Island was once the home of the Vanderbilts and a more picturesque setting for this exclusive retreat would be hard to find. The estate was built in the 1920's for entertaining America's elite and today it has been restored to its original grandeur offering the ultimate in luxury recreation and accommodation. There is nearly a mile of private manicured beach, two deepwater marinas, spectacular championship golf links, and 18 tennis courts offering clay, grass and hard surfaces. The club itself is the epitome of style and offers an extensive choice of accommodation from newly restored 1 and 2 bedroom Vanderbilt cottages, to luxurious courtyard villas with private patios and spas, or a choice of de luxe suites overlooking the Atlantic ocean. There are five choices of restaurant; from the cool Beach Club on the front, to the Italian Café Porto Cervo, or the more formal Vanderbilt Mansion. The Spa Internazionale offers the latest in European and American health and beauty treatments and the great Kids Club enables parents to really take advantage of this and all the other recreational facilities. The legendary Miami nightlife and shopping experience is only 5 minutes away after taking the ferry but the seclusion and beauty of the island itself is such that most guests will move little from this quite unique destination.

Our inspector loved: The Spa Internazionale is an oasis of unparelled luxury.

FLORIDA - NAPLES

HOTEL ESCALANTE
290 FIFTH AVENUE SOUTH, NAPLES, FLORIDA 34102

A red brick drive and terracotta tiles set the scene for this friendly, sophisticated and discreet Mediterranean-style hotel situated in the heart of Naples. Surrounded by lush tropical gardens overflowing with more than three hundred species of native and exotic shrubs, trees and beautiful butterflies flying everywhere, the hotel is an oasis of tranquillity. The peaceful atmosphere of the elegantly furnished en suite bedrooms is enhanced by embroidered Frette bedlinen, stylish colour co-ordination and subtle furnishings. Fabulous showers in the marble bathrooms create a luxurious feel. Breakfast is served in a quiet courtyard by the pool, or can be enjoyed on the terrace of your stunning garden suite. Health enthusiasts will enjoy the well equipped fitness centre and the superb spa and health treatments. Guests can unwind in the wonderful oak-panelled library bar, or simply relax and sunbathe on comfortable sun loungers around the pool or at the seven mile beach, a mere two-minute walk away. Nearby are Naples' finest golf courses, whilst the famous Fifth Avenue and Third Street provide pleasurable shopping. Delicious food and wine can be sampled in the many bistros and restaurants within easy walking distance of the hotel and the area has museums and theatres for entertainment.

Our inspector loved: *This mystical Mediterranean villa cloistered within lush tropical gardens just minutes from the beach and Fifth Avenue..*

Directions: In the heart of Old Naples; 2 hours from Miami Int'l Airport.

Web: www.johansens.com/hotelescalante
Tel: 1 941 659 3466
Fax: 1 941 262 8748

Price Guide:
rooms $195-$360
suites $250-650

Georgia
Hotel location shown in red with page number

GEORGIA - PERRY

HENDERSON VILLAGE

125 SOUTH LANGSTON CIRCLE, PERRY, GEORGIA 31069

A collection of charming cottages in the style of 19th century southern plantation houses, graced with wide shady porches, nestle in the village which is situated in the historic heartland of Georgia. Authentic southern hospitality can be enjoyed in these 12 historic homes, beautifully restored and relocated to create a charming country resort with thousands of acres to relax, unwind and recuperate in traditional southern style. The Langston House Restaurant serves gormet cuisine which was voted "the absolute best dining experience in Georgia" by Georgia Trend Magazine. Serpentine brick paths lead to rolling pastures and formal gardens which feature a swimming pool and twin gazebos. For those who wish to relax, fishing for bass in the sun, taking a massage or lazing by the pool set amongst the tranquil gardens can be savoured, alternatively, guests can unwind whilst horse riding alongside cotton fields and pecan orchards. Shooting sporting clays can be arranged. Henderson Village is a rare find and exceptional value for money. Local points of interest include President Jimmy Carter Historic site, Museum of Aviation, Peach Packing, Camellia Gardens, Antique Trails and Civil War Museum.

Directions: From Atlanta, take I-75 south to exit 127. Turn right, travel approx. 1 mile to 1st intersection. Henderson Village is on the right.

Web: www.johansens.com/hendersonvillage
E-mail: info@hendersonvillage.com
Tel: 1 478 988 8696
Fax: 1 478 988 9009
US Toll Free: 1888 615 9722

Price Guide: (incl. breakfast)
rooms $165–$235
suites $285–$325

Our inspector loved: *The combination of southern charm and gourmet food set amongst beautiful gardens.*

THE ELIZA THOMPSON HOUSE
5 WEST JONES STREET, SAVANNAH, GEORGIA 31401

The Eliza Thompson House, built in 1847, offers a delightful fusion of past and present times with traditions and customs of the last century and the comforts and amenities of today. Set on a quiet residential street, the house is one of the oldest inns in the heart of Savannah's historical district and is an architectural landmark. Meticulous restoration work has resulted in the superb interior, enhanced by heart pine floors and antique furnishings. Guests may stay in either the 12 stately rooms in the main house or in the Carriage House, which boasts a further 13 rooms. All the bedrooms are furnished in an exquisite style with en suite facilities and colour televisions. In addition, some main house rooms have charming fireplaces. The soft bathrobes and make-up mirrors are thoughtful extras. The breakfast is imaginative and extensive, comprising home-made recipes with fresh, local ingredients. Other delightful traditions include an afternoon wine and cheese reception and evening dessert & coffee. Guests may relax in the beautifully landscaped courtyard, where the air is scented with southern fragrances and the gentle sound of the Ivan Bailey fountain may be heard. Savannah is a wonderful town to explore with many antique shops, museums and old churches nearby.

Our inspector loved: *The peaceful courtyard with the soft sound of the fountain in which to breakfast or read a book by.*

Directions: Travel east on I-16, towards Savannah. Exit at Montgomery Street, turn right at traffic lights on Liberty Street. Turn right on Whitaker Street and left onto Jones Street.

Web: www.johansens.com/elizathompsonhouse
E-mail: innkeeper@elizathompsonhouse.com
Tel: 1 912 236 3620
US Toll Free: 800 348 9378
Fax: 1 912 238 1920

Price Guide:
rooms $149–$269

GEORGIA - SAVANNAH

GRANITE STEPS

126 EAST GASTON STREET, SAVANNAH, GEORGIA 31401

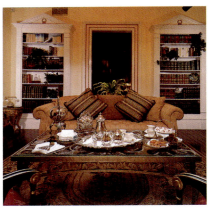

Directions: From I-16, head towards Liberty Street, then turn right on to Abercorn. Granite Steps is on the right, on the corner of Gordon Street.

Web: www.johansens.com/granitesteps
Tel: 1 912 233 5380
Fax: 1 912 236 3116

Price Guide: (incl. breakfast)
rooms $275
suite $500

Considered by many to be Savannah's most elegant B & B inn, Granite Steps was built in 1881 and is an imposing Italianate building situated very close to beautiful Forsyth Park. The charming owners, Donna and Randy Sparks, have spared no expenses and their attention to detail is clearly evident. The house has an interesting history and its restoration began in the mid-1980s when it was owned by Jim Williams. The impressive twin mirrors above the marble fireplaces may be attributed to this time. High ceilings, attractive mantles, original hard-wood floors and an oriental screen, popular in the late 1800s, add to the appeal of this friendly inn. The rooms and suites are all individually decorated and feature top quality linen and luxurious amenities such as balconies, Jacuzzis and canopy beds. The bathrooms are designed in stylish marble and some have televisions. Before breakfast, coffee and muffins are served. This is followed by a gourmet meal of shrimp eggs Benedict with citrus hollandaise, apple pancakes in pork tenderloin or raspberry stuffed French toast. Each evening, hors d'oeuvres are served in the beautiful parlour and recommendations and reservations are made for the best restaurants in town.

Our inspector loved: The opulent marble bathrooms definitely the piece de resistance.

The President's Quarters
225 EAST PRESIDENT STREET, SAVANNAH, GEORGIA 31401

Residing on Oglethorpe Square, these authentic Federal-style town houses were constructed by the estate of W. W. Gordon in 1855. Fashioned in the likeness of Savannah's Davenport House and as a neighbour of the renowned Owens-Thomas House, The President's Quarters opened its doors in 1987 after a careful restoration. With a long history of famous inhabitants and guests such as Robert E. Lee, each room is individually decorated celebrating 19 Presidents known to have enjoyed Savannah's southern hospitality. The spacious guest rooms feature regal wallcoverings and carefully chosen historic colours exclusive to grand homes of Savannah. Selected suites have balconies, romantic loft bedrooms and hand-painted ceilings. The inn is renowned for its fine service and hospitality. Those accustomed to pampering will enjoy the thoughtful extras such as soft bathrobes, a chilled bottle of wine and fresh fruit. Other delights include breakfast served in the rooms, sumptuous afternoon hors d'oeuvres and a nightly turndown service with bedside cordials and local sweets. Concierge service is available 24 hours for dining and entertainment suggestions and reservations. The night-life of River Street is only three blocks away! The many quaint shops will please those with an interest in curio

Our inspector loved: *The central location and large rooms, plus the small adjoining town house with its historic decor.*

Directions: Take I-16 to Montgomery, right on Oglethorpe, left on Abercorn, right on York. Off-street parking

Web: www.johansens.com/prsidentsquarters
Tel: 1 912 233 1600
Fax: 1 912 238 0849

Price Guide:
rooms $137–$177
suites $187–$250

Illinois

Hotel location shown in red with page number

THE SUTTON PLACE HOTEL
21 EAST BELLEVUE PLACE, CHICAGO, ILLINOIS 60611

At 23 storeys high this elegant hotel, built of French-Canadian granite, strikes an impressive balance of contemporary and traditional design amidst the red and brown brickwork of late 19th and early 20th century neighbouring buildings. Situated in the heart of Chicago's downtown, The Sutton Place Hotel is considered an architectural jewel. The interior décor is stunning art deco graced with over 100 originals and numerous reproductions of Robert Mapplethorpe's dramatic floral still-life photography – the largest acquisition of the artist's works. Lake and city views abound from the 246 spacious guest rooms, which include 34 junior suites and six luxurious duplex penthouse suites, some of which feature balconies or terraces. Room amenities include air conditioning, sound proofing, CD and 25-inch television, three telephones with voicemail, data port and high speed Internet connections, mini bar, and 24-hour service. Imaginative cuisine is served in The Whiskey Bar and Grill and in the elegant function rooms. There are seven naturally-lit meeting rooms which can accommodate up to 150, plus a business centre. Courtesy transport is available to loop businesses.

Our inspector loved: The quiet neighbourhood and old brownstones that surround this lovely hotel.

Directions: One block from Lake Michigan, minutes from the Loop business district and the Magnificent Mile, 17 miles from O'Hare International Airport and 12 miles from Midway Airport.

Web: www.johansens.com/suttonplace
E-mail: info_chi@suttonplace.com
Tel: 1 312 266 2100
Fax: 1 312 266 2103

Price Guide:
rooms $305-$360
suites $395-$1500.

LOUISIANA
Hotel location shown in red with page number

Madewood Plantation House
4250 HIGHWAY 308, NAPOLEANVILLE, LOUISIANA 70390

Madewood, a great plantation house in Louisiana, has been so authentically restored that several films have been made with the mansion in the star role. A National Historic Landmark, its beauty is accentuated by its setting – extensive parkland encompasses the original slave quarters, kitchen and family graveyard. The classic façade, with its pillars, is magnificent and the interior has the same aristocratic grace. Guests stay in one of the original bedchambers in the main house, where modern facilities blend harmoniously with period antiques whilst retaining the character of the house. Here you will experience a refreshing return to the art of conversation, as there are no televisions or telephones in the bedrooms. Non-smoking prevails throughout. Original artworks from the owner's collection are omnipresent, particularly in the drawing room with its exquisite pieces. Residents gather in the handsome Library at 6.00pm for a preprandial wine and cheese, before a Southern-style dinner, round the immense oak table. Coffee and brandy are served in the Parlour, where guests mingle and converse. Exploring the Bayou country, boat trips down the Mississippi and antique-hunting in shops along the Bayou are popular pastimes.

Our inspector loved: *To step back in time and feel the charm of the Ole South.*

Directions: I-10 West, exit 182, cross Sunshine Bridge, then Highway 70 to Spur 70, signed Bayou Plantations. Left for 1 mile then left onto Highway 308. The hous eis 2.2 miles south of Napoleanville.

Web: www.johansens.com/madewood
E-mail: madewoodpl@aol.com
Tel: 1 985 369 7151
Fax: 1 985 369 9843

Price Guide:
$225–$285
$245–$235

LOUISIANA - NEW ORLEANS

Hotel Maison De Ville
727 RUE TOULOUSE, NEW ORLEANS, LOUISIANA 70130

Directions: In the heart of the French Quarter.

Web: www.johansens.com/maisondeville
E-mail: tyoung@dal.meristar.com
Tel: 1 504 561 5858
Fax: 1 504 528 9939

Price Guide:
rooms $215–$395
cottages $245–$980

Situated in the heart of the Vieux Carre, the French Quarter that so typifies New Orleans, lies this wonderfully preserved and charming building. Its character is totally of the period, when New Orleans was a French colony and America still a British colony, with high elegant ceilings and pretty ensconced courtyards. The bedrooms can be found either in the main building or within the Audubon Cottages, so named after the naturalist John James Audobon who created many of his masterpieces here. Each has its own unique charm and style and in both the main house and the cottages the utmost care has been taken to restore everything to historical accuracy. Original paintings, antiques and individual décor feature in all of the bedrooms and the twice-daily housekeeping service ensures an unflinching attention to detail. The Bistro Restaurant is rapidly gaining a wide reputation for its innovative cuisine and unpretentious atmosphere and has been included in Conde Nast's top 100 restaurants. The heart of New Orleans remains just outside the front door and has a relaxed and infectious ambience. There are numerous antiques stores to visit, as well as delicious restaurants exuding the buzz and attractions of the sidewalk.

Our inspector loved: The true feeling of the old French Quarter ambience.

MARYLAND
Hotel location shown in red with page number

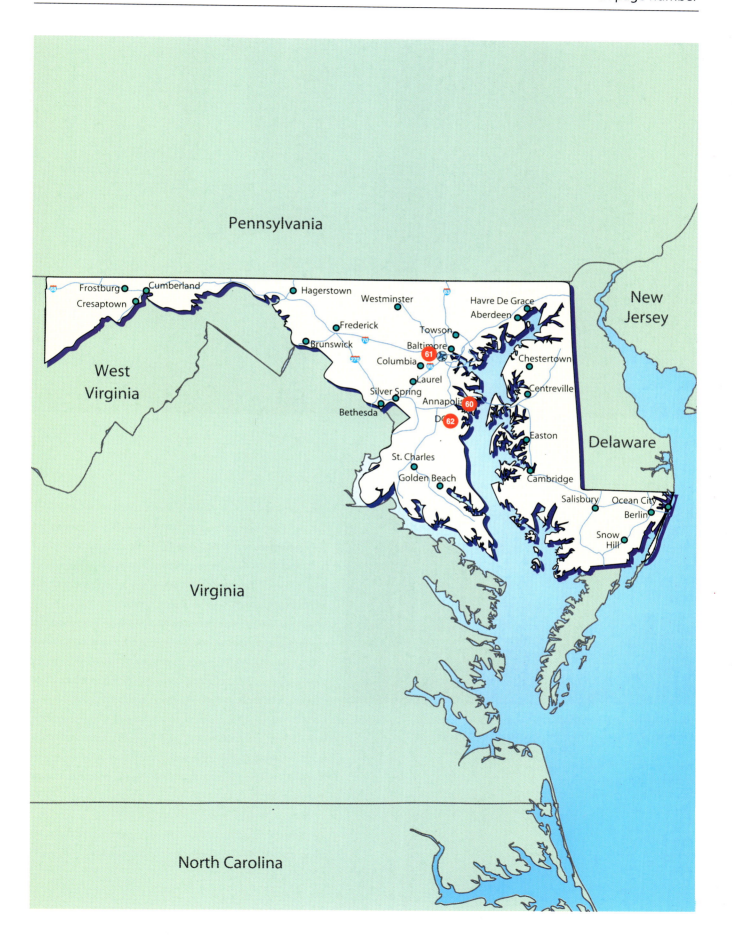

MARYLAND - ANNAPOLIS

THE ANNAPOLIS INN

144 PRINCE GEORGE STREET, ANNAPOLIS, MARYLAND 21401-1723

Directions: From Baltimore take 97 south to RT 50 east to exit 27. Follow signs to the Naval Academy, at main entrance take right then right again.

Web: www.johansens.com/annapolisinn
E-mail: info@annapolisinn.com
Tel: 1 410 295 5200
Fax: 1 410 295 5201

Price Guide:
rooms $250–$310
suites $375–$475

Lying between the U.S. Naval Academy, city harbour and State Capital, The Annapolis Inn is surrounded by buildings of exciting and diverse architecture and built circa 1770, this is a classic example of the Georgian and Greek revival. It holds just 3 guest bedrooms that really do exude the expansive opulence of a bygone age, with the accompanying attentive levels of service. Each room in the Inn has been painstakingly designed to maximise on the classical mouldings, ceiling roses and elaborate wooden carvings of the time and the result is a truly romantic retreat. The bathrooms have heated marble floors, towel warmers and jacuzzi baths; the overwhelming ambience is one of unadulterated luxury. Going outdoors seems like re-entering the real world although there is much to see in the surrounding area; the Boat Building School and Naval Academy are 2 suggestions; and there are some excellent boat trips and walking tours that are ideally followed by a seafood lunch in one of the delightful nearby restaurants.

Our inspector loved: *The beautiful silverware, porcelain and cut crystal glasses that were used to serve breakfast at this unique Inn.*

Antrim 1844

30 TREVANION RD, TANEYTOWN, MARYLAND 21787

Built in 1844, this elegant plantation was once the headquarters of General George Meade prior to the Battle of Gettysburg, only 12 miles away. Owners Dorothy and Richard Mollett have recreated that era at Antrim 1844, a classical Greek revival mansion, which won the Johansens Most Excellent Inn Award in 1999. The romantic guest rooms within the mansion have delicate linens, jacuzzis and fireplaces while the luxurious suites are imaginatively transformed in secluded outbuildings throughout the property. Wooden butlers outside each door offer newspapers in the morning and roses at night! Guests may dine on the veranda overlooking the lovely formal gardens, or in the charming Smokehouse-Restaurant with overstuffed chairs and brick floors. The acclaimed 6 course menu boasts the highest Zagat ratings, along with DiRONA and Wine Spectator's coveted 'The Best of Award of Excellence.' Guests may stroll the 23 acre estate or enjoy the pool with its gazebo, croquet, target golf or tennis. There are multiple facilities for corporate events, and the Glass Pavilion is ideal for weddings. Washington DC is one and a half hours (70 miles) away, and Balto with its inner harbour is 45 miles to the east.

Our inspector loved: The attention to detail in room decoration, historical preservation and fine dining.

Directions: Route 140 east to Taneytown, cross railroad tracks and bear right at fork. After 150' turn right, parking is signed.

Web: www.johansens.com/antrim1844
E-mail: antrim1844@erols.com
Tel: 1 410 756 6812
Fax: 1 410 756 2744
US Toll Free: 1 800 858 1844

Price Guide:
rooms $225
suite $375

MARYLAND - WASHINGTON D.C.

THE GEORGE WASHINGTON UNIVERSITY INN

824 NEW HAMPSHIRE AVENUE, N.W. WASHINGTON D.C., DISTRICT OF COLUMBIA 20037

Directions: Located one block from The George Washington University & one block from the Potomac River.

Web: www.johansens.com/georgewashingtoninn
E-mail: info@gwuinn.com
Tel: 1 202 337 6620
Fax: 1 202 298 7499

Price Guide:
rooms $160–$180
suites $180–$220

Whether travelling to Washington for business or pleasure The George Washington University Inn is an ideal place to stay. The Inn is located on a quiet residential street in the heart of the prestigious district of Foggy Bottom, yet the university from which it takes its name, is just 2 blocks away and the State Department and Kennedy Centre are also close by. This boutique-style, Williamsburg-inspired Hotel boasts a standard of excellence that even the most discerning traveller will relish. With a reputation for elegant, impeccable service and unsurpassed attention to detail the guest leaves feeling totally pampered. Each of the deluxe rooms and suites have excellent views, is furnished in restful pastel colour schemes and all suites have complete kitchens. The new restaurant, Nectar, due to open in October 2002, will serve nouveau California-style cuisine created by chef Jaminson Blankenship, formerly of Tahoga Restaurant in Georgetown, and will provide the ideal venue for pre-theatre diners going to the nearby Kennedy Centre. Breakfast (full American), lunch and dinner will be available together with room service. Georgetown is just a short walk and the Foggy Bottom metro is just 1 block away where guests can board to reach The White House, Smithsonian Institution, Washington Cathedral and Capitol Hill.

Our inspector loved: The panoramic views of the capital and the Potomac River from some of the bedroom suites.

Mississippi

Hotel location shown in red with page number

MISSISSIPPI - BILOXI

GREEN OAKS

580 BEACH BOULEVARD, BILOXI, MISSISSIPPI 39530

Directions: Upon request

Web: www.johansens.com/greenoaks
E-mail: greenoaks4@aol.com
Tel: 1 228 436 6257
Fax: 1 228 436 6225

Price Guide:
rooms $120–$160

Steeped in American history, Green Oaks was one of the original beach houses built by wealthy New Orleans planters in the early 19th century. With its deep verandas and traditional clapboarding it is a fine example of period architecture and is recognised as being one of Mississippi's oldest remaining beachfront residences. Today, it is a magnificent place to stay, the owners have taken care to preserve the integrity of its heritage with an impressive collection of heirlooms and antiques, as well as all the original beams, mouldings and fixtures. The gourmet breakfast is a delight, served on antique china accompanied by the finest silver, crystal and table linens. Each of the 5 bedrooms is airy and spacious with deep windows, elegant crystal chandeliers and enveloping four poster beds, as well as modern day facilities: telephone and computer ports; mailbox and access to fax machine. The House retains 2 of its original 64 acre grounds, which are breathtakingly landscaped and have wonderful views of the Gulf Coast making it in ideal place to relax although the frenetic city life of New Orleans is just 2 hours away. There is plenty to see and do great shopping, fine dining and many tourist attractions within walking distance as well as the great beach and nearby golf links.

Our inspector loved: That Green Oaks is the perfect spot for a wedding.

FAIRVIEW INN
734 FAIRVIEW STREET, JACKSON, MISSISSIPPI 39202

This gracious pillared white house with its sweeping driveway and beautifully landscaped gardens is reminiscent of George Washington's Mount Vernon residence. Situated in the exclusive Belhaven District of Jackson, it is a grand Colonial Revival house listed in the National Register of Historic Places. From the moment guests step into the traditional hallway, the charm and luxurious atmosphere of this property is apparent, with reception rooms to left and right, sparkling chandeliers and polished wooden floors scattered with antique rugs. The Simmons family has owned the house since 1930: there are old family portraits, photographs and crests tracing the history of the family name. The house has three luxurious bedrooms and fifteen opulent suites. All incorporate the original characteristics of 1908 when the house was built combined with every accessory and comfort that today's visitor expects. Two of the suites are very private and have their own entrances and car parking. There is a large, elegant dining room where co-owner Carol Simmons and her executive chef serve excellent gourmet meals. The hotel is close to the centre of Jackson and its historical attractions, art galleries, museums and theatres.

Our inspector loved: *The family feeling that you get from the minute you walk in.*

Directions: From I-55 exit at 98A into Woodrow Wilson Drive. Turn left at the second traffic lights into North State Street and Fairview Street is first left after the second traffic lights.

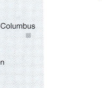

Web: www.johansens.com/fairviewinn
E-mail: fairview@fairviewinn.com
Tel: 1 601 948 3429
Fax: 1 601 948 1203
US Toll Free: 1 888 948 1908

Price Guide:
rooms $100–$250
suite $225–$350

Dunleith Plantation

84 HOMOCHITTO STREET, NATCHEZ, MISSISSIPPI, 39120

Directions: From US61 exit onto US84 (John R. Junkin Drive) towards Mississippi Bridge. Homochitto Street is on the right.

Web: www.johansens.com/dunleithplantation
E-mail: Dunleith@bkbank.com
Tel: 1 601 446 8500
Fax: 1 601 446 8554

Price Guide:
rooms $145–$250

With its fantastic array of towering white columns, impressively high windows, wrought-iron edged wrap-around verandahs and general air of majesty, Dunleith Plantation is without doubt one of the most attractive, grand old houses of the south. Situated in the heart of Natchez and surrounded by 40 acres of magnificently maintained landscaped gardens and wooded bayous, it is a perfect example and reminder of an era when people and occasions were typified by elegance and style. Built in the 19th century, Dunleith has been lovingly restored and refurbished to the house's full glory and is listed on the National Register of Historic Places and is a National Historic Landmark. Inside, the décor is superb and all modern comforts have been considered without compromising the building's architectural splendour. Each of the spacious en suite guestrooms has their own personality and charm; the rooms in the main house have exquisite, large period beds and working fireplaces. Acclaimed chef John Martin Terranova, produces excellent and imaginative cuisine in the Castle Restaurant which, with an English type pub, is located in a restored 1790's carriage house. Dunleith Plantation is part of the famous annual autumn and spring Pilgrimage Tours and is conveniently situated near to all historic sites and museums.

Our inspector loved: Stepping back in time to the grandeur of "The Ole South"

Monmouth Plantation

36 MELROSE AVENUE AT, JOHN A QUITMAN PARKWAY, NATCHEZ, MISSISSIPPI 39120

Monmouth Plantation is truly one of the grand old ladies of the South, lovingly restored by owners Ron and Lani Riches to how she would have been in her full glory when built in 1818. Listed as a historic landmark, the Hotel has won numerous awards and welcomed many distinguished guests, including former President and Mrs Clinton. Set in 26 immaculately maintained acres with a rose garden, ponds and walking trails, the building is surrounded by the scent of jasmine and wisteria which hangs in the air. Inside, each of the 30 well appointed rooms and suites have their own distinct personality and charm. The décor is beautiful, and every modern comfort has been considered without compromising the building's architectural values, resulting in a perfect blend of comfort and Southern splendour. A five-course dinner is served by chandelier and candlelight each evening, and renowned chef Regina Charboneau plans daily menus which incorporate traditional favourites and regional ingredients. The downtown district of Natchez, the oldest city on the Mississippi river, is just five minutes away and with its mansion tours, carriage rides, antique shops and air of pre-Civil War elegance is well worth exploring.

Our inspector loved: *The feeling of stepping back to The Civil War, you can feel Scarlet O'Hara sitting on the beautiful lawns with all her admirers around her.*

Directions: Five minutes from downtown Natchez; 90 miles north of Baton Rouge off Highway 61.

Web: www.johansens.com/monmouthplantation
E-mail: luxury@monmouthplantation.com
Tel: 1 601 442 5852
Fax: 1 601 446 7762

Price Guide:
rooms $150–$220
suites $215–$375

MISSISSIPPI - VICKSBURG

ANCHUCA HISTORIC MANSION & INN

1010 FIRST EAST STREET, VICKSBURG, MISSISSIPPI 39183

'Happy Home,' the native American translation for Anchuca, is part of Mississippi history; an impressive, columned mansion and one of the most significant antebellum properties in Vicksburg. Anchuca was a hospital during the siege of the town in 1863 and the site of one of Jefferson Davis' last public addresses following the 'War between the States'. Built in 1863 for a local politician and now on the National Register of Historic Places, the mansion has been extended and refurbished. It not only has a bold and impressive exterior but also an elegant, refined and inviting interior delightfully furnished with 18th and 19th century antiques and paintings. There is excellent en suite accommodation in The Main House, The Carriage House and The Quarter Apartment and facilities are of the highest standard. The Master Suite in the Main House has an 1850 hand-carved rosewood canopy bed and private dressing area and The Quarter Apartment, the former kitchen and servants' quarter, features original brick floors and fireplaces. All guestrooms have every modern amenity. Hearty Plantation breakfasts are served in a formal dining room and for relaxation guests can enjoy the tranquillity of a New Orleans style courtyard, walks through mature grounds or swimming.

Directions: From I-20 take exit 4B (West Clay Street). Go 1.7 miles to Cherry Street, turn right, and continue for 5 blocks to First East Street. The mansion is immediately on your right..

Web: www.johansens.com/anchuca
E-mail: Reservation@AnchucaMansion.com
Tel: 1 601 661 0111
Fax: 1 601 661 0111

Price Guide:
rooms $95–$175

Our inspector loved: *The gardens, patio, décor, warm, friendly welcome and the best breakfast in the south.*

MISSISSIPPI - VICKSBURG

THE DUFF GREEN MANSION
1114 FIRST EAST STREET, VICKSBURG, MISSISSIPPI 39180

A long, wide stairway leads onto the wrought-iron fenced porch fronting the white doorway of this magnificent mansion situated in the historic district of Vicksburg. Considered to be one of the finest examples of Palladian architecture in the State, it escaped destruction during and after the Civil War's siege by serving as a hospital for Confederate and Union soldiers. Beneath its high ceilings and richly decorated walls of cardinal reds, deep blues and rich greens the polished floors carry bloodstained marks from wounds. In one room, the ceiling beams show where a cannon-ball struck. Original works of art hang throughout and most of the furniture is antique. Duff Green contains five luxurious bedrooms with amenities to satisfy the expectations of the most discerning visitor. All have an individual character, open fireplaces and porches where guests can relax in the evening air. Guests may enjoy a drink at the free bar in one of the charming reception rooms, before sampling the extensive menu at the Duff's Tavern & Grille. During the day, sunbathing on the secluded patio surrounds of a swimming pool is a popular pastime. Vicksburg is famous for its battlefield where Civil War skirmishes are re-enacted.

Our inspector loved: *This Ante-bellum house, the Queen of Vicksburg, you can almost hear the cannons going off from the river.*

Directions: From Jackson, take I-20 west and exit at 4B into Clay Street. After approximately 2 1/2 miles turn into Cherry Street. First East Street is on the right.

Web: www.johansens.com/duffgreenmansion
Tel: 1 601 636 6968
Fax: 1 601 661 0079

Price Guide:
rooms $95–$125

Missouri

Hotel location shown in red with page number

MISSOURI - ST LOUIS

Chase Park Plaza Hotel

212 NORTH KINGSHIGHWAY BOULEVARD, ST LOUIS, MISSOURI 63108

Uniquely situated in the heart of the Central West End and perfect for downtown St Louis lies the Chase Park Plaza, affectionately known as "The Chase is the place." Originally built in 1922 the vast art-deco building stands testament to a bygone era where grace and style were paramount and its marble halls and lofty chandeliers gleam today as they did then. Recent modifications have resulted in 251 elegantly furnished suites that come equipped with the very latest in modern luxury; fully-fitted kitchens, coffee-makers, data ports, voicemail, access to a 24 hour concierge and an 18,000 foot, fitness centre. Views over Forest Park and the city skyline from the bedrooms are spectacular and the dining facilities are extensive. The newly opened Marquee Café serves breakfast, lunch and dinner, whilst The Tenderloin Room provides an elegant backdrop to traditional steaks, seafood specialities and seasonal salads. The newly opened Chasers Lounge serves a choice of over 250 martinis and drinks and the Eau Bistro and Café has a lighter Californian feel. Functions from 5 to 2,500 can be accommodated either within a range of elegant panelled rooms, or within the spectacular and truly elegant ballroom; the setting for all of St Louis' major social events! The shopping at the heart of the West End, the Zoo and Forest Park are all within a stone's throw.

Our inspector loved: Seeing The Grand Dame of St Louis looking so good.

Directions: At the crossroads of Forest Park and Kingshighway Boulevard.

Web: www.johansens.com/chaseparkplaza
Tel: 1 314 633 3000
Fax: 1 314 633 1133

Price Guide:
rooms $189–$209
suites $209–$350

NEW ENGLAND
Hotel location shown in red with page number

Copper Beech Inn
46 MAIN STREET, IVORYTON, CONNECTICUT 06442

Directions: 1¾ miles west of route 9, from exit 3 follow signs to Ivoryton.

Web: www.johansens.com/copperbeechinn
Email: info@copperbeechinn.com
Tel: 1 860 767 0330

Price Guide:
rooms $125–$325

Superb country and antique furnishings, dazzling décor, a multitude of fresh flower displays and a homely atmosphere make this attractive Inn the perfect, peaceful escape from a busy world. Once the home of an ivory comb and piano keyboard manufacturer, it stands behind a magnificent Copper Beech tree in beautiful turn-of-the-century gardens in a quiet little village that is part of the town of Essex. Just 2 hours from New York City. Recent renovations have resulted in delightful decoration throughout. The 13 guest rooms are superb and extremely comfortable; 4 in the Main House have old-fashioned baths and 9 in the Carriage House have whirlpool baths and lead onto decks. Some have four poster or canopy beds under soaring cathedral ceilings where original beams are exposed. An exquisite plant-filled, Victorian-style conservatory is a relaxing venue for a quiet read or chat over an aperitif before dining in hearty, French country style. The lobster bisque is spectacular, the fish excellent and the veal so tender. Sparkling silver and soft candlelight create an atmosphere of romance and warm elegance that has helped earn the restaurant an AAA 4 Diamond Award, complemented by the Wine Spectator national Award of Excellence for its wine list. Places to visit include the Ivoryton Playhouse, Godspeed Opera House, the quaint villages of Essex and Old Lyme.

Our inspector loved: The romance of the garden porch.

NEW ENGLAND / CONNECTICUT - MYSTIC

THE INN AT MYSTIC

US1 & STATE 27, PO BOX 216, MYSTIC, CONNECTICUT 06355

Overlooking Mystic Harbour and Long Island Sound, this award-winning Inn is spread across 5 buildings and surrounded by 15 acres of bird watching and hiking trails. The best rooms are housed within the Katherine Haley Mansion, a Colonial Revival building dating back to 1904. Humphrey Bogart and Lauren Bacall stayed here on honeymoon and it features English panelling, original bird motif wallpaper in the Dining Room as well as modern therma-cuzzi spas and whirlpool tubs. The tranquil Gate House, with its period antiques, fireplaces and imported mantels, has views across the orchards, while up a sweeping driveway The Motor Inn sits close to Pequotsepos Cove. Individually furnished rooms have colonial wallcoverings and some offer private balconies, providing guests with an idyllic spot to relax and enjoy the sunset. Excellent cuisine is served at the Flood-Tide Restaurant and visitors can experience the elegant breakfast buffet, lunch al fresco and complimentary afternoon tea. Dinner menus include the freshest local fish and seafood such as colossal sea scallops and native lobster and after-dinner drinks can be taken in the classic wine and piano lounge. Every season has something to offer at Mystic and activities and places of interest include kayaking, golf, the Mystic Seaport Museum, Marinelife Aquarium, sailboat cruises and cross-country skiing.

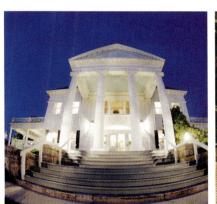

Directions: From Boston I-95 to exit 90, 2 miles on Route 27, left onto Route 1, 1st driveway on left.

Web: www.johansens.com/innatmystic
Tel: 1 860 536 9604
Fax: 1 860 572 1635

Price Guide:
rooms $65–$235

Our inspector loved: The 15 acres of bird watching and hiking trails.

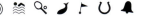

NEW ENGLAND / CONNECTICUT - MYSTIC

STONECROFT COUNTRY INN

515 PUMPKIN HILL ROAD, LEDYARD, CONNECTICUT 06339

Directions: Leave the I-95 at Exit 89, Allyn Street

Web: www.johansens.com/stonecroftcountryinn
E-mail: innkeeper@stonecroft.com
Tel: 1 860 572 0771
Fax: 1 860 572 9161

Price Guide:
rooms $150–$350

Listed on the National Historic Register, Stonecroft is an early 19th century sea captain's colonial country house situated in six acres of lovely meadows and woodland. Peace and tranquillity abound and every modern comfort is offered, combined with an old world charm, elegance and atmosphere. The main, pale yellow clapboard house, built in 1807, has 4 superb public rooms, 6 open fireplaces and 4 exceptional en suite guest rooms. The oldest has the original ceiling beams and doors; another features a colourful wraparound wall mural. 4 more luxury bedrooms and 2 premier suites are in the nearby two-storey converted post and beam. All rooms are air-conditioned and superbly decorated and furnished in American, English or French style. Breakfast and dinner are served in a magnificent granite-walled dining room decorated in English country manor style and featuring a comfortable lounge and French windows opening onto a terrace for outdoor dining, overlooking manicured lawns, a water garden and grapevine pergola. Excellent cuisine is delightfully and imaginatively prepared by chef Drew David Egy who trained and perfected his expertise under award-winning international chefs such as Raymond Blanc, owner of the famed Le Manoir Aux Quat' Saisons, Oxfordshire, England, Marco-Pierre White, Pierre Kauffman and the Roux brothers.

Our inspector loved: *The wonderful cuisine.*

THE BOULDERS INN

EAST SHORE ROAD, ROUTE 45, NEW PRESTON, CONNECTICUT 06777

This enchanting Inn is in the Berkshire Hills with spectacular views of Lake Waramaug. The sound of water lapping on the shore and the sight of this lovely Victorian house will add to guests' anticipation of a perfect stay. The hotel has just 21 guest rooms, all filled with a melange of antiques and country furniture, patchwork quilts and cushions adding colour. Six rooms in the main inn, seven are in the Carriage House and others are in four guest cottages behind the Inn with their own decks overlooking the Lake. Several of the cottages have double whirlpool baths. The lounge at the foot of the elegant staircase is the focal point of The Boulders, where guests gather for apéritifs. The big sofas are in American Buffalo, the polished floors gleam and charming ornaments add a personal touch. Residents change for dinner as it is a memorable occasion, for not only has the restaurant won much acclaim for its imaginative interpretation of New England dishes, but the wine list has also won many awards. The Inn has its own beach, a private trail to Pinnacle Mountain, its own boats and canoes, bikes, a games room and skating on the lake in winter. Golf, riding, antique hunting and exploring nearby villages are alternative activities.

Directions: From New Milford, Rt. 202 to New Preston, turning left onto Route 45 to Boulders Inn.

Web: www.johansens.com/bouldersinn
E-mail: boulders@bouldersinn.com
Tel: 1 860 868 0541
Fax: 1 860 868 1925

Price Guide: Upon application

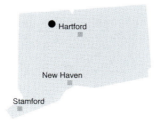

Our inspector loved: The view of the lake from the living room, matched only by the exquisite furnishing and decor of this wonderful room.

NEW ENGLAND / CONNECTICUT - OLD MYSTIC

THE OLD MYSTIC INN

52 MAIN STREET, OLD MYSTIC, CONNECTICUT 06372-0733

Directions: Two miles north of Mystic.

Web: www.johansens.com/oldmysticinn
E-mail: omysticinn@aol.com
Tel: 1 860 572 9422
Fax: 1 860 572 9954

Price Guide: (incl. tax rooms $128–$196)

Built in 1784, this picturesque historic inn, which used to be the Old Mystic Bookshop, offers a truly warm welcome to its guests. It has been carefully transformed to provide a comfortable stay, preserving much of its old charm, which blends perfectly with modern day conveniences. A carriage house was built in 1988 to provide additional accommodation. The Old Mystic Inn is the ideal place to unwind and soak up the peaceful surroundings. Guests can enjoy a lazy afternoon in a hammock under a huge maple tree, while the common rooms provide a cosy setting at all times; one of them is warmed by a crackling fireplace during the colder months. Each of the eight comfortable and individually designed bedrooms is named after a New England author; all rooms are en suite and have queen-sized beds; six have fireplaces and two feature whirlpool tubs. One of the inn's highlights is the sumptuous country breakfast, prepared by your host, Michael Cardillo, graduate of the Culinary School of America. It is served in a candlelit and welcoming breakfast room and might include special dishes such as scrambled eggs with fine herbs and banana-stuffed French toast with warm maple pecan syrup. Mystic with its numerous shops, museums and restaurants is just minutes away, whilst Foxwoods, the world's largest casino, is within easy driving distance.

Our inspector loved: *The tucked away setting in a very convenient location.*

West Lane Inn

22 WEST LANE, RIDGEFIELD, CONNECTICUT 06877

This is a charming and truly splendid inn conveniently situated in an historic town, a region considered to be one of the most treasured in all of Connecticut. Its buildings are architecturally superb, its open spaces wonderfully tranquil, its cultural venues marvellous and its entertainment, leisure and shopping facilities of the highest standard. The Inn is as attractive inside as it looks from the outside. The special thoughtfulness of its intimacy lies in both the décor and the commitment of a friendly and attentive staff. A welcoming, relaxing ambience with sophisticated overtones, charm and character are its hallmarks. Magnificent highly polished wood panelling combines delightfully with a wealth of period details and sumptuous furnishings. There is elegance at every turn with original style blending impressively with the best of 21st century facilities and amenities. Bedrooms are extremely comfortable and luxuriously decorated and appointed. Each has one or two queen size beds, individual climate control, colour television and telephone. All have private baths. Some have open fireplaces for cosiness and warmth on chilly nights. Guests start the day hearty breakfasts in a bright and cheery room and excellent lunches and dinners are available if required. There are a number of good restaurants nearby and golf, tennis and walking routes are just minutes away.

Directions: From the Merritt Pkwy. Take route 35 south.

Web: www.johansens.com/westlaneinn
Tel: 1 203 438 7323
Fax: 1 203 438 7325

Price Guide:
rooms $145
suites $195

Our inspector loved: The wicker front porch it's so relaxing.

BLACKBERRY INN
82 ELM STREET, CAMDEN, MAINE 04843

Blackberry Inn is Maine's only 'Painted Lady' as recognised by the editors of 'Daughters of Painted Ladies: America's Resplendent Victorians' and has in the past welcomed esteemed guests such as Bette Davis during filming of the movie 'Peyton Place.' The Inn's exterior features distinctively coloured clapboards and grand bay-windows, while inside its 3 beautifully decorated public rooms include original mouldings reminiscent of wedding cake designs on the breakfast room walls, ornately painted tin ceilings and a fine collection of oriental rugs. Light, airy bedrooms also reflect the grace and elegance of the Victorian era but incorporate modern facilities such as en suite bathrooms, cable television and air conditioning. 3 newly furnished and well-appointed suites in the Carriage House have sinks from the Sheepscott potters. Outside, guests can relax and socialise in the lovely gardens, which of course boast a large blackberry patch. Owner Jim creates mouth-watering breakfasts such as buttermilk waffles with maple syrup or herb baked eggs and fresh muffins, while wife Cyndi takes care of the gardens and the Inn's special touches. Camden, with its harbour shops, galleries, restaurants and boat trips to nearby islands is just a walk away and in winter, skiing and tobogganing are available nearby.

Directions: Exit 24 off I-95, Route 196E to Route 1N left onto Route 90 in Waldoboro, left onto Route 1 in Rockport.

Web: www.johansens.com/blackberryinn
E-mail: blkberry@midcoast.com
Tel: 1 207 236 6060
Fax: 1 207 236 9032

Price Guide:
rooms $85–$175
suites $145–$225

Our inspector loved: The romantic gardens.

CAMDEN MAINE STAY

22 HIGH STREET, CAMDEN, MAINE 04843

Camden Maine Stay is a grand old home, perfectly situated for those who prefer to stay in the centre of town close to good shopping, with excellent restaurants and easy access to the waterfront. A former early 19th century progressive farm building, it stands regally in Camden's historic district with an attractive white frontage being highlighted by a magnificent pillared entrance. Now a prestigious bed and breakfast Inn consisting of a main house, attached carriage house and four-story barn, Maine Stay provides a relaxed, cosy and friendly atmosphere. The delightful sunporch overlooks the surrounding 2 acres of magnificently landscaped grounds on which hearty breakfasts of home-baked goods, egg dishes, waffles, french toast or pancakes can be enjoyed. Alternatively, guests can be served at an antique harvest table in the dining room. They are always welcome to visit the kitchen and can raid the cookie jar without feeling they are imposing. Two parlours with wood burning stoves are tastefully decorated with oriental rugs and period pieces. The Inn's 8 themed bedrooms are beautifully decorated and have an eclectic collection of furnishings that include wonderful old beds, 4 of the rooms are warmed by gas fires. Sailing, kayaking, walking, cycling and windjammer cruising lead the list of local activities.

Our inspector loved: *The delightful sunporch where breakfast is served.*

Directions: Exit 24 off I95 N to Rt 196E to Rt 1 N. Left on 90 in Waldboro. Left on Rt1 in Rockport.

Web: www.johansens.com/camdenmainestay
E-mail: innkeeper@camdenmainestay.com
Tel: 1 207 236 9636
Fax: 1 207 236 0621

Price Guide:
rooms $105–$195

NEW ENGLAND / MAINE - CAMDEN

HARTSTONE INN

41 ELM STREET, CAMDEN, MAINE, 04843

Directions: I95 exit 24, Route 196E to Route 1N left onto Route 90 in Waldoboro. Left on Route 1 in Rockport.

Web: www.johansens.com/harstoneinn
E-mail: info@hartstoneinn.com
Tel: 1 207 236 4259
Fax: 1 207 236 9575

Price Guide:
rooms $115–$225

This is one of Camden's grandest historic homes, famed for its comfort, friendliness, fine dining and collection of orchids cultivated by Mary Jo Salmon who owns and runs the inn with her husband, award-winning chef Michael. Her prime blooming specimens adorn the front parlour. Built in 1835, the architecturally splendid Hartstone Inn is an enchanting, Mansard-style Victorian hideaway in the heart of Camden, perfectly situated for those who prefer staying in the middle of town close to good shopping and with easy access to the waterfront. Beyond the hotel's pillared entranceway is a quiet world of peace, charm and elegance with rooms sprinkled with period antiques, family heirlooms and interesting collections creating a romantic atmosphere. Each guest room is en suite, air-conditioned and decorated and furnished to a high standard. Some feature wood-burning fireplaces, four-poster and Queen-size, lace canopy beds jacuzzi's. Three spacious suites at the rear of the inn have private entrances and outdoor patios. Chef Michael is famed for his New England cuisine, beautifully presented on the inn's porch or in the elegant dining room. Creative menus feature the freshest seafood and 5-course dinners change to reflect the seasons.

Our inspector loved: The exquisite dining experience.

THE LODGE AT MOOSEHEAD LAKE
UPON LILY BAY ROAD, BOX 1167, GREENVILLE, MAINE 04441

The North Woods of Maine have a rugged beauty, dense forests, and more moose than anywhere else in New England. The Lodge is typical Cape Cod colonial, in brown shingle. The façade may be rustic, the interior is not. Sonda and Bruce Hamilton have great style – their imaginative use of colour, light, raw materials and local folklore has created a friendly ambience with sophisticated overtones. The spectacular views over the lake are focus points. The guest rooms have handcarved Queen-sized beds, with individual themes. They are all luxuriously appointed and every bathroom has a Jacuzzi. Attention to detail includes concealed television and full ice-buckets! Guests recount their day over drinks in the charismatic Great Room, adjacent to the charming dining room which has a wall of windows overlooking the shimmering water. There is also a minute Library, the snug Toby Room and colourful Moosehead Games Room. Breakfast is a small feast, dinner a candlelit gastronomic experience. One of the most popular activities is a 3-hour guided "Moose Safaris" aboard the Discovery on Moosehead Lake. Other activities include fly fishing, canoeing, seaplane expeditions, exploring national parks, and winter sports when the snows come.

Our inspector loved: *That you know you're in Maine.*

Directions: Interstate 95N to Newport then Route 7 North, then Route 23 North to Route 15 North.

Web: www.johansens.com/lodgeatmooseheadlake
E-mail: innkeeper@lodgeatmooseheadlake.com
Tel: 1 207 695 4400
Fax: 1 207 695 2281

Price Guide:
rooms $185–$350
suites $250–$425

THE CAPTAIN LORD MANSION

6 PLEASANT STREET, KENNEBUNKPORT, MAINE 04046-0800

Built in 1812 by wealthy shipbuilder Nathaniel Lord, the Captain Lord Mansion is as impressive today as it was then and is listed on the National Register of Historic Places. It is beautifully situated within manicured grounds and has the most gracious and welcoming of entrance halls, as well as enveloping and cosy public rooms. The hotel lies just three short blocks from Dock Square, where there are many charming art galleries, restaurants, boutiques and gift shops; and just two miles further is Kennebunkport, Maine's quintessential fishing village. This is a great place for seafood lovers, the freshly caught and boiled lobster is something every visitor should try! The hotel has been thoughtfully designed and appointed with the owners' love of antiques very much in evidence, each bedroom has its own unique blend of character and style. The curtains and bedspreads are all made by the owner herself, and the elegant bathrooms have the ultimate luxury of heated floor tiles! Breakfasts are a source of great pride at the Captain Lord, and make a hearty start to day's sightseeing at the Rachel Carson wildlife preserve or L.L.Bean, the home of President George Bush.

Directions: I-95N to exit 3, Left onto RT9 east, right on to Ocean Avenue, left onto Green Street.

Web: www.johansens.com/captainlordmansion
E-mail: innkeeper@captainlord.com
Tel: 1 207 967 3141

Price Guide:
rooms $99–$349
suites $269–$399

Our inspector loved: The gracious public areas.

GREENVILLE INN

PO BOX 1194, NORRIS STREET, GREENVILLE, MAINE 04441

Once inside this delightful inn visitors are transported to an era of elegance, charm, friendly service and traditional luxury living. Built for a timber baron in 1895, Greenville Inn rises majestically above manicured gardens overlooking Moosehead Lake and the distant Squaw Mountains. It has been beautifully restored and refurbished with modern comforts that combine excellently with period pieces. A large spruce tree painted on a leaded glass window highlights the stairway landing, stunning panelling adorns the public rooms, and Tiffany lamps from 1910 can be found throughout. There are open fireplaces, comfortable chairs and wicker furniture, and porches from which to savour the views over morning coffee or cocktails prior to enjoying superb cuisine in either of two candle-lit dining rooms. Guests have a choice of four individually appointed en suite bedrooms, a Master Suite with king-size bed, lake views and sitting room with fireplace, a Carriage House Suite with queen-size and full-size bed, sitting area, woodstove and private deck, or one of the inn's cottages surrounded by gardens and woods. Leisure activities include moose safaris, canoeing, fly-fishing and boating on the lake.

Our inspector loved: *The magnificent Tiffany lamps dating back to 1910.*

Directions: I-95 North to Newport (exit 39) then Route 7/11 north to Dexter, Route 23 north to Sangerville, then Route 15 north to Greenville. 2nd street on the right after flashing traffic light is Norris Street.

Web: www.johansens.com/greenvilleinn
E-mail: gvlinn@moosehead.net
Tel: 1 207 695 2206
Fax: 1 207 695 0335

Price Guide:
rooms $135–$195
suites $175–$255

NEW ENGLAND / MAINE - NEWCASTLE

The Newcastle Inn

60 RIVER ROAD, NEWCASTLE, MAINE 04553

Directions: I295N to Brunswick, Rt1N (25 miles). Right on River Road, ½ mile to the Inn.

Web: www.johansens.com/newcastleinn
E-mail: innkeep@newcastleinn.com
Tel: 1 207 563 5685
Fax: 1 207 563 6877
US Toll Free: 1 800 832 8669

Price Guide:
rooms $125–$300

This is an attractive- country inn renowned for its wonderfully relaxing atmosphere, ambience, charm, cuisine and the attentive, welcoming hospitality of owners Rebecca and Howard Levitan. It is an unpretentious and traditional New England country inn situated in an idyllic setting overlooking the Damariscotta River. The interior is beautifully decorated and furnished with modern comforts, complemented by fine antiques and sumptuous fabrics. Guests have a choice of 15 individually styled and uniquely furnished en suite bedrooms that provide every home comfort. Some are in an adjoining carriage house, several have fireplaces and many have river outlooks. 2 elegant dining rooms offer an intimate, fireside experience of savouring 4 star gourmet cuisine accompanied by an extensive wine list. There is a cosy living room in which to relax over a pre-dinner drink or to enjoy reading a book from the Inn's fabulous collection. A popular common room has an exquisite stencilled floor. Summer days and evenings can be delightfully whiled away and the perennial gardens viewed from a wicker chair or couch in the Sun Porch or on its deck. Among places of interest in this quiet corner of Maine's Mid Coast are lighthouse-crowned ocean points, islands in the bay and authentic seaside villages.

Our inspector loved: The picture-perfect setting.

CAPTAIN LINDSEY HOUSE
5 LINDSEY STREET, ROCKLAND, MAINE 04841

In 1832 Captain George Lindsey fired the bricks for his home that five years later, he then turned into the town's oldest inn. Today it still has the warm and inviting atmosphere that it had then, offering guests a rare combination of modern day comforts combined with the owner's personal collection of antiques from around the world. The parlour is particularly evocative with deep down-filled sofas, rich plaids and roaring fires; whilst the library snug has a fascinating collection of books as well as a chess game always laid ready to fill the idle moment. The charming breakfast room, known as the Scottish Snug, has been lovingly restored with elegant oak panelling, and it is here that breakfast is served in the winter months, or alternatively in summer on the terrace. There is much to see and do in the area, the famous Farnsworth Museum is within walking distance, and the Shore Village Lighthouse Museum and Owls Head Transportation Museum are also nearby. There are numerous shops, galleries and antiques centres within a stone's throw, and for the more adventurous there is kayaking, hiking, skiing and windjammer cruises, as well as ferry trips to the offshore islands.

Our inspector loved: *The parlour.*

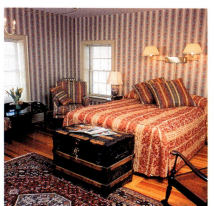

Directions: I-95N, Exit 22. Coastal Route 1N to Rockland. Lindsey Street is off Main Street.

Web: www.johansens.com/captainlindsey
E-mail: lindsey@midcoast.com
Tel: 1 207 596 7950
Fax: 1 207 596 2758

Price Guide:
rooms $120–$175

A CAMBRIDGE HOUSE

2218 MASSACHUSETTS AVENUE, CAMBRIDGE, MASSACHUSETTS 02140–1836

A Cambridge House is a most prestigious Inn offering impeccable service. The house is glorious, Colonial revival built in 1892 and its fin de siècle grace has been meticulously restored. This is a most superior bed and breakfast establishment, nothing but the best clearly being the rule (also no smoking) The guest rooms are exquisite, delicately patterned papers and fragile toiles, lots of cushions and bolsters, period furniture, porcelain ornaments and fresh flowers all creating a romantic ambience. Breakfast is a nourishing experience served early for professional guests and later for those on vacation – fresh fruits and/or seductive pastries, and also waffles/omelettes cooked to order for those who want it. Every evening, distinguished guests gather in the parlour, an elegant room filled with burnished antiques and gleaming silver, relaxing over delicious fresh hors d'oeuvres, with jazz playing quietly in the background. Both Boston and Cambridge have excellent restaurants, famous universities, a busy waterfront, harbour cruises, galleries, theatres, bookstores, museums and diverse sporting facilities not too far away.

Directions: The hotel has a parking lot – Boston's airport is 20 minutes away. The rapid transit subway is recommended for visitors heading for campuses or financial and high technology districts.

Web: www.johansens.com/cambridgehouse
E-mail: InnACH@aol.com
Tel: 1 617 491 6300
Fax: 1 617 868 2848

Price Guide:
rooms $129–$275

Our inspector loved: All the trimmings of a bygone era.

THE CHARLES STREET INN
94 CHARLES STREET, BOSTON, MASSACHUSETTS 02114-4643

This is a charming inn conveniently situated in the heart of Beacon Hill just 2 1/2 blocks from the Boston Public Garden and subway and a 10 minutes cab ride from the airport. It has an elegant facade featuring small, neat decorative windows and two really beautiful overhanging bedroom bow windows. Inside is elegance and luxury. Built in 1860 as a 'Model Home', the Inn has been extensively and sympathetically renovated and refurbished to preserve and enhance its original style while combining the very best in 20th century facilities and amenities. There are nine superb guest rooms decorated and furnished in exquisite Victoria style, complete with King or Queen-size four poster or canopy beds, linen presses, authentic period pieces, working marble fireplaces and plaster ceiling medallions. Each room is named after a famous Boston writer or artist and holds literature about the rooms. Some have rooftop views, all have luxury cherry wood and white tile bathrooms and fittings which include extra large whirlpool tub, sub-zero refrigerator, two-line phone service with voice mail, fax, DSL Internet access, radio/CD, cable television and VCR, safe, minibar and coffeemaker. Owners Louise Venden and Sally Deane provide warm and attentive service and set guests off on a day's shopping, touring or exploring with an excellent breakfast

Directions: Leave I93 at Storrow Drive exit and follow signs to Charles Street/Government Centre

Web: www.johansens.com/charlesstreetinn
Tel: 1 617 314 8900
US toll free: 877 772 8900
Fax: 1 617 371 0009

Price Guide:
rooms $250–$340

Our inspector loved: This little gem in the centre of Old Boston.

NEW ENGLAND / MASSACHUSETTS - BOSTON

THE LENOX HOTEL

710 BOYLSTON STREET, BOSTON, MASSACHUSETTS 02116-2699

Directions: One block from Massachusetts Turnpike Exit 22, Copley Square. Shuttle service from hotel to Logan Int'l Airport.

Web: www.johansens.com/lenox
Tel: 1 617 536 5300
US Toll Free: 1 800 225 7676
Fax: 1 617 236 0351

Price Guide:
rooms $284–428
suites $508–$695

Since opening in 1900, The Lenox has been synonymous with elitism, style and luxury. A Who's Who of the famous, from opera singer Enrico Caruso and former President George Bush to film stars Judy Garland, John Travolta and Kenneth Branagh, have driven up to its terra cotta brick exterior and entered into the lavish interior. Sympathetic modernisation has taken place over the past century, and today this AAA Four Diamond, award-winning Back Bay hotel is the epitome of personal attention, understated elegance and the quiet, intimate atmosphere of a boutique-style establishment. Standing 11 storeys high at the corner of Boylston and Exeter Streets in Copley Square, The Lenox is within walking distance of Boston's finest shops, attractions and business area. All en suite guest rooms and suites, blending old world charm with 21st-century amenities, are equipped with the luxuries expected from a hotel of this caliber, and a few you may not, such as fireplaces found in 12 of the rooms. Acclaimed 4-Star chef Robert Fathman holds court with superb dinner cuisine in the Azure restaurant, whilst the Solas Irish Pub offers more casual dinners and lunches. There is a fully equipped fitness centre and valet parking.

Our inspector loved: The handpainted ceiling in the lobby and the great location to downtown Boston.

THE CAPTAIN'S HOUSE INN

369–377 OLD HARBOR ROAD, CHATHAM, CAPE COD, MASSACHUSETTS 02633

What better name for a fine hotel in Chatham, still a busy port today with yachtsmen, private craft and its fishing fleet. Captain Harding, a famous sailor in the 1800s, built this graceful white neo-classic home and some guest rooms are named after the ships he skippered. The inn, surrounded by splendid old trees, is peaceful and secluded. The interior has period wallpapers, Queen Anne chairs, Williamsburg antiques and Oriental rugs on polished floors – a grand country house ambience with a no smoking rule. The guest quarters are extremely comfortable and wonderfully different, each with its own elegant Colonial style. Luxurious suites are in the Carriage House beyond the English Garden, The Stables, or the romantic Captain's Cottage. Disabled travellers have not been forgotten. The dining room is exquisite with floor length windows, hanging plants and pristine linen. A delicious breakfast starts the day; a full English afternoon tea appears at 4 o'clock. The friendly hosts have a list of recommended restaurants for dinner. The Inn has a croquet lawn and outdoor swimming pool. Chatham has its fascinating harbour, a Friday night band, sailing, fishing, galleries, golf and glorious sunsets.

Our inspector loved: *The opportunity to enjoy good old traditional comfort.*

Directions: Route 28 to Chatham Centre, continuing towards Orleans. After 1/2 mile the Inn is on the left.

Web: www.johansens.com/captainshouse
E-mail: info@captainshouseinn.com
Tel: 1 508 945 0127
Fax: 1 508 945 0866

Price Guide:
rooms $235–$350
suite $235–$425

NEW ENGLAND / MASSACHUSETTS - CAPE COD

WEDGEWOOD INN

83 MAIN STREET, ROUTE 6A, YARMOUTH PORT, MASSACHUSETTS 02675

Directions: Interstate 3, over Sagamore Bridge on Route 6, exit 7, turning right, at halt sign right onto Route 6A, finding Inn 75yds on right.

Web: www.johansens.com/wedgewoodmassachusetts
E-mail: info@wedgewood-inn.com
Tel: 1 508 362 5157
Fax: 1 508 362 5851

Price Guide:
rooms $135–$225

Yarmouth Port flourished in Cape Cod in the 19th century, and Main Street, the most fashionable street in this historic town, is the address of the Wedgewood Inn, a fine colonial house built in 1812. The mansion is lovely, with its white façade, green shutters and graceful lines, and stands in formal gardens, ablaze with chrysanthemums in the Autumn. The interior is faultless – polished floors, attractive wall coverings, colourful rugs, nautical prints, comfortable chairs, flowers and intriguing bibelots. The lounges have a warm elegance. The three stunning guest rooms in the modern extension, the Carriage Barn, are romantic with traditional quilts, wooden bedsteads and luxurious bathrooms. Some have garden patios and others a private, sheltered terrace. In winter the aroma of burning wood fires adds to the joy of staying here. Breakfast and afternoon tea are served in the sunny dining room, but the Inn does not have a licence – residents should 'bring their own', and hosts Milt & Gerrie Graham will suggest where to dine in the evenings. Guests enjoy the beaches, swim, fish, sail, play golf and tennnis, explore the Cape on bikes and hunt for antiques. Nantucket and Martha's Vineyard are close by.

Our inspector loved: The wonderfully warm welcome extended to guests by Milt & Gerrie Graham.

THE WHALEWALK INN

220 BRIDGE ROAD, EASTHAM (CAPE COD), MASSACHUSETTS 02642

Whales have always had an important role in Cape Cod and this prestigious 1830's mansion was built by one of the famous Whaling Masters. It is set in the unspoiled Outer Cape, near the 40 mile long National Seashore. Owners, Kevin and Elaine Conlin, welcome their guests to this distinguished house, in which authentic 19th century antiques and Waterford Crystal abound and meticulous attention to detail is evident. The romantic guest rooms are immaculate and inviting, with delicate drapes in soft colours. All are light and airy and the luxurious suites have charming sitting rooms. Guests relax on the colourful patio or in the pleasant sitting room, which has original contemporary paintings hung on the walls. Breakfast is an inspired feast, "put your diet on vacation" is one of the Inn's maxims, although the light repast is equally delicious. The Inn is unlicensed but hors d'oeuvres are served each evening. Good places to dine are nearby. Residents are able to watch whales, follow the nature trails, explore the sandy beaches and salt marshes, swim, sail, bike through the lovely countryside, play golf and tennis, hunt antiques or visit Martha's Vineyard, a nearby island.

Our inspector loved: This Cape Cod Inn close to the national seashore.

Directions: Having crossed Sagamore Bridge, follow Route 6 past exit 12 to the Orleans rotary. Take the third exit onto Rock Harbour Road, find Bridge Road on the right and watch for Whalewalk Inn sign, also on the right.

Web: www.johansens.com/whalewalkinn
E-mail: information@whalewalkinn.com
Tel: 1 508 255 0617
Fax: 1 508 240 0017

Price Guide:
rooms $175–$300
suite $255–$300

NEW ENGLAND / MASSACHUSETTS - DEERFIELD

DEERFIELD INN
81 OLD MAIN STREET, DEERFIELD, MASSACHUSETTS 01342-0305

Directions: Exits 24/25/26 from Interstate 91, then routes 5 and 10, marked to Historic Deerfield

Web: www.johansens.com/deerfieldinn
E-mail: frontdesk@deerfieldinn.com
Tel: 1 413 774 5587
Fax: 1 413 775 7221

Price Guide:
rooms $128–$241

Step back in time and stay in this select country inn in the centre of Deerfield, a three hundred years old New England village, nominated a National Historic Landmark. The Inn is an enchanting, classical building with its tall pillars and balcony over the entrance. The drawing rooms are elegant, with lovely curtains draped round the tall sash windows, yielding sofas and chairs and old rugs. The guest rooms are gorgeous – decorated in soft colours, with antique wooden bedsteads. Some are in the South Wing, reached by a covered walkway. All are wondrously peaceful and inviting. The host, Karl Sabo, trained as a chef, also has a great interest in wines, which is displayed in the renowned restaurant, an exquisite room with graceful chandeliers and authentic period furniture. Breakfast is generous, country-style and dinner is by candlelight. The menu is cosmopolitan New American and the cellar houses some great vintages. Non-smoking prevails throughout the Inn. Deerfield is ideal for discreet strategy meetings and magical for special celebrations. The fourteen 'museum' dwellings in the village should be visited. Nearby golf, tennis, hiking, cycling, and white water rafting occupy athletic residents; others may go antique hunting.

Our inspector loved: The atmosphere of the unique historic village of Deerfield.

NEW ENGLAND / MASSACHUSETTS - LENOX

WHEATLEIGH

HAWTHORNE ROAD, LENOX, MASSACHUSETTS 01240

Wheatleigh is the perfect marriage of the grandeur of a 16th-century Florentine palazzo with the elegance and comfort of the 21st century. Set within 22 acres overlooking the Berkshire mountains and lakes, this enchanting country house hotel is 2½ hours by car from New York City and Boston. Built in 1893, Wheatleigh has completed a 4-year, multimillion dollar renovation to create this unique, luxurious small hotel. The 19 suites, guest rooms and baths set a new standard of style and sophistication, exquisitely combining antique and custom furnishings with original museum quality contemporary art. The internationally renowned dining room offers a striking contemporary interpretation of classic French cuisine, an award-winning wine list and the highest level of service. The Library provides an intimate lounge for cocktails, lunch and dinner. Wheatleigh has a state-of-the-art fitness centre, heated outdoor pool, tennis and massage facilities. Golf is five minutes away, whilst hiking, biking, riding fishing, skiing and hot air ballooning are available nearby. The hotel is within walking distance to Tanglewood, summer home of the Boston Symphony Orchestra. The area is known for its vast array of cultural attractions, art, antiques, jewellery and speciality shops.

Our inspector loved: The thrill of a Florentine palazzo in the heart of the Berkshires.

Directions: Route 183 leads to Lenox.

Web: www.johansens.com/wheatleigh
Tel: 1 413 637 0610
Fax: 1 413 637 4507

Price Guide:
rooms $425–$1400

95

NEW ENGLAND / MASSACHUSETTS - MARBLEHEAD

THE HARBOR LIGHT INN

58 WASHINGTON STREET, MARBLEHEAD, MASSACHUSETTS 01945

Directions: Located approximately 15 miles north of Boston and within 15 miles of Rte I-95 and Rte 128.

Web: www.johansens.com/harborlightinn
Tel: 1 781 631 2186
Fax: 1 781 631 2216

Price Guide:
rooms $150–$275

The Inn stands in the heart of one of the few remaining seacoast towns along historic Massachusetts Bay's North Shore; a grand and dramatic setting. The Harbor Light reflects this with its distinct character, charm and the tranquil atmosphere of a bygone era. It is reminiscent of a slower, more gentle and less hectic time. The sun's rays, through small paned windows highlight deep rich Oriental carpets covering mellowglow pine floors, glint-off sparkling chandeliers and brasswork and accentuate lovely hand-carvings, finely tooled furnishings, paintings, etchings and prints. Each guest room is an individual delight, beautifully decorated, exquisitely furnished and with every modern day facility. There are four poster beds, magnificent open fireplaces, double tubs, and beamed ceilings, every luxury the discerning visitor could wish for. One room even has a private deck that provides superb panoramic viewing over sea and harbour. Excellent, freshly baked breakfasts send guests fulfilled and happily away on excursions, tours and explorations of the countryside and coastline or for leisurely beach relaxation or active water sports. The Harbor Light is within walking distance of the harbour, antique and speciality shops, art galleries and a wide range of restaurants. Available to corporate clients for midweek meetings.

Our inspector loved: *The sumptuous home-baked Continental breakfasts served in the elegant breakfast room.*

HOB KNOB INN

128 MAIN STREET, PO BOX 239, EDGARTOWN, MASSACHUSETTS 02539

The Hob Knob Inn takes its name from the owners' grandparents, the "Knob" being the hill upon which their country estate in Ohio was sited and the "Hob" standing for the initials of its matriarch figure Helen Osborne Bruch. It is a piece of detail that illustrates the care and attention that has been given to establishing this pretty gothic revival style home as one of the key hotels on the island. Once, just the summer retreat for the rich and famous (John F. Kennedy has sought shelter at the Hob Knob), Martha's Vineyard is rapidly becoming a popular destination during spring and autumn, where the days are warm and sunny and the nights just cool enough to enjoy a drink by the fireside. The Inn has just 20 guest bedrooms, each with a vast bed and beautifully decorated with English chintz, cotton linens, down comforters and pillows. These rooms either overlook the Inn's pretty gardens or across into Edgartown with its quintessentially New England clapboard façades. Food is also given careful consideration at the Hob Knob and the full farm breakfasts are legendary, as are the delightful afternoon teas; freshly baked scones and home-made preserves are served on the spacious porch accompanied by pitchers of fresh frosty lemonade. Those guests who choose to go aboard the Inn's Boston Whaler may also have their catch specially grilled for their evening dinner!

Directions: Located in the heart of Edgartown. 10 minutes from Martha's Vineyard airport..

Web: www.johansens.com/hobknobinn
E-mail: hobknob@hobknob.com
Tel: 1 508 627 9510
Fax: 1 508 627 4560
US Toll Free: 1 800 696 2723

Price Guide:
rooms $225–$550 (in season)
rooms $125–$350 (off season)

Our inspector loved: The sunny interior of the Inn.

NEW ENGLAND / MASSACHUSETTS - MARTHA'S VINEYARD

Thorncroft Inn

460 MAIN STREET, PO BOX 1022, VINEYARD HAVEN, MASSACHUSETTS 02568

A welcome addition to the Guide's Massachusetts family of properties is this pretty Martha's Vineyard Inn. A perfect vacation spot, the Inn is situated just out of town and set in 3 acres of secluded, wooded grounds. Its 2 restored houses comprise of 14 antique furnished guest rooms each with its own private bathroom and some boast 2 person jacuzzis or hot tubs. Romantic canopied four poster beds and a discreet evening turndown service are available and working fireplaces can be used all year round. Real wood is provided and guests simply add logs when needed although staff are always on hand to assist. Each morning the Boston Globe newspaper is delivered to the door and a full country breakfast is served in 2 intimate dining rooms. Continental breakfast in bed can be requested while those seeking further retreat can find it in the private guest cottage. Thorncroft Inn is not an appropriate setting for young children or large groups and is strictly non-smoking but is particularly ideal for honeymooners or for those celebrating anniversaries and engagements. Bicycle and car hire can be arranged locally and the Island's ferries to Nantucket and Cape Cod operate nearby.

Directions: From Vineyard Haven ferry, go left onto Water Street. Take the next right then the first right onto Main Street, the Hotel is one mile up on the left.

Web: www.johansens.com/thorncroftinn
E-mail: innkeeper@thorncroft.com
Tel: 1 508 693 3333
Fax: 1 508 693 5419

Price Guide:
rooms $180–$550

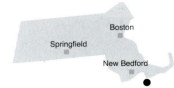

Our inspector loved: The personalised check-in given to guests, planning their holiday with them.

THE VICTORIAN INN
24 SOUTH WATER STREET, EDGARTOWN, MASSACHUSETTS 02539

The picturesque Victorian Inn is one of the most elegant buildings in an island community awash with architectural splendour. Justifiably listed in the National Register of Historic Places, it stands majestically on the South Water Street where many early 19th-century sea captains built their mansions. The Victorian itself was once the home of a whaling captain, Laffayette Rowley, and reflects the charm, style and grandeur of his era. Voted 'Best B&B on Martha's Vineyard' 1996-2002 consecutively by readers of Cape Cod Life Magazine, it offers comfort, hospitality, relaxation and the highest standards of service. Each bedroom with either twin, double, canopied, queen or king-sized bed is spacious, tastefully decorated and furnished with cherished antiques. Several offer private decks or balconies with views of the harbour or the English garden framed with a picket fence. The Inn's award-winning gourmet breakfast and excellent, complimentary afternoon tea are served in a delightful breakfast room or in the garden. Edgartown's fine shops, restaurants, galleries, museums, and the sands and watersports of Lighthouse Beach are just a short walk away. Golf, tennis and riding are also close by. Smoking permitted only on the balconies and porches.

Our inspector loved: Being so close to Edgartown with it's wonderful shops, galleries & restaurants.

Directions: From Vineyard Haven Dock take the Edgartown/Vineyard Haven Road south to Edgartown for 6.5 miles.

Web: www.johansens.com/victorianinn
E-mail: victorianinn@vineyard.net
Tel: 1 508 627 4784

Price Guide:
rooms $180–$385

NEW ENGLAND / MASSACHUSETTS - NANTUCKET

The Pineapple Inn
10 HUSSEY STREET, NANTUCKET, MASSACHUSETTS 02554

Directions: Just a few minutes from the Steamship Authority Ferries.

Web: www.johansens.com/pineappleinn
E-mail: info@pineappleinn.com
Tel: 1 508 228 9992
Fax: 1 508 325 6051

Price Guide:
rooms $185–$325

Whaling has always had an important role here and this stylish Inn is an authentic 1838 whaling captain's house. Nantucket is recognised by many as a town of tasteful, refined and understated elegance and The Pineapple reflects this. The Inn is ideally located in a narrow lane, in the historic district, 4 blocks from the ferry docks and just a short walk to some excellent shops and restaurants. Resident hosts, Caroline and Bob Taylor, offer the friendliest and warmest of welcomes to their Inn which has been subject to a 1 million dollar restoration and renovation programme. The upgraded property, complemented by the Taylors seasoned innkeeping skills has brought such critical acclaim as: 'The island's most elegant B&B,' from Yankee Magazine's Travel Guide to New England; 'Easily one of the best places to stay,' from Lonely Planet, New England and 'Nantucket's most comfortable and stylish B&B,' from New England's Best, 2002. Elegant furnishings and antiques abound and meticulous attention to detail is evident. Décor is superb and the guest rooms are immaculate and inviting. Each is named after a whaling captain and has every facility and comfort; from luxurious white marble bathroom and air conditioning to cable television and telephone with voice mail. The Taylors were formerly restauranteurs so their gourmet breakfast really is a treat.

Our inspector loved: The elegant marble bathrooms and the truly delightful Innkeepers.

Union Street Inn
7 UNION STREET, NANTUCKET, MASSACHUSETTS 02554

This great Inn, standing in a quiet residential area, just off Main Street, boasts historic Nantucket style. Built in about 1770, it has been completely restored and decorated to highlight its Colonial period charm and update all amenities. Guestrooms have air conditioning, private baths, original panelling, pine floors and are decorated with beautiful antique furniture and fittings. Many have canopied or four poster beds and half have wood-burning fireplaces. For extra comfort, the beds are made-up with Frette linens of 100 per cent Egyptian cotton and fluffy Pique-woven duvets complemented by opulent bathrobes and large, soft towels. A delicious home-cooked breakfast is enjoyed in the intimate dining room or at handsome tables on a shady garden patio beneath an ivy-covered hillside. The menu selection is extensive and includes French toast and sausages, apple cinnamon pancakes, croissants and fresh fruit. During the afternoon there are usually home-baked cookies or other goodies to sample. Owners Deborah Withrow and husband Ken, former manager of The Royalton in New York and Chicago's Ambassador East Hotel, are very welcoming and provide full concierge service. Nantucket's restaurants, museums, beaches and ferry services are comfortable walks away.

Our inspector loved: The combination of Nantucket charm and sophistication.

Directions: Union Street Inn is a short distance from the ferry terminal.

Web: www.johansens.com/unionstreetinn
E-mail: unioninn@nantucket.net
Tel: 1 508 228 9222
Fax: 1 508 325 0843
Price Guide:
rooms $195–$395

Seacrest Manor

99 MARMION WAY, ROCKPORT, MASSACHUSETTS 01966

Directions: From Boston, take the Interstate 93 north to Interstate 95 east. Then take State Route 128 east to Route 127 North into Rockport.

Web: www.johansens.com/seacrestmanor
Tel: 1 978 546 2211

Price Guide: (incl. breakfast and tea):
rooms $98–$180;

This historic building is situated in the heart of the charming hamlet of Rockport, a town dramatically perched on the Cape Ann peninsula in the north east of Massachusetts, commanding unbelievable views of the austere Atlantic Ocean. A small and intimate Inn, the Seacrest Manor is surrounded by a 2 acre sculpted garden and is stunningly positioned on a tree-lined residential shoreline drive. The Inn is reminiscent of a slower, less hectic era. Several of the comfortably decorated rooms have decks overlooking the tranquil grounds and the 'Twin Lights' lighthouses on Thatcher's Island in the ocean beyond. Described by "Town and Country" as one of the 'great American breakfasts,' these home-made meals are served in a very pleasant breakfast room with a crackling log fire illuminating dark mornings. Rockport is a positive haven for marine fanatics and maritime activities abound. Visitors can embark on whale watching cruises or view the spectacular coastline from a yacht. The Seacrest Manor can also organise deep-sea fishing and sea kayaking expeditions. The town is a hive of activity, with concerts and festivals celebrating the region's unique heritage all year around. If Rockport's many shops and restaurants are not enough, Boston is a mere hour's drive away.

Our inspector loved: Being in Rockport, surrounded by gardens and overlooking the Atlantic Ocean.

CHESTERFIELD INN

ROUTE 9, PO BOX 155, CHESTERFIELD, NEW HAMPSHIRE 03443-0155

With breathtaking views over the Connecticut River Valley and the Green Mountains of Vermont, this delightful New England Inn nestles gently into the sweeping hillside and instantly evokes a sense of tranquillity and escapism. It is, however, extremely easy to reach, being less than 2 hours from Manchester, Boston and Hartford airports, minutes from route I-91 and a scenic drive from Brattleboro, Vermont and Keene, New Hampshire. With just 15 guest bedrooms, the sense of traditional charm is very much in evidence and is carefully blended with modern convenience. The dark oak beams and period furniture of the bedrooms are charmingly complemented by pretty floral wallcoverings and drapes; some rooms include wood-burning or gas fireplaces. The bathrooms contain deep and luxurious whirlpool baths and each room has its own sun deck or terrace from which to enjoy the dramatic views or take in the fragrance of the Inn's cottage gardens. It is here in the gardens that herbs are produced for use in the Inn's kitchens, whose team pride themselves on their contemporary and locally-produced cuisine. The dining room has views of the setting-sun over the mountains and with the sweetly- scented fresh flowers and intimate candlelight an extremely special atmosphere is created.

Our inspector loved: This wonderful location with views of the Connecticut River Valley.

Directions: The Inn is located between Brattleboro & Keene and is a 2 hour drive from Boston.

Web: www.johansens.com/chesterfieldinn
E-mail: chstinn@sover.net
Tel: 1 603 256 3211
Fax: 1 603 256 6131

Price Guide:
rooms $150–$275
suites $200–$225

THE MANOR ON GOLDEN POND

ROUTE 3, PO BOX T, HOLDERNESS, NEW HAMPSHIRE 03245

Directions: I-93 North to Exit 24, take Route 3 South for 4.7 miles.

Web: www.johansens.com/manorongoldenpond
E-mail: info@manorongoldenpond.com
Tel: 1 603 968 3348
Fax: 1 603 968 2116
US Toll Free: 1 800 545 2141

Price Guide:
rooms $175–$395

Built in the early 1900's this beautiful inn is situated in the Squam Lake area, backdrop of the famous movie 'On Golden Pond', starring Jane and Henry Fonda. The Manor and its 14 acre estate provides a stunning all year round location for relaxing breaks and romantic getaways; in summer the tranquillity of the lake can be enjoyed from the private sandy beach, in fall the brilliant colours of the surrounding trees are reflected in its clear waters, and in winter, skiing in the White Mountains is just 20 minutes away. Each individually named guest room reflects the Manor's English heritage and is decorated in a different theme using exquisite country furnishings. Many have superb views and wood burning fireplaces, while some feature a whirlpool tub big enough for two. Four o'clock tea is served in the library, living room or on the patio overlooking the Lake, and every evening unique New American cuisine and an award winning wine list are on offer in the relaxed yet elegant dining room. Other activities available in the region include hiking, ice fishing, golf and skating, while The Manor has its own delightful outdoor pool.

Our inspector loved: The unique decor in each exquisite bedroom.

NEW ENGLAND / NEW HAMPSHIRE - JACKSON

THE INN AT THORN HILL

THORN HILL ROAD, JACKSON VILLAGE, NEW HAMPSHIRE 03846

Jackson can only be reached through the 'Honeymoon Covered Bridge' – a delightful introduction to this enchanting village and the inn stands high above it, looking across to the dramatic Presidential Mountain Range. This idyllic retreat was built in 1895 and Victoriana is the theme throughout the Main Inn, with its lace curtains and fine antiques. The Parlour has a grand piano and board games, cards and books await guests' pleasure. The romantic guest rooms have old world charm and have been totally renovated and now feature gas fireplaces and spas. Other accommodation is country style in The Carriage House, while three recently renovated cottages offer more privacy. The cosy Bar resembles a small pub, alternatively residents relax in the charming lounges or settle in the wicker chairs on the porch overlooking the gardens and mountains. The restaurant is joyous, the aroma of marvellous home cooking pervading the air. Hungry diners appreciate the rich seasonal dishes, fabulous soups and glorious pastries, accompanied by fine wines. In summer the Inn has a pool; tennis, golf and riding are nearby. The Appalachian Mountain Club gives hikers and climbers good routes. In winter Jackson offers cross country and downhill skiing, skating and sleigh rides.

Our inspector loved: *The view from the Jacuzzi in the Presedential Suite, which overlooks the mountains.*

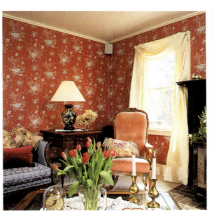

Directions: From Montreal, Can-10 to Can-55, I-91 to I-93, Exit 40, take Route 302 to Route 16 North to Jackson

Web: www.johansens.com/innatthornhill
E-mail: thornhll@ncia.net
Tel: 1 603 383 4242

Price Guide:
rooms $190–$345

105

NEW ENGLAND / RHODE ISLAND - BLOCK ISLAND

The Atlantic Inn

PO BOX 1788, BLOCK ISLAND, RHODE ISLAND 02807

This splendid Victorian inn stands on six acres of landscaped grounds overlooking the Atlantic Ocean and historic Old Harbour village. The views over the island's windswept bluffs, hollows and beaches are splendid, and the surrounds of rolling green lawns and colourful flowerbeds are exquisite and peaceful. Built in 1879 and owned by Brad and Anne Marthens since 1994, the Atlantic Inn is the ideal place to just laze around with the occasional exploration of countryside and seashore. The Marthens' hospitality is the most welcoming one can imagine. The 21 comfortable guest rooms are individually and tastefully decorated, many with period antiques and family heirlooms. Children are welcome (with supervision), and parents can relax on the verandah while watching their offspring enjoying the garden playhouse, a replica of the inn. There are also two all-weather tennis courts. Relaxed dining is enjoyed in the dining room; Chef Edward Moon's cuisine is considered the best in the region, and accompanied by wines from an extensive wine list. Local seafood predominates, whilst the inn's gardens provide many of the herbs and vegetables used. A fully-equipped conference room in a charming old outbuilding accommodates up to 30 delegates. Closed November–April.

Directions: By ferry from Point Judith, R1, New London, Connecticut, or Montauk, New York.

Web: www.johansens.com/atlanticinn
E-mail: atlanticinn@iebiri.com
Tel: 1 401 466 5883
Fax: 1 401 466 5678

Price Guide:
rooms/suites $130–$400

Our inspector loved: The view of the Atlantic Ocean from this splendid Victorian Inn.

NEW ENGLAND / RHODE ISLAND - NEWPORT

CLIFFSIDE INN

2 SEAVIEW AVENUE, NEWPORT, RHODE ISLAND 02840

In the 19th century East Coast tycoons built magnificent weekend retreats in fashionable Rhode Island. Today Newport is a major yachting centre. Cliffside Inn is the epitome of the style and grace of the late 19th century, standing on a tree lined avenue, close to the famous Cliff Walk and the Gilded Age mansions. The interior is sumptuous Victoriana – the spectacular carved stairway, the elaborate (and comfortable) sofas, the lamps and chandeliers, self portraits of the esteemed previous owner, painter Beatric Turner, adorning the walls, grand antique sideboards, even the plants in the patios and decks are evocative of that era. Past residents might not approve of the no-smoking regime, however. The guest rooms are glorious, wonderfully peaceful, romantic floral fabrics at the windows and covering the generous-sized beds. The opulent bathrooms are a joy! Three of the luxurious suites are in the adjoining delightful Seaview Cottage. A lavish breakfast is served and a fabulous Victorian tea is offered later in the day. There is no bar, but guests may bring their own beverages. Guests stroll along the cliffs, go to the beach, sail, play tennis, golf or fish nearby and explore Newport's fascinating old buildings and shops.

Our inspector loved: The delicious pastries and finger sandwiches, served on fine china on the porch in the afternoon.

Directions: Seaview Avenue is off Memorial Boulevard (Route 138). Abundant parking.

Web: www.johansens.com/cliffsideinn
E-mail: innkeeper@legendaryinnsofnewport.com
Tel: 1 401 847 1811
Fax: 1 401 848 5850
US Toll Free: 1 800 845 1811

Price Guide:
rooms $235–$325
suites $325–$495

NEW ENGLAND / RHODE ISLAND - NEWPORT

THE FRANCIS MALBONE HOUSE

392 THAMES STREET, NEWPORT, RHODE ISLAND 02840

Directions: Into Newport via the Sakonnet River or Newport Bridges. Once on Thames Street continue and turn left onto Brewer Street. Take the first right off of Brewer Street to park at the Inn.

Web: www.johansens.com/francismalbone
E-mail: innkeeper@malbone.com
Tel: 1 401 846 0392
Fax: 1 401 848 5956
US Toll Free: 1 800 846 0392

Price Guide:
rooms $165
suites $455

Built in 1760 for the shipping merchant Francis Malbone and with a unique downtown harbourfront location, this delightful Inn was designed by the architect responsible for some of Newport's most esteemed buildings, including the famed Touro Synagogue and the Redwood Library. Its 20 spacious en suite guest rooms are furnished with wonderful antiques and period décor and many have spa baths and working fireplaces. A gourmet breakfast is served in the colonial dining room and coffee and afternoon tea can be enjoyed on the secluded courtyard with its views across the pretty, manicured garden. Guests can choose a book from the library and relax by an open fire in one of the comfortable parlours, or explore Newport's historic sites, mansions, shops, restaurants and of course, the harbour. Rhode Island's many beaches are also nearby with excellent sailing on offer. An award-winning, non-smoking Inn, The Francis Malbone House is happy to extend its exuberant welcome and relaxed, yet luxurious ambience, to leisure and business guests alike as a range of corporate conference facilities can be organised upon request.

Our inspector loved: *The serenity of the courtyard even in the centre of Newport.*

THE INN AT SHADOW LAWN

120 MIANTONOMI AVENUE, NEWPORT, RHODE ISLAND 02842

A sense of wonder hits you as you arrive at this elegant Italianate stick-style house – one of the first to be built in the USA by Richard Upjohn. Set in acres of parkland, this truly elegant mansion has been carefully restored to lose none of its Victorian charm with original frescoes, colours and lofty ceilings. The magnificent ballroom with its inlaid floor is the perfect venue for memorable parties. Each of the bedrooms is named after a female author of the period, and all have original fireplaces and are furnished in authentic style. The bathrooms are also generous and crisply decorated in fresh, light colours and tiles, and the upstairs rooms have kitchenettes. The location just outside Newport and the surrounding acres of parkland make this an extremely peaceful and tranquil place to stay, although the concierge will tailor a programme of sightseeing around the area. There are a number of period mansions in Newport, as well as the town and beach itself and various museums, such as the Naval Museum. Further attractions are the numerous historical sites nearby reminiscent of the rum and slave trades.

Our inspector loved: Browsing the antiques and paintings in this wonderful family house.

Directions: The Inn is located just outside Newport.

Web: www.johansens.com/innatshadowlawn
Tel: 1 401 847 0902
Fax: 1 401 848 6529
US toll free: 1 800 352 3750

Price Guide:
$125–$225

109

NEW ENGLAND / RHODE ISLAND - PROVIDENCE

HISTORIC JACOB HILL INN

PO BOX 41326, PROVIDENCE, RHODE ISLAND 02940

Directions: 10 minutes drive from downtown Providence and 1 hour from Boston and Cape Cod and 45 minutes from Newport .

Web: www.johansens.com/jacobhill
Email: host@jacobhill.com
Tel: 1 508 336 9165
Fax: 1 508 336 0951

Price Guide:
rooms $199–$299

This is a splendid, peaceful and friendly retreat. Behind the attractive, brilliant white façade is an elegant home-from-home ambience that has everything caring owners Bill and Eleonora Rezek can possibly provide. Built in 1722 and situated on a country estate just across the river from the East Side of Providence its charm and character have grown with the years. Although modernised to cater for 21st century trends the Inn retains the atmosphere, grace and appeal of past, less stressful eras. Today, it has received many prestigious awards: it is the only bed and breakfast in Providence to acquire 4 Diamonds from the AAA and to be appointed into the select registry of 'Distinguished Inns of North America.' Beautifully decorated and furnished with fine antiques, the Inn has had some of America's most prominent families enjoy its hospitality, including the legendary Vanderbilts. The recently renovated barn rooms have king or queen size beds which are superb; each room is extremely comfortable, individually and tastefully decorated with polished wood floors and original fireplaces making them truly authentic and romantic. Breakfasts are feasts; the Rezeks take great pride in their award winning stuffed French toast and pumpkin pancakes. The garden boasts a swimming pool and tennis court and horse riding can be arranged.

Our inspector loved: The renovated barn rooms are truly spectacular! If you want peace and friendliness you will find it here.

Fox Creek Inn

49 DAM ROAD, CHITTENDEN, VERMONT 05737

Deep in seclusion, surrounded by the lush green backdrop that has made Vermont known throughout the world, the Fox Creek Inn is a hideaway for the more discerning holidaymaker. A country house that is redolent of style, guests could almost walk right past it, nestled as it is in a veritable forest of foliage. Once inside, a tranquil ambience relaxes the visitors with simple yet refined furniture providing a comfortable environment in which to escape the hectic pace of a modern lifestyle. The nine bedrooms are superbly designed in their own individual way, elegantly styled to make each stay as comfortable as possible. They all feature every necessity that today's traveller may desire. Dinner is more of an experience than just a meal; served by candlelight whilst classical music plays soothingly in the background. The food is sumptuous and wholesome, prepared using only the freshest of ingredients. Guests can indulge in some horse-riding, visit the many museums nearby or peruse the glassworks. For those wishing to immerse themselves in the glorious natural surroundings, why not take a stroll around the stunning grounds, go hiking in the mountains and if all else fails simply relax in style at this beautiful resting spot.

Our inspector loved: *The amazing breakfasts.*

Directions: North or east of Rutland, follow signs from Route 4 or 7.

Web: www.johansens.com/foxcreekinn
E-mail: foxcreek@sover.net
Tel: 1 802 483 6213
Fax: 1 802 483 2623
US Toll Free: 1 800 707 0017

Price Guide: (incl. breakfast & dinner)
rooms $190–$409

NEW ENGLAND / VERMONT - CHITTENDEN

Mountain Top Inn & Resort

195 MOUNTAIN TOP ROAD, CHITTENDEN, VERMONT 05737

Directions: Route 7, then Route 4, left onto Meadowlake Drive and follow road to the very top.

Web: www.johansens.com/mountaintopinn
E-mail: info@mountaintopinn.com
Tel: 1 802 483 2311
Fax: 1 802 483 6373

Price Guide:
rooms $168–$226
suite $226–$268

Mountain Top, known as 'Vermont's best kept secret' is a marvellous resort, famous for its cross country ski-ing but also delightful in summer – and the Inn plays an important role in its success. This enchanting small hotel enjoys spectacular views in all seasons. Purpose built, it has every modern comfort. The spacious guest rooms are charming, decorated in soft colours, with country style furniture. Some are in the adjacent cottages and chalets. The lounges are also simple and attractive, looking out onto the mountains. The games room is the social centre. The elegant restaurant has big picture windows, and offers New England cooking at its best. Good wines are listed. The Inn is no smoking throughout. Mountain Top has its own ski instructors and shop. Skating and sleighrides are other popular winter diversions. In summer the Golf School is active, with tuition for all handicaps. The enormous estate has excellent facilities for shooting, riding, fishing, tennis, swimming, while the lake has a sandy beach and opportunities for water sports. A great location for exploring Vermont.

Our inspector loved: *This great mountain resort, a true vacation for all seasons.*

NEW ENGLAND / VERMONT - LOWER WATERFORD

RABBIT HILL INN

48 LOWER WATERFORD ROAD, LOWER WATERFORD, VERMONT 05848

Rabbit Hill Inn is a luxurious and historical escape from the pressures of today's busy world. The property is truly romantic: from the soft strains of music welcoming visitors as they step across the entrance porch to the restful glow of candles pervading the bedrooms as they retire for the night. Innkeepers Brian and Leslie Mulcahy are dedicated to pampering guests in a stylish and comfortable environment. Overlooking the beautiful White Mountains and the Connecticut River Valley, the Inn was built in 1795 to serve the needs of travellers journeying between Canada and the New England harbours. The property has been completely restored and modernised but has retained many of its classic features, antique furnishings and its historical atmosphere. The stylish bedrooms are enhanced by original artworks, whirlpool baths and magnificent King and Queen-sized canopy beds. The whimsical use of rabbits is delightful: from bunny-shaped butter to sculpted rabbits tucked into the beams, these animals are scattered throughout. Guests relax in the parlours or the Snooty Fox Pub before indulging in the superb cuisine offered in the candlelit dining room. The exquisite dishes are made with fresh ingredients and include produce from the Inn's own greenhouse and garden. On site activities include canoeing, hiking and sledding.

Directions: From I93 north, exit 44, onto Rt18 north, 2 miles to the inn.

Web: www.johansens.com/rabbithill
E-mail: info@rabbithillinn.com
Tel: 1 802 748 5168
Fax: 1 802 748 8342

Price Guide: (incl. breakfast tea dinner & all service charges):
rooms $260–$295
suites $360–$375

Our inspector loved: The pretty hilltop location.

1811 House

PO BOX 39, ROUTE 7A, MANCHESTER VILLAGE, VERMONT 05254

Directions: On the historic Route 7A.

Web: www.johansens.com/1811house
E-mail: house1811@adelphia.net
Tel: 1 802 362 1811
Fax: 1 802 362 2443
US Toll Free: 800 432 1811

Price Guide:
rooms $140–$280
suite $280

Pretty Manchester Village is proud of its enchanting inn, the 1811 House which has extensive gardens filled with daffodils in Spring and its own Scottish pub appreciated as much by the locals as by the hotel guests! Loving restoration work has resulted in the joyous interior of this Federal house – a fine collection of American and English antiques sits well on rich Persian carpets, handsome paintings adorn the walls while silver photograph frames and other memorabilia add a personal touch. Discreet air conditioning controls the atmosphere. It is a non-smoking house. The attractive guest rooms are filled with gracious period furniture, and many have spectacular views of the Green Mountains. A few bedrooms are in the adjacent cottage. Marnie and Bruce Duff, good Scottish names, have their individual skills. Marnie is a superb cook and her breakfasts are fabulous. Bruce is a great gardener. He is also 'mine host' of the traditional 'snug' which offers good company, well-kept ale and 75 malt whiskies. The parlour is an elegant rendezvous, the library peaceful and residents relax over a game of snooker in the games room. Restaurants abound for dinner, and in the day antique shops, boutiques, galleries, museums, fishing, cycling, good golf, tennis are but a selection of local activities.

Our inspector loved: *The history and antiques in this well kept original Inn with wonderful views of the whole estate.*

THE VILLAGE COUNTRY INN

ROUTE 7A, PO BOX 408, MANCHESTER VILLAGE, VERMONT 05254

This quaint village Inn is built in traditional New England style and due to its proximity to a wealth of attractions it is also a perfect summer or winter retreat. The building itself is charmingly furnished in a romantic style with each of the 32 bedrooms being individually decorated with pretty spring prints and florals, as well as delicate lace and canopied beds. The long veranda that stretches along the front of the house makes a chocolate box scene with autumnal leaves and pumpkin lanterns, and with thick snow at Christmas time. In the winter months there is an array of sports available including cross-country skiing and romantic sleigh rides, whilst the summer months can be spent visiting the many museums, galleries and antique centres or meandering around the Inn's most charming gardens. Here, long sweeping lawns are interrupted by delicate borders of stocks and delphiniums, as well as interesting pieces of architecture and sculpture. The elegant swimming pool is a delightful spot in which to relax with a cocktail or two. For the dedicated shopper there is also a range of outlet stores nearby and there is a regular selection of romantic break packages.

Our inspector loved: This traditional New England Inn, so close to shopping & winter sports.

Directions: I-87 to route 7 east. At Manchester take Route 7A. The Inn is one mile ahead on the right.

Web: www.johansens.com/villagecountryinn
Tel: 1 802 362 1792
Fax: 1 802 362 7238

Price Guide:
rooms $149–$345

NEW ENGLAND / VERMONT - NEWFANE

Four Columns Inn

PO BOX 278, NEWFANE, VERMONT 05345

Directions: From I-91, take Exit 2 in Vermont. Turn left towards Brattleboro and after approximately ½ mile left onto Cedar Street. At 3rd stop sign turn left again and travel 11 miles to Newfane.

Web: www.johansens.com/fourcolumnsinn
E-mail: innkeeper@fourcolumnsinn.com
Tel: 1 802 365 7713

Price Guide:
rooms $115–$175
suite $190–$340

This elegant inn with its imposing entrance columns is a luxurious and romantic retreat that exudes warmth and the wonderful hospitality of innkeepers Pam and Gorty Baldwin. Situated in 150 wooded acres, Four Columns is appealing in every respect for those seeking luxury accommodation in a quintessential New England village. The interior décor is exquisite, there are wonderful open fires and a wealth of antiques. In the grounds are a swimming pool, two ponds, a stream, award-winning perennial garden beds and hiking trails. The fifteen pristine guest rooms offer every home comfort, eleven have gas log fireplaces, and the bathrooms in the suites boast two-person Jacuzzi bathtubs. Dining is a delight, and Chef Greg Parks has been dazzling guests at the inn's Four Diamond gourmet restaurant with his creative flair since 1976. His menus are a blend of New American, Asian and French and as well as being honoured by the Distinguished Restaurants of North America, Greg has prepared a gourmet dinner for the exclusive James Beard Foundation. Nearby sporting activities include golf, fishing, canoeing, tennis, riding and in winter skiing, ice-skating and snowmobiling.

Our inspector loved: This elegant Inn and it's beautiful - not to mention the exceptional wine list.

The Mountain Road Resort At Stowe

PO BOX 8, 1007 MOUNTAIN ROAD, STOWE, VERMONT 05672

The Mountain Road Resort is a vibrant, cosmopolitan and stylish hotel surrounded by seven acres of landscaped gardens. The complex is pristine and the accommodation includes commodious bedrooms with comfortable country-style furnishings, air conditioning, modern bathrooms and many gas-powered fireplaces. There are also luxurious studios and split level suites with full kitchens, large windows and Jacuzzis. No smoking is the rule. A lavish continental breakfast is served in The Library. There is no restaurant but afternoon refreshments are served. Children have a Games Room. Billy's Wine Bar has excellent vintages, several beers, 'munchable' snacks and Ben & Jerry's ice cream. The Mountain Road has a 'Dine Around' option and the Stowe Trolley transports guests into town – babysitters available. The Resort has a splendid outdoor pool, tennis and boules – indoors a marvellous Aqua-Centre with fitness facilities. The sun terraces are great for doing nothing! Special green fees have been organised at local golf clubs and other summer sports are tennis, canoeing, fishing, hiking and riding. Winter sports include downhill and cross-country skiing. Boat trips on Lake Champlain and gondola rides up the mountain are leisure activities.

Our inspector loved: *The pretty views atop the Mountain Road visible from this splendid, friendly Inn.*

Directions: Interstate 89 to Junction 10, then Route 100 to Stowe.

Web: www.johansens.com/mountainroad
E-mail: stowevt@aol.com
Tel: 1 802 253 4566
Fax: 1 802 253 7397
UK Freephone 0800 894 581

Price Guide:
rooms $135–$215
suites $225–$425

WINDHAM HILL INN

WEST TOWNSHEND, VERMONT 05359

Directions: Route 30, at West Townshend turn off opposite county store, finding Windham Hill sign 1 1/4 miles on right.

Web: www.johansens.com/windhamhillinn
Tel: 1 802 874 4080
Fax: 1 802 874 4702

Price Guide:
rooms $195–$345

The first settlers came to Vermont in 1720, and how thrilled they would have been had this enchanting country house inn been at the end of their journey. The Green Mountains country is some of the most spectacular in New England, whether snowclad in winter or lush and green in summer. Today's travellers arriving at this haven, with its welcoming facade, relax instantly. The parlours are inviting, filled with antiques, jewel coloured oriental rugs on the polished wood floors and comfortable locally made furniture. The Music Room has an 1888 Steinway! The pristine guest rooms have big beds and some have decks or window seats. Some are in the attractive White Barn, adjacent to the Main House. The dress code is casual, a little smarter for the delicious four-course candle-lit dinner in the Frog Pond Dining Room and many of the excellent wines listed are available by the glass. In winter guests skate on the pond, ski downhill or cross country; in summer they use the hotel pool and tennis court, golf, maybe take a picnic and and follow – on foot, bike or horse – the main trails through forests and flower filled meadows. South Vermont is fascinating: country fairs, art and craft shows, picturesque villages, antique dealers, music festivals.

Our inspector loved: The gourmet dinners served in the elegant dining room.

NEW ENGLAND / VERMONT - WESTON

THE INN AT WESTON

SCENIC ROUTE 100, WESTON, VERMONT 05161

This is an elegant inn whose owners strive to provide a friendly and comfortable environment in which to unwind and relax. The inn is centrally located in Southern Vermont in the heart of the Green Mountains in the picture perfect village of Weston. Nestled in six acres of property next to the West River with wonderful seasonal views, it is composed of two houses and a barn that are typical of the mid-19th century. The original building was built in 1848 as a working farmhouse with connecting stable and bar, and was converted to a guest house 50 years ago. The Coleman House, built as a farmhouse in 1830, is across the street and was renovated in 1988. Bob and Linda Aldrich have substantially renovated the inn since purchasing it in 1998 and have sympathetically combined modern facilities with traditional character and ambience. Guests enjoy luxurious rooms and suites, many offering whirlpool tubs, fireplaces, four-poster pine beds and televisions hidden in armoires. Fine cuisine, complemented by an extensive wine list is served in the delightful dining room, where piano music is played. Gallery quality photographs are on display in the public areas. An integral part of the property is a new orchid greenhouse, which is open for viewing. A renowned summer theatre is in strolling distance; golf, tennis and skiing are nearby.

Directions: On Route 100 North, 30 miles from I-91, Exit 6.

Web: www.johansens.com/innatweston
E-mail: inweston@sover.net
Tel: 1 802 824 6789
Fax: 1 802 824 3073

Price Guide:
rooms and suites $155–$255

Our inspector loved: The orchids placed in each guestroom.

NEW ENGLAND / VERMONT - WOODSTOCK

THE JACKSON HOUSE INN

114-3 SENIOR LANE, WOODSTOCK, VERMONT 05091

Directions: 1 ½ miles west of the village, just off Route 4.

Web: www.johansens.com/jacksonhouse
E-mail: innkeeper@jacksonhouse.com
Tel: 1 802 457 2065
Fax: 1 802 457 9290

Price Guide:
single $195–$260
suite $340

Amidst 5 acres of enchanting landscaped gardens with a delightful pond, this beautiful late Victorian Inn is listed in the National Register of Historic Places and offers uncompromising quality and understated elegance. Excellently crafted woodwork, stunning wooden floors, traditional light fixtures and stained-glass add to the warm ambience of the interior, which has been carefully decorated with period furniture. Lovingly restored bedrooms and suites are extremely luxurious with huge hand-carved wooden beds, fireplaces and opulent bathrooms. Some of the rooms overlook the gardens and attention to detail includes fresh flowers, the finest toiletries, Italian linens and plush terry robes to make your stay as comfortable as possible. The award winning restaurant, which has a remarkable granite hearth, offers outstanding New American gourmet cuisine to tempt the most discerning of palates and is considered to be one of the best in Vermont. Woodstock is a beautiful New England village and offers all-year-round adventure from kayaking and skiing to antiquing and visiting art galleries, historic architecture and museums. Other outdoor pursuits available include golf, horse riding, cycling and swimming. The Hotel has a spa with weights, aerobic equipment, steam room, and large-screen satellite TV.

Our inspector loved: *The spring-fed pond by which guests can relax or take a cool dip.*

WOODSTOCK INN & RESORT

FOURTEEN THE GREEN, WOODSTOCK, VERMONT, 05091-1298

Historic Woodstock has been frequently referred to as one of the most beautiful villages in New England. It's the personification of a picture postcard scene. Pristine white frame and traditional brick houses edge its green, delicate church spires reach skywards from a patchwork of colourful country stores. And all around is the unspoiled lush green grandeur that has made Vermont known throughout the world. The Woodstock Inn and Resort is at its heart, a luxury retreat of colonial charm and understated elegance where guests can't help but perceive and appreciate the unmistakable feeling of quality and exclusiveness. A huge open fire in the lobby welcomes winter visitors, the public rooms are elegant, spacious, tranquil and provide a comfortable environment in which to relax and forget cares, worries and any aches and strains received during a hard activity day. There is a choice of 144 guest rooms, 23 with fireplaces. All are superbly designed in their individual way and feature every necessity, from air conditioning and colour television to specially designed furniture and colourful handmade bed quilts. Relaxed dining is enjoyed in any of four restaurants where the menus are extensive and the service of the highest standard. Summer and winter activities abound, from tennis, swimming golf, riding and hiking to alpine skiing, nordic skiing and sleigh riding.

Directions: Take I-95 North to I-91 North take exit 10 N onto I-89 North. After 3 miles get off at exit 1 for Woodstock.

Web: www.johansens.com/woodstockinn
Tel: 1 802 457 1100
Fax: 1 802 457 6699

Price Guide:
rooms $129–$589

Our inspector loved: The special location, opposite the village green.

NEW MEXICO
Hotel location shown in red with page number

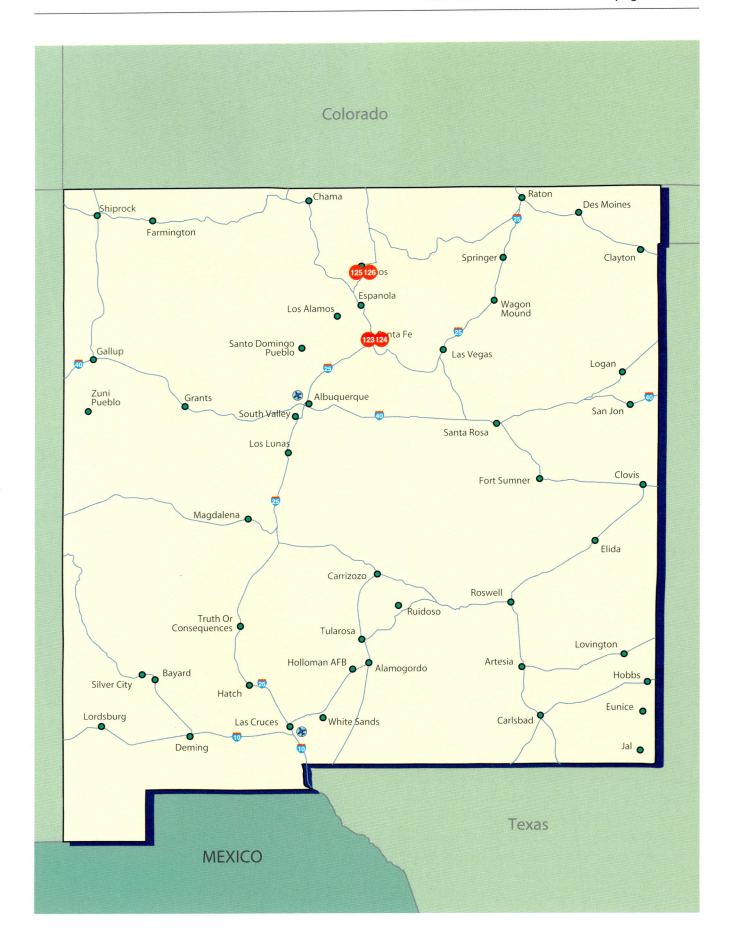

Hotel St Francis
210 DON GASPAR AVENUE, SANTA FE, NEW MEXICO 87501

Built before the Wall Street Crash, this elegant 3 storey building is a classic example of the grandiose structures of its time. High ceilings, ornate fireplaces and elegant mouldings around windows and doors has led the Hotel to become known as one of Santa Fe's most historic hotels and the staff today are anxious to preserve this reputation. The combination of 1920's style and south-western elements create an unusual ambience, with Mexican clay floor tiles and contemporary wrought-iron chandeliers in the lobby. In recent refurbishment programme much care has been taken to ensure that the period furnishings were fully-restored and authentic reproductions were ordered to maintain the period character. Each guest room has its own unique theme with different bedspreads and has been carefully furnished. The veranda is a recognised spot for people-watching; afternoon tea is served daily which includes finger-sandwiches, scones, clotted cream and pastries accompanied by sherry, port or champagne. The Club Restaurant and Artist's Pub with large windows and views of the foothills are frequented by locals and hotel guests. The hotel offers a special historic ambience throughout as well as friendly and courteous service. Places of interest nearby: Native American Pueblos, Georgia O'Keeffe Country.

Our inspector loved: Afternoon tea served in the mellow ambience of the lobby.

Directions: Follow area signs to Downtown Plaza. The Hotel is 1 block south-west of Plaza.

Web: www.johansens.com/hotelstfrancis
E-mail: david.stone@hotelstfrancis.net
Tel: 1 505 983 5700
Fax: 1 505 992 6340

Price Guide:
rooms $80–$220

BISHOP'S LODGE
PO BOX 2367, SANTA FE, NEW MEXICO, 87504

Built in 1851 for Jean Baptiste, first Bishop of Santa Fe, and converted into a hotel in 1922, this luxurious oasis retreat encompasses lush gardens and lawns among 450 acres of desert serenity, rolling foothills and tranquil valley just beside the Sante Fe National Forest. At an altitude of 7,300 feet the resort enjoys crystal clear days and crisp cool nights, with snowfalls in the lofty Sierra Mountains in excess of 100 inches. Bishop's Lodge is ideal for everything from family vacations and romantic breaks to weddings and corporate events. An intriguing variety of guest accommodation is located in 11 Spanish colonial style lodges. Rooms are opulently equipped with every comfort and modern amenity and all have lovely Kiva fireplaces and private patios from which to enjoy superb panoramic views while relaxing over a cooling drink or pre dinner aperitif. A newly opened spa features an extensive range of facilities. Among the many body and beauty treatments popular with guests is the Tesque Clay Wrap and a Herbal Detoxification Wrap with herbal infused sheets that envelope the body. Horseback riding and hiking trails lead to the canyons and foothills of Sangre de Cristos or to the campground of Mesa Vista. For sports enthusiasts there are two all weather tennis courts and a skeet and trap shooting range.

Directions: From downtown Santa Fe, north on Bishop's Lodge Road for 3 miles.

Web: www.johansens.com/bishopslodge
Tel: 1 505 983 6377
Fax: 1 505 989 8739

Price Guide:
rooms $229–$749
suites $279–$899

Our inspector loved: *The peace and tranquility of this high desert oasis well saturated with Santa Fe history and traditions.*

CASITAS AT EL MONTE
125 LA POSTA ROAD, PO BOX 20, TAOS, NEW MEXICO 87671

Dotted throughout the mountain town of Taos, El Monte Casitas are renovated, historic landmark guest homes offering the utmost privacy, luxury. Against a backdrop of the spectacular Sangre de Cristo Mountains the Casitos are within a comfortable walk of the town's best galleries, art museums, restaurants and shops and just a short drive to a testing golf course, rafting, rock climbing, wildlife viewing and winter skiing. Owner Tom Worrell redeveloped the Casitas to preserve and restore these historic properties, most of which are on the National Register. Each of the nine adobe-style casitas was authentically created with a specific theme in mind. From tribal African and Caribbean to Tibetan and Spanish hacienda they feature exquisite artifacts of the chosen culture. Comfort and luxury are supreme, from custom bed covers and duvets, wood burning fireplaces and overstuffed sofas to Jacuzzi-style baths and outdoor tubs. All rooms have dining areas. Some have mini-kitchens, reading rooms and libraries. Most have a washer/dryer, private courtyard and satellite television. Concierge services are available and can arrange astrological, tarot and psychic readings. Pilates, yoga or meditation sessions. Each home is stocked with guests' food and wine requests.

Our inspector loved: The rich vibrant interiors.

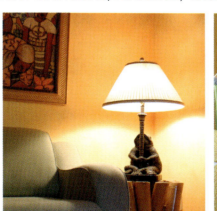

Directions: Twenty minutes from Taos, Private airfield for small aircraft 15 minutes away.

Web: www.johansens.com/casitaselmondo
Tel: 1 800 828 8267
Fax: 1 505 758 5089

Price Guide:
rooms $150–$945

NEW MEXICO - TAOS

THE INN ON LA LOMA PLAZA

315 RANCHITOS ROAD, TAOS, NEW MEXICO 87571

Directions: From the southwest corner of the Plaza (downtown) take Ranchitos Road and continue through the next stoplight (approximately 2 blocks). After this intersection with Salazar Road, the Inn is a short distance on the right.

Web: www.johansens.com/lalomaplaza
E-mail: laloma@vacationtaos.com
Tel: 1 505 758 1717
Fax: 1 505 751 0155

Price Guide:
rooms $100 – 220
suites $195 – 300

This traditional Santa Fe style hacienda lies in its own walled estate just 2½ blocks from Taos Plaza. The setting is immensely tranquil with lofty trees and staggering views of the mountain ranges, whilst the building itself dates back to 1800 and is listed in the National Register of Historic Places. Each of the 7 bedrooms is individually designed and perfectly captures the southwestern atmosphere with a combination of Mexican tiles, Kiva fireplaces and splashes of Taos blue or cheery yellow on sponged and rag-rolled walls. Many of the rooms can be linked to create 2 bedroomed suites and the views of the mountain ranges from many, are outstanding. This is strong skiing territory with 3 ski valleys located nearby, as well as white water rafting and the Hotel's gourmet breakfast will set up any guest for a day of such adventures. Equally accessible from the Hotel is Taos Indian Pueblo and other art galleries which are fascinating and a more sedate way to spend some vacation, there is also great shopping nearby.

Our inspector loved: The romantic rooms with fireplaces in this authentic southwestern hacienda.

NEW YORK
Hotel location shown in red with page number

NEW YORK - CAZENOVIA

THE BREWSTER INN

6 LEDYARD AVENUE, CAZENOVIA, NEW YORK 13035

Surrounded by secluded lawned grounds, The Brewster Inn stands elegantly on the southern shore of Cazenovia Lake close to a quaint village which was founded in 1793. It is a perfect venue for carefree relaxation. The inn was built as the summer home for financier Benjamin Brewster who, with John D. Rockefeller, Sr, established the Standard Oil Company. Its elegance is enhanced by rich décor, fine drapes and impressive woodwork, including solid mahogany and antique quartered oak. Guests choose from bedrooms in the main inn or in the completely renovated carriage house. Each one has a private bath, air conditioning, television and telephone. Four rooms have Jacuzzi baths and there is one three-room de luxe suite. The attractive dining rooms offer dinner menus of superb, classic American cuisine to please every palate. The inn's lake view tavern and terrace are excellent spots in which to relax and browse the award-winning wine list. Guests are welcome to tour the impressive climate-controlled wine cellar. After a complimentary Continental breakfast guests can enjoy a leisurely stroll along the inn's extensive shoreline, swim in the clear lake waters, fish off the private docks or explore Cazenovia's many shops. Lorenzo historic mansion is worth a visit, as is the picnic area at the nearby, spectacular Chittenango Falls.

Directions: The Brewster Inn is on US Route 20, 20 miles east of Syracuse

Web: www.johansens.com/brewsterinn
Tel: 1 315 655 9232
Fax: 1 315 655 2130

Price Guide:
rooms $110–$170
suite $205–$235

Our inspector loved: The extraordinary wine cellar.

ROYCROFT INN

40 SOUTH GROVE STREET, EAST AURORA, NEW YORK 14052

The Roycroft Inn is in every sense an American National Landmark. It was founded over a hundred years ago by the philosopher and writer Elbert Hubbard to provide congenial accommodation for devotees of the local Arts and Craft movement. His influence and memory live on at the Roycroft, thanks largely to the Margaret L Wendt Foundation who enabled the inn to be renovated and reopened in 1995 in a style worthy of the founder's highest beliefs and aspirations. The décor and furniture are either original or authentic reproduction examples of the celebrated movement of which the inn is a shrine. The bedrooms at the Roycroft conform to the original structure whilst enhancing and conserving the historic character of the entire building. All rooms are furnished in traditional Roycroft style and feature modems, televisions and video equipment. The Roycroft inn restaurant is open for lunches, dinners and on Sunday for brunch. In summer there is dining out of doors. Private facilities are available for meetings and parties for as few as 10 or as many as 200 people. Attractions in the locality are museums, golf courses, nature walks, tennis and in season, many downhill and cross-country skiing areas

Our inspector loved: The noble simplicity of an historic Inn.

Directions: From Buffalo follow Route 190 south to Route 90 heading west. Take exit 54 to Route 400 and exit onto route 20A East Aurora, becoming Main Street. Pass through village, turn left into South Grove Street.

Web: www.johansens.com/roycroftinn
E-mail: info@roycroftinn.com
Tel: 1 877 652 5552
Fax: 1 716 655 5345

Price Guide:
Suite $120–$260

NEW YORK - GENEVA

GENEVA ON THE LAKE

1001 LOCHLAND ROAD (ROUTE 14 SOUTH), GENEVA, NEW YORK 14456

Directions: 47 miles drive from Rochester and Syracuse airports, the hotel is on Route 14 South.

Web: www.johansens.com/genevaonthelake
E-mail: info@GenevaOnTheLake.com
Tel: 1 315 789 7190
Fax: 1 315 789 0322

Price Guide:
rooms $113–$700

This beautifully romantic villa overlooking Seneca Lake was built between 1910 and 1914 as a faithful replica of the Italian Villa Lancellotti in Frascati. The Italian marble fireplaces and wood-coffered ceilings are just a few of the features that have been lovingly maintained throughout this time, and carefully incorporated into the elegant hotel that it is today. There is a romantic ambience throughout, with each suite having its own unique décor, some with original fireplaces, each with a ready kitchen and ten having two bedrooms. The setting itself makes this an ideal venue for a wedding or conference, and the restaurant is renowned locally, serving to residents and non-residents alike. The Colonnade Pavilion is ideal for al fresco dining in the summer months, while the splendid Lancellotti Dining Room is delightfully romantic, with live music from piano, vocalist or string ensemble. This is fine antiques area, but guests can also fish from the hotel dock, go on a canoeing trip or ice-skate and ski in the winter months. Guests may enjoy scenic drives through the picturesque countryside and visit Geneva's historic district and Seneca Lake's wine trail. Niagara Falls could make a wonderful day trip.

Our inspector loved: The perfect match of Villa and Gardens.

William Henry Miller Inn
303 NORTH AURORA STREET, ITHACA, NEW YORK 14850

This delightful building takes its name from Cornell University's first student of architecture, William Henry Miller, who built it in 1880. It has since been lovingly restored and now offers nine spacious guest bedrooms that retain much of their period style with high ceilings and American chestnut woodwork. Extremely close to the town centre, this is an ideal destination for the business traveller or family alike – the intimate music room with its feature fireplace is a welcoming environment for small meetings, and data ports are available in all the bedrooms. A range of hot drinks or a complimentary evening dessert await guests after an eventful day at the nearby shops or museums. Situated in the Finger Lakes district, there is a range of local wineries to visit, but the committed traveller will hire a car and visit the waterfalls, gorges, lakes and gardens where the breathtaking scenery will be just reward for his efforts. The winter months also turn the William Henry Miller into a great skiing destination – and a welcome retreat at the end of the day with its warm, relaxing ambience.

Our inspector loved: The perfect balance of history & hospitality.

Directions: In downtown Ithaca, just a few blocks away from the Ithaca Commons and down the hill from both Cornell University and Ithaca College

Web: www.johansens.com/williamhenrymiller
E-mail: millerinn@aol.com
Tel: 1 607 255 4553
Fax: 1 607 256 0092
US Toll Free: 1 877 256 4553

Price Guide:
rooms $95–175

NEW YORK - NEW YORK CITY

BRYANT PARK HOTEL
40 WEST 40TH STREET, NEW YORK, NEW YORK 10018

Directions: Between 5th and 6th, just off 5th Avenue on 40th near midtown Manhattan, the theatre district, Times Square, 5th Avenue shopping and Soho.

Web: www.johansens.com/bryantpark
E-mail: jpalmer@phgmc.com
Tel: 1 212 869 0100
Fax: 1 212 869 4446

Price Guide:
rooms $265 – $425
suites $495 – $695

The historic American Radiator Building exterior does not prepare you for the vibrant red leather walls of the lobby and contemporary interior. Every aspect of this very smart hotel is cutting edge, luxurious and vibrant with energy. Guest rooms create a special sensuality, with 400 thread count Egyptian linens and goose down comforters, step on Tibetan rugs and snuggle under Cashmere blankets. Share the Travertine bathroom featuring custom designed tubs and marble showers. In-room entertainment is provided by Bose CD Wave Radio, 27" television and digital films. If you insist on keeping in touch with the office there is a fax machine and T-1 high speed internet connectivity or, if you wish to be left alone, simply press the bedside privacy button. Award winning chef, Rick Laakkonen, takes care of your culinary requirements at his 3 star ILO restaurant. Private guest room dining is available 24 hours a day. The Cellar Bar is definitely the place to meet and be seen, with clever illuminations to match the mood and an extensive list of cocktails. There is also a relaxing Lobby Bar with stunning views of the park. The Screening Room is available for private viewings and functions for those wishing to mingle with the stars!

Our inspector loved: *The overwhelming sense of intimacy and fun.*

THE KITANO NEW YORK

66 PARK AVENUE NEW YORK, NEW YORK 10016

This elegant hotel is an attractive fusion of American and Japanese style, ideally located on fashionable Park Avenue within minutes of Grand Central Station, the Empire State Building and the best of Manhattan shopping. First opened in 1973 as the Kitano Hotel, it reopened in 1995 after a 3 1/2-year, $55million reconstruction and refurbishment programme. The magnificent, mahogany and marble entrance lobby features a tea room, superb paintings, photographs and sculptures are displayed throughout. The individually designed guestrooms and suites are equipped with all comforts and facilities for the discerning leisure and business travellers, including soundproof windows, large desks, dual line speaker telephones, fax machines, data ports, cable television and high speed internet access and luxurious bathrooms. An authentic Tatami Suite comes complete with a Japanese tea ceremony room. The mix of East and West continues in the hotel's choice of dining. The informal, sun-lit Garden Cafe serves contemporary American cuisine whilst the Nadaman Hakubai offers award-winning Japanese gastronomy. Two banqueting rooms with adjoining terraces can accommodate up to 150 people for parties, meetings and presentations.

Our inspector loved: *The quiet atmosphere with its Japanese decor and most attentive staff.*

Directions: On Park Avenue and 38th Street in the Murray Hill district, a 5-minute walk from Grand Central Terminal.

Web: www.johansens.com/kitano
E-mail: reservations@kitano.com
Tel: 1 212 885 7000
Fax: 1 212 885 7100

Price Guide:
rooms $460-$605
suites $630-$2100

NEW YORK - NORTHERN CATSKILL MOUNTAINS

ALBERGO ALLEGRIA

#43 ROUTE 296, WINDHAM, NEW YORK 12496

Directions: Leave New York State Thruway (I-87) at exit 21 (Catskill), take Route 23 west for 23 miles, then turn left onto Route 296. The hotel is on the left.

Web: www.johansens.com/albergoallegria
E-mail: mail@AlbergoUSA.com
Tel: 1 518 734 5560
Fax: 1 518 734 5570

Price Guide:
rooms $73–$189
suites $169–$299

This superb bed and breakfast inn stands on two acres of immaculate lawns and beautiful country gardens. It is a meticulously cared for registered historic site in the picturesque hamlet of Windham, and the perfect place to unwind. Italian for the 'Inn of Happiness' Albergo Allegria, which dates from the late 19th century, is located in the heart of the scenic Northern Catskill Mountains. Inside its attractive, pillared exterior enhanced with shady verandahs there is a welcoming atmosphere reminiscent of a family home. Furniture, furnishings, décor, handcrafted woodwork and original stained glass windows add an elegance that rewarded owners Leslie and Marianna Leman with an award as Inn of the Year 2000. The delightful rooms and suites are individually decorated and offer every facility from air conditioning, television and videos to en suite tubs and king-size beds. Five spacious Carriage House Suites behind the main house offer guests extra privacy, a whirlpool, gas log fire, outdoor deck, 15-foot cathedral ceiling and private entrance. Breakfasts are magnificent; the chef's imaginative repertoire includes gourmet omelets, sautéed herb frittata's and stuffed French toast. Golf and two alpine ski areas are nearby.

Our inspector loved: The experience of feeling at home.

NEW YORK - SARATOGA SPRINGS

SARATOGA ARMS
495–497 BROADWAY, SARATOGA SPRINGS, NEW YORK 12866

This attractive late 19th-century Second Empire red brick hotel stands in the heart of the historic downtown district of Saratoga Springs. Gently rising steps with superb, ornamental balustrades ease visitors onto a magnificent wraparound porch with colourful hanging baskets – the perfect place on which to while away a lazy afternoon. Hospitable owners Kathleen and Noel Smith have magnificently restored the hotel to award-winning status, and its elegance is enhanced by beautiful custom décor, fine drapes, impressive woodwork, period pieces, wicker porch furniture and family treasures all designed to carry out the refined style of Saratoga tradition. Guests choose from a variety of delightful en suite bedrooms. Each is individually and tastefully decorated and has every home-from-home comfort. There are some with a fireplace and two with a double whirlpool. The hotel also has excellent business facilities. The President Grant conference room along with the Kaydeross and Walton Rooms are perfect for getaway board and committee meetings, seminars and training sessions. Within a short stroll are a number of superb restaurants, shops, museums, colleges and cultural activities including jazz, opera and orchestral concerts and ballet festivals throughout the year. Guests can enjoy horse racing from July to September.

Directions: Centre of Saratoga Springs.

Web: www.johansens.com/saratogaarms
E-mail: hotel@saratoga-lodging.com
Tel: 1 518 584 1775
Fax: 1 518 581 4064

Price Guide:
rooms $150–$450

Our inspector loved: Watching the world from the wonderful verandah.

NORTH CAROLINA

Hotel location shown in red with page number

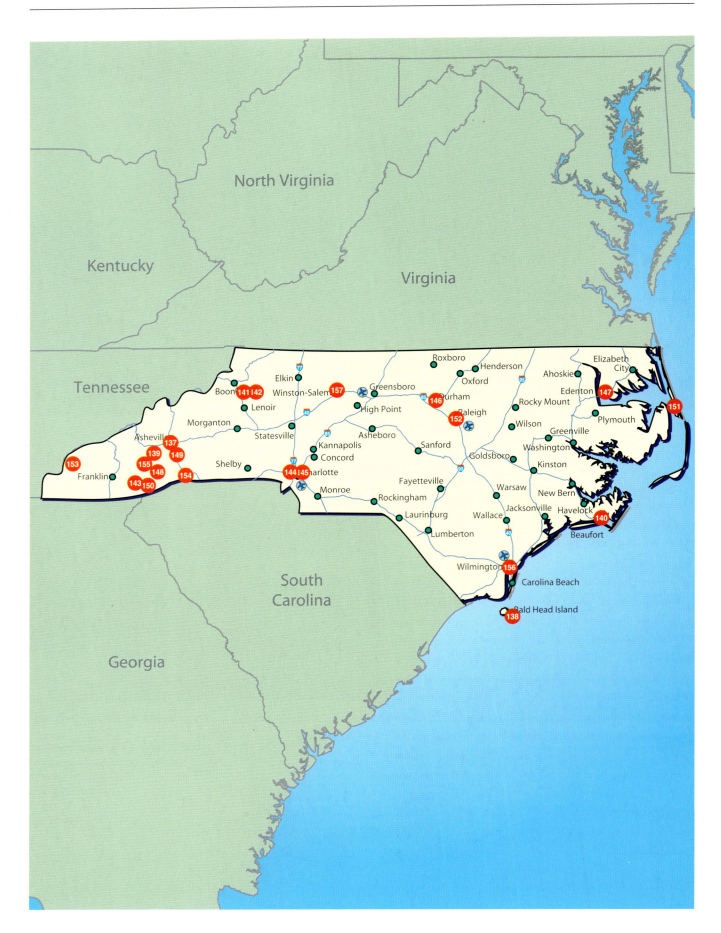

THE WRIGHT INN & CARRIAGE HOUSE

235 PEARSON DRIVE, ASHEVILLE, NORTH CAROLINA 28801

A private residence in 1899 during America's industrial and real estate boom years, The Wright Inn is now considered by many to be one of the finest examples of Queen Anne architecture to be found in the Montford District of historic Asheville and all of Western North Carolina. Elegant and imposing, this three-story Bed & Breakfast Inn is surrounded by attractive tree-lined streets and stately Victorian homes which are welcome reminders of a graceful and peaceful era. With its adjoining Carriage House the restored Wright Inn is deservedly on the National Register of Historic Places. Among many impressive features are its superb antiques, wide wrap-around porch and award-winning gardens. Visitors have the choice of 11 distinctive suites and guest rooms that are delightfully decorated and furnished in an early turn of the century style that blends excellently with every modern facility. Bedrooms boast luxurious queen-size beds, fine linens, family heirlooms, central heating, television and telephones with modem sockets. 2 suites have their own entrances and one has fireplace and double jacuzzi. Afternoon social hour can be enjoyed before an open-fire in the elegant Willows Drawing Room, on the wrap-around porch or in the formal dining room. The perfect venue for sumptuous gourmet breakfast and wine and cheese social gatherings.

Directions: I-26 to 240, Exit 4C (Montford Avenue)

Web: www.johansens.com/wrightinn
Tel: 1 828 251 0789
Fax: 1 828 251 0929

Price Guide:
rooms $140–$210
suites $210–$225

Our inspector loved: The antiques, gardens and wrap-around porch.

NORTH CAROLINA - BALD HEAD ISLAND

Theodosia's Bed & Breakfast
PO BOX 3130, 2 KEELSON ROW, BALD HEAD ISLAND, NORTH CAROLINA 28461

Directions: Accessible by ferry from Indigo Plantation Ferry Terminal.

Web: www.johansens.com/theodosias
E-mail: stay@theodosias.com
Tel: 1 910 457 6563
Fax: 1 910 457 6055

Price Guide:
rooms $180–$300

Situated on historic Bald Head Island, at the mouth of Cape Fear River, 2 miles off North Carolina's coast, Theodosia's is a picturesque, Victorian-style, bed and breakfast Inn offering immense charm, total relaxation and superb views from the porches and balconies of its exquisite rooms. Surroundings are quiet and peaceful and enable guests to read or chat about the day's events whilst sipping drinks and resting in comfortable outside rocking chairs, swings or white wicker sofas, enjoying the panoramic scenery encompassing the harbour, river, lighthouse and island marshes. Hosts, Garrett and Donna Albertson, are renowned for their welcoming hospitality and their beautifully decorated and furnished Inn is dotted with personal pieces, from an extensive collection of blue and white china to the dress Donna's grandmother wore for her wedding 120 years ago. Each guestroom has every facility and the individual décor and furnishings reflect the Inn's grace and attractiveness. 8 guestrooms are in the main house, 2 in an adjoining carriage house, and 3 with a 2 room suite are in a nearby 3 storey island cottage. Gourmet breakfasts serving old favourites such as eggs benedict, are eaten on the porch or in a cosy breakfast room. Golf carts and bicycles are complimentary with each room for island exploring.

Our inspector loved: Everything: the rooms, the Albertsons and the Swiss chocolates.

Balsam Mountain Inn
PO BOX 40, BALSAM, NORTH CAROLINA 28707

Built in 1908 and tucked away amongst lush trees, the magnificent Balsam Mountain Inn stands at 3500 feet and is enveloped by the spectacular Great Balsam Mountains. The welcoming staff creates a homely atmosphere enhanced by the large comfortable living area with wicker chairs, two fireplaces, marvellous foliage and an abundance of light from the many windows. Large porches on the front of the building have old oak rockers to gaze over the beautiful views. Original hardwood floors, beaded board walls and Victorian trim add to the authentic charm. Local artwork adorns the corridors and the library of this unique building, which has a wonderful collection of books. There are games available and a gift shop and on the ground floor. The individually decorated bedrooms have an old-fashioned feel with antique features, local twig furniture, colourful fabrics and no television or telephone to disturb the tranquil ambience. Delicious Southern fare featuring simple, honest dishes is served in the lovely, brightly decorated restaurant with mosaic floor. Outdoor enthusiasts will enjoy hiking, tennis, golf and the thrill of white water rafting. The Biltmore Estates, Great Smoky Mountain Park and Blue Ridge Parkway are nearby.

Our inspector loved: The 'get away from it all' feel at this historic Inn.

Directions: From Highway 74/23 take Balsam exit. Follow signs to Balsam Mountain Inn (35 miles south-west of Asheville).

Web: www.johansens.com/balsammountaininn
E-mail: balsaminn@earthlink.net
Tel: 1 828 456 9498
Fax: 1 828 456 9298
US Toll Free: 1 800 224 9498

Price Guide:
rooms $120
suites $175

NORTH CAROLINA - BEAUFORT

The Cedars Inn

305 FRONT STREET, BEAUFORT, NORTH CAROLINA 28516

Directions: In the heart of Beaufort's historic district.

Web: www.johansens.com/cedarsinn
Tel: 1 252 728 7036
Fax: 1 252 728 1685

Price Guide:
rooms $125
suites $150–$165

Situated in the heart of Beaufort's historic district, The Cedars is two charming traditional clapboarded houses that have stood watch over the city's harbour for over 200 years. Just steps away from all restaurants, shops and attractions, the complex has been lovingly transformed into a delightful hotel by the current owners, who have carefully chosen antiques and delicate furnishings to complement its period charm. There are just 11 bedrooms and suites, five of which are located in the main house, and the remainder in the adjacent house. Each has been beautifully decorated and feature special touches for guests' comfort. Some rooms have romantic four poster beds and Victorian claw-footed baths. The Carolina Cottage room even features hand-painted murals around the relaxing jacuzzi bath. Fires glow in the elegant fireplaces in the winter months and the smell of freshly cut flowers is always in the atmosphere. Breakfast is a sumptuous buffet of creative southern dishes that are the hallmark of the Inn. Menus change daily and are complimented by aromatic coffees presented in a silver service.. The Cedars also offers a wine bar with a selection of beer, wine, soft drinks and bottled waters. The Inn makes a great destination for intimate wedding services and romantic honeymoons. Business travellers will find an office centre with internet, fax and copying services.

Our inspector loved: The Carolina Cottage.

CHETOLA RESORT

PO BOX 17, NORTH MAIN STREET, BLOWING ROCK, NORTH CAROLINA 28605

This is North Carolina's High Country and Chetola Resort is one of its gems. Whether seeking action, adventure, challenges or just plain relaxation it is a real family treat with everything for everyone, all year round. Chetola encompasses 87 acres of glorious countryside surrounded by the Blue Ridge Parkway, the Blue Ridge Mountains and a 3,600 acre National Park. The mountain village of Blowing Rock with its attractive traditional and rustic shops, galleries, restaurants and artisan populace is a comfortable walk away. Chetola Lodge overlooks a picturesque lake and features beautifully appointed guestrooms and suites. If privacy is premier there is a choice of 1, 2 and 3 bedroom condominiums; all are comfortably furnished, have fully-equipped kitchens, fireplaces, outdoor decks and every facility expected in first-class accommodation. Excellent cuisine is served in the beautiful Manor House Restaurant and mountain specialities can be enjoyed in any of the 3 vintage dining rooms or on a patio overlooking the lake. A multitude of activities are available; from the resort's magnificent swimming pool and fitness centre to mountain-biking, riding, fly-fishing, boating, whitewater rafting at all levels, hiking, skiing and golf. An Adventure Camp offers exciting activities and trips for children.

Our inspector loved: The gorgeous setting on the lake and the first-class family atmosphere.

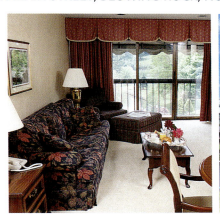

Directions: Located just off the Blue Ridge Parkway in the High Country.

Web: www.johansens.com/chetoaresort
E-mail: info@chetola.com
Tel: 1 828 295 5500
Fax: 1 828 295 5529
US Toll Free: 1 800 243 8652

Price Guide:
rooms $86–$190
suites $139–$235
condos $125–$395

Gideon Ridge Inn

PO BOX 1929, BLOWING ROCK, NORTH CAROLINA 28605

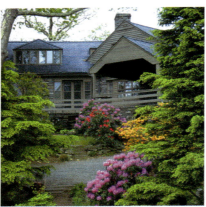

Directions: From Raleigh, Durham and Chapel Hill take Interstate 40 west to Greensboro-Winston-Salem, then take 421 north and up the mountain. Go south on Blue Ridge Parkway to Blowing Rock then take the 321 south. Turn right onto Rock Road, then the first left into Gideon Ridge Road.

Web: www.johansens.com/gideonridge
Email: innkeeper@ridge-inn.com
Tel: 1 828 295 3644
Fax: 1 828 295 4586

Price Guide:
rooms $150–$280
suites $220–$300

Built in 1939 as a secluded residence for a Boston family, Gideon Ridge Inn stands amidst some of the most breathtaking North Carolina scenery, with sweeping views of the Blue Ridge Mountains and surrounding countryside. Owned and operated by the same family since 1984, today, it is a welcoming and individual inn that prides itself on its personal levels of service and keen attention to detail. Each of the sunny bedrooms and suites are carefully furnished with antique pieces and welcoming décor, nine have private fireplaces and six open on to delightful terraces or gardens. Cuisine is a real delight at Gideon Ridge and a special touch is the pre-dinner chat with chef, Randy Plachy, who will take the time to explain the menu and preparations to each guest and advise on wine selections from the French and Californian list. The surrounding scenery can be explored by hiking, riding or even white water rafting and this is great skiing territory in winter. In summer there are many concerts and theatrical performances and art lovers can explore the many galleries in the area.

Our inspector loved: The breathtaking view of the mountains from the Inn.

Millstone Inn
119 LODGE LANE, HWY 64 WEST, CASHIERS, NORTH CAROLINA 28717

Built as a private home in 1933 and tucked away amongst lawns and lush greenery, Millstone Inn offers guests superb views of Whiteside Mountain and the Nantahala Forest, considered by many to be the finest scenery in North Carolina. A short hike away is the impressive Silver Slip Falls, part of the wild headwaters of the Chattooga River. Many other challenging hikes and picturesque waterfall are nearby together with some fine fly fishing, river rafting boating, horse back riding and mountain golf. You can explore the local antique and craft shops The Inn's seclusion and relaxing, mountain atmosphere are enhanced by the luxurious and comfortable accommodations, making it an ideal place for a restful or romantic getaway. Millstone Inn has been selected as one of Country Inns Magazine's '12 best inns.' The 7 guest rooms and 4 suites and one 2 bedrroom cottage have private bathrooms, charming and cheerful ambience, tasteful décor, period and antique furnishings, original art work and every up-to-date amenity; some have sitting rooms, kitchen, gas fireplaces, deck and all offer mountain views. The main sitting room has an open fireplace and an assortment of antique furniture, which makes it a popular rendezvous with guests. Guests dine in the Inn's scenic view dining room which is rustically elegant with old world Blue Willow china..

Our inspector loved: *The breathtaking views of the mountains from every room.*

Directions: Take Highway 64 west, at crossroads in Cashiers turn off at the Millstone Inn sign onto Wildriver Road and then take second right onto Lodge Lane.

Web: www.johansens.com/millstoneinn
E-mail: office@millstoneinn.com
Tel: 1 828 743 2737
Fax: 1 828 743 0208
US Toll Free: 1 888 645 5785

Price Guide:
rooms $170–$250
suites $220–$290
cottage $400–$520

NORTH CAROLINA - CHARLOTTE

BALLANTYNE RESORT

10000 BALLANTYNE COMMONS PARKWAY, CHARLOTTE, NORTH CAROLINA 28277

Tall, wide, impressive. Ballantyne soars seven stories high at the heart of 2,000 beautiful acres in the rolling hills just outside Charlotte. It is a vibrant, stylish and luxurious community complex - pristine and prestigious. A superb porte entrance leads guests into a gorgeous, flower-filled, marble-floor lobby with a library on one side and an intimate bar on the other. At the rear, a magnificent two-story palladian window overlooks the 18th fairway of the Par 71, golf course, voted 'Best New Golf Course of 1998'. Dana Rader, named by Golf Digest as one of 'America's Hundred Top Teachers', leads its team of PGA and LPGA instructors. Each guestroom and suite has every modern facility, from superb bathrooms with marble baths, oval soaking tubs and heated mirrors to two shelf marble vanity units, double telephone lines and electric safe. Sarah Bissel, the owner's wife, decorated the rooms herself after travelling the world to decide which custom made furniture would be best. She chose English. Mrs Bissel also commissioned original paintings depicting some of Charlotte's renowned sites from famed artist Tom Veith to hang throughout the hotel. Excellent cuisine is enjoyed in the Grill Room, Club Room and Ballroom. Extensive fitness and leisure facilities include a state-of-the art Spa, gymnasium, indoor swimming and wave pools.

Directions: Take I 485 to Exit 61, then route 521.

Web: www.johansens.com/ballantyneresort
E-mail: spa@ballantyneresort.com
Tel: 1 704 248 4000
Fax: 1 704 248 4005
US Toll Free: 1 866 248 4824

Price Guide:
rooms $180
suite $1200

Our inspector loved: The balcony overlooking the 18th green.

THE PARK

2200 REXFORD ROAD, CHARLOTTE, NORTH CAROLINA 28211

The Park was the first hotel in the prestigious South Park area of Charlotte and over the years has gained a reputation for comfort and privacy. It has the elegant look and quiet ambience of a grand European residence, with exquisite, classic style furnishings and a level of unobtrusive and attentive service associated with a leading luxury establishment. It's southern style hospitality has helped earn membership in Preferred Hotels and Resorts Worldwide as well as Mobil Four Star and AAA Four Diamond ratings. Each beautifully decorated and furnished guestroom has every amenity and feature, original artwork, marble bathroom, desk, two-line telephones with internet access and voice mail. For those preferring a little more pampering, luxurious suites have one or two bedrooms and a dining room. Complimentary services such as full-time concierge, nightly turndown and valet parking add to the pleasure of a stay. The hotel's Smoky's Grill is a favourite with locals. Prime chops and seafood head an excellent menu which is complemented by a selection of fine wines. An adjoining Piano Bar brings lively entertainment to weekends at the hotel. Leisure and fitness facilities include an outdoor pool, indoor and outdoor whirlpools, steam room and gym. Golfers can take on the challenge of the Par-71 course at Ballantynes Resort, The Park's nearby sister hotel.

Directions: Located in the SouthPark area of Charlotte and just a 20 minute drive from the international airport.

Web: www.johansens.com/thepark
Tel: 1 704 364 8220
Fax: 1 704 365 4712

Price Guide:
On application.

Our inspector loved: The extraordinary attention to service.

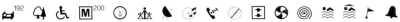

Morehead Manor Bed & Breakfast

914 VICKERS AVENUE, DURHAM, NORTH CAROLINA 27701

This elegant Colonial style home is ideally located for the heart of the downtown area. The Durham Bulls Athletic Park, historic Brightleaf Square and the universities are all moments' away, whilst the airport and interstates are also within easy access. The house itself is a veritable feast of style and maximises the owner's expertise with colour coordination. The entrance hall features the most dramatic chandelier, whilst throughout the Inn there are bold colour combinations that bring a contemporary twist to the period setting, and make strong accents of the furniture. The bathrooms feature specially commissioned tiles and luxurious fittings, and each of the guest rooms bears a unique and striking name – the Tiger Room or the Eagle's Inn, Magnolia Suite and Jasmine. Upon arrival, guests are served complimentary refreshments by their hosts, who use this time to assist with any queries over sightseeing or special plans, and to help with dinner reservations. There is a range of pampering packages available as well as Murder Mystery Weekends and a pre-wedding Bridesmaids' Package

Directions: Accessible from Interstates 85 and 40. RDU international airport nearby.

Web: www.johansens.com/moreheadmanor
E-mail: moreheadmanorbnb@aol.com
Tel: 1 919 687 4366
Fax: 1 919 687 4245

Price Guide:
rooms $135–$210

Our inspector loved: The Tiger Room.

NORTH CAROLINA - DURHAM

The Lords Proprietors' Inn

300 NORTH BROAD STREET, EDENTON, NORTH CAROLINA 27932

The Lords Proprietors' Inn is a collection of three beautifully restored turn-of-the-century buildings that open onto a delightful central patio with potted plants and trees adorned with fairy lights. Each house retains original characteristics such as hardwood floors and has individually decorated bedrooms with lovely bright colours and furniture made by a skilled local craftsman. The parlours have coal fireplaces, cosy sofas and fresh flowers to create a relaxing environment. A kitchen is available for drinks, tea and coffee and delicious freshly baked cookies. Stained glass is a stunning feature in Satterfield House, which has two suites with whirlpool tub, wet bar and king-size beds. The Pack House is a renovated tobacco warehouse that displays original old beams and a vaulted lounge with internal gallery wrapped by stairs. In the centre of the grounds is the Whedbee restaurant, which serves a superb gourmet dinner with distinctive regional flavours and fresh ingredients. Colourful checkerboard floors and matching décor create a charming, cheerful ambience. Guests can discover Edenton's slave history and visit Hope Plantation and other colonial houses. There is a wonderful cruise of Edenton Bay, an 18-hole golf course, sailing and the waterfront.

Our inspector loved: The historic rooms - the elegant dinners and the wonderful hostess.

Directions: Take Route 17 or 32 into downtown Edenton. The inn is on the corner of East Albemarle and Broad Street.

Web: www.johansens.com/lordsproprietors
E-mail: stay@edentoninn.com
Tel: 1 252 482 3641
Fax: 1 252 482 2432

Price Guide:
rooms $135–$190
suites $260

INNISFREE VICTORIAN INN AND GARDEN HOUSE
PO BOX 469, GLENVILLE, NORTH CAROLINA 28736

Web: www.johansens.com/Innisfreevictorianinn
Tel: 1 828 743 2946

Price Guide:
rooms $119–$150
suites $249–$290

Summer, winter, sunshine or snow, whatever the season or the weather this picturesque, 2 storey hillside Inn offers the most friendly and warmest of retreats combined with the utmost comfort and fantastic scenic views from each bedroom or porch. The scenic splendour appears to get better every year and the majestic surrounding Blue Ridge Mountains never disappoint with their stark magnificence. It is difficult not to succumb to the clear and crisp air, the deep greens of thousands of wooded acres and the hospitality of Innisfree owner Henry Hoche. He is a master host, catering for every guest individually, entertaining royally and cooking mouth-watering meals. He is also a celebrated ballroom dancer who can be coaxed into showing a few steps! Guestrooms in the Inn and its Garden House have everything that can be desired; from television and CD players to huge jacuzzis and fluffy bathrobes. They are all en suite, extremely spacious, individually and elegantly decorated, luxuriously furnished and boast superb panoramic views over the gardens and Lake Glenville. Delicious Irish Coffee is served in front of crackling open fires in the high ceiling parlour but for real relaxation little can better than taking afternoon refreshments on the high sweeping veranda.

Our inspector loved: *The special theme parties that keep guests coming back year after year. Truly a gem in the mountains.*

Claddagh Inn

755 NORTH MAIN STREET, HENDERSONVILLE, NORTH CAROLINA, 28792

Owners, Vanessa Mintz and Eric McDowell, have aimed to infuse the essence and spirit of the word 'Claddagh,' which means, 'loyalty, love and friendship,' into the Inn itself. Newly renovated, the Inn has stood in Hendersonville, North Carolina for over 100 years and has offered traditional hospitality to guests throughout American history. Its cheerful classical revival exterior boasts a wraparound veranda with comfortable chairs, affording guests and innkeepers alike conducive surroundings to sit and share stories of their day. The interior has been restored to the original look of the late 1800's and features an eclectic array of antiques, oriental rugs and rich wallcoverings, while a library holds a wide selection of books for visitors to use. Here, a relaxing glass of sherry is served nightly and in the mornings a full home-cooked breakfast includes eggs, grits, muffins, Hendersonville-baked apples or pancakes. Each of the unique guest rooms is comfortable with delightful décor and a range of facilities is on offer, including a suite suitable for families. The Inn has a business centre for corporate guests and also caters for private parties and luncheons. Its location means it is an ideal base for exploring the Great Smoky Mountains National Park and the Blue Ridge Parkway.

Our inspector loved: The wraparound porch with rocking chairs.

Directions: I-26 to exit 18b, turn right onto Main Street.

Web: www.johansens.com/claddaghinn
E-mail: innkeepers@claddaghinn.com
Tel: 1 828 697 7778

Price Guide:
rooms $105–$150

NORTH CAROLINA - HIGHLANDS

Inn at Half Mile Farm

PO BOX 2769, 214 HALF MILE DRIVE, HIGHLANDS, NORTH CAROLINA 28741

Tucked away on the outskirts of town, this lovely rambling inn is a paradise for nature lovers and those who hanker for fresh mountain air, forests, ponds, streams and the great outdoor life. There's hiking, fly-fishing, lake canoeing, white water rafting and just about every mountain activity. All can be arranged by a friendly and helpful staff. Originally a mid-19th century farmhouse the Inn is surrounded by beautiful grounds which feature a lake, swimming pool and an abundance of wild flowers and deep greenery. All of which can be viewed and enjoyed from comfortable whicker rocking chairs on the shaded porch. Sit and watch the sun rise and set over the mountain peaks while an early morning coffee is sipped or an evening complimentary wine and hors d'oeuvres savoured. Tennessee fieldstone fireplaces, soft sofas, polished pine floors, local wood decorations and Rattan stick furniture in the breakfast room are particularly attractive features of the four guestrooms in the main house and those surrounding a colourful courtyard and fountain. All fifteen rooms are spacious, individually decorated and have every comfort and amenity. Soft muted tones and locally crafted beds, tables and lights provide a calm, relaxing rustic atmosphere. Most rooms have decks and jetted tubs with king suites boasting fireplaces and sitting areas.

Directions: A two-hour drive from Atlanta and in close proximity to interstates 40, 77 and 85

Web: www.johansens.com/halfmilefarm
E-mail: halfmilefarm@aol.com
Tel: 1 828 526 8170
Fax: 1 828 526 2625

Price Guide:
rooms $180–$285

Our inspector loved: The light and airy rooms.

THE WHITE DOE INN & WHISPERING BAY

PO BOX 1029, 319 SIR WALTER RALEIGH STREET, MANTEO, NORTH CAROLINA 27954

Originally built in 1898 and extended in 1910, this elegant building has become one of the most photographed houses on the island of Roanoke. Renowned for its beautiful architecture and wrap around porch, it takes its name from a local legend. The legend has it that the first English child born to settlers on the island was turned into a white doe by a powerful medicine man and hunted and killed by Indians. The story goes that rare glimpses of fleeting white shadows can still be seen on late evenings. The hotel verandah is a fine place from which to while away summer's evenings. There are just 8 bedrooms and 3 suites, each has its own style and character, embracing modern luxury incorporating the period charm of turrets and garrets. The dining room serves a delicious southern style breakfast every morning and afternoon tea and refreshments. There is a great deal to see and enjoy on the island – indeed, the harbour front is only minute's away – including Fort Raleigh National Historic Site, The Wright Brothers Memorial Museum and the Lost Colony Outdoor Drama offering a range of sports and leisure pursuits.

Our inspector loved: *The legend of the White Doe.*

Directions: US 64/264 onto Sir Walter Raleigh Street. One block down turn left onto Uppowac Street.

Web: www.johansens.com/whitedoe
E-mail: whitedoe@whitedoeinn.com
Tel: 1 252 473 9851
Fax: 1 252 473 4708
US Toll Free: 1 800 473 6091

Price Guide:
rooms $150–$230
suites $275–$375

THE SIENA HOTEL

1505 E. FRANKLIN STREET, CHAPEL HILL, NORTH CAROLINA 27514

Directions: 15 miles from Raleigh Durham Airport on I40 West to 15-501 South.

Web: www.johansens.com/siena
E-mail: msherburne@sienahotel.com
Tel: 1 919 929 4000
Fax: 1 919 968 8527

Price Guide:
rooms $180–$235
suites $230–$325

Named after a small, beautiful Italian town cradled in the Northern hills of Tuscany, The Siena Hotel embodies the spirit of Italy in the heart of North Carolina. A personalised check-in service surrounded by authentic marble is overshadowed only by the sight and aroma of roses grown in the gardens. The décor is luxurious, with grand European antiques, elaborate furnishings, rich textured fabrics, majestic columns, warm colours and soft lighting. The hallways and rooms are a picture of grandeur reflected by the Renaissance paintings together with the Hotel's overall ambience, floral aromas and excellent service. Based on a Tuscan villa, The Siena is considered by many to be North Carolina's finest luxury boutique hotel and has been a AAA Four Diamond holder since 1989. Each of the 68 guest rooms and 12 suites are individually appointed with rich fabrics and elaborate artwork; they have magnificent marble bathrooms, the latest technology and lovely additional touches such as a nightly turndown service, Belgian Siena chocolates, soft bathrobes and European toiletries. Exceptional cuisine can be enjoyed in Il Palio, the only AAA Four Diamond Italian restaurant in the State.

Our inspector loved: *Feeling as if you are in Italy.*

NORTH CAROLINA - ROBBINSVILLE

SNOWBIRD MOUNTAIN LODGE

275 SANTEETLAH ROAD, ROBBINSVILLE, NORTH CAROLINA 28771

The views get better and better as guests ascend 3,000 feet up a winding road to this magnificent two-storey chalet lodge nestling in 100 acres of undisturbed hilltop drenched in the clearest and crispest of air. The view culminates in an awe-inspiring panoramic picture through 12-feet-high windows of the unspoilt mountain ranges and thousands of wooded acres in the magnificent Nantahala National Forest. These windows are in the Great Room, distinguished by its 21-feet-high cathedral ceiling with chestnut beams, wrought-iron chandeliers, butternut panelling, a 2,000-volume library, two massive stone fireplaces and comfortable rocking chairs, overstuffed sofas, leather chairs, local artwork and colourful fresh flowers from the garden. It is a popular relaxing venue for every guest who just wants to chat about their day, view the scenery or stargaze through binoculars and viewfinders helpfully placed around the room. The guest rooms are superb. There are 15 in the rustic main lodge, two with decks in nearby Wolfe Cottage and six in Chestnut Lodge, each with private porch. All are panelled in hardwood, have local crafted furniture and every facility from ceiling fan to coffeemaker, but no telephone or television. Delicious buffet breakfasts and gourmet dinners are served in a lovely dining room warmed in winter by a crackling log fire

Directions: From Robinsville take North Carolina Highway 143 West

Web: www.johansens.com/snowbirdmountainlodge
E-mail: innkeeper@snowbirdlodge.com
Tel: 1 828 479 3433
US Toll Free: 800 941 9290
Fax: 1 828 479 3473

Price Guide: (full board)
rooms $170
suite $350

Our inspector loved: The warmth and friendliness of the Lodge.

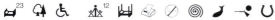

NORTH CAROLINA - TRYON

PINE CREST INN

85 PINE CREST LANE, TRYON, NORTH CAROLINA 28782

Directions: From I-26, exit 36 to Tryon. Follow Rte 108/176 to town of Tryon. Turn on New Market Rd. Follow signs to Inn.

Web: www.johansens.com/pinecrestinn
E-mail: info@pinecrestinn.com
Tel: 1 828 859 9135
US Toll Free: 1 800 633 3001
Fax: 1 828 859 9135

Price Guide:
rooms $135–$190
suite $190–$550

Situated at the foot of the Blue Ridge Mountains, this traditional English-style inn was once a popular haunt for some of America's finest 20th-century authors including F Scott Fitzgerald and Ernest Hemingway. Its beautiful location makes Pine Crest Inn an ideal choice for enthusiasts of outdoor pursuits. The interior is furnished in a quaint style with stone fireplaces, wooden floors and oriental rugs. The charming owners have aimed to create a "home away from home" ambience, with books to read beside the fire, games to play and areas for guests to commune. The choice of accommodation is delightfully varied with rooms, suites and cottages; all individually decorated. There is a wide array of amenities such as cable television, telephones, bathrobes and sherry. Guests relax with a drink in the Fox and Hounds Bar before dining in the superb restaurant; serving imaginative dishes and a fine selection of wines. The Pine Crest Inn is renowned for its excellent cuisine and a breakfast is the highlight of every morning, with blueberry muffins, Belgian waffles, eggs Benedict and other specialities. After a hearty meal, guests may wish to ramble through the surrounding woods or explore the many nearby hiking trails. Volleyball may be practised on site whilst golf, tennis, swimming and riding is arranged nearby.

Our inspector loved: The variety of rooms and country cottages nestled around the grounds.

THE SWAG COUNTRY INN
2300 SWAG ROAD, WAYNESVILLE, NORTH CAROLINA 28785

Nestled in a secluded position atop a breathtaking 5,000 foot ridge overlooking the Smoky Mountains, The Swag Country Inn is a peaceful, relaxing hideaway on the boundary of the Great Smoky Mountains National Park. It is a paradise for nature lovers who seek the finest amenities in a romantic and natural setting. Superb cuisine and a house-party environment help create the Smokies' great Country Inn. It has a Mobil 4 Star and has been listed annually by Andrew Harper's Hideaway Report since 1993, when it was named 'Hideaway of the Year.' 15 exquisite, individually decorated guest rooms have beautiful handcrafted interiors, quilts, fireplaces, porches and spectacular views. Comfortable, hickory bark and rhododendron beds all boast hypo-allergenic feather mattress toppers and the natural materials of hand-picked fieldstone and hand-hewn logs complement the surrounding 250 unspoilt acres. Breakfasts are magnificent and superb picnics can be arranged. "Town and Country" calls the meals at The Swag 'sophisticated,' guests dine together by candlelight, enjoying sumptuous 4 courses. The estate has its own entrance into the Great Smoky Mountains National Park. Guests can follow wilderness trails, relax in a hammock, lounge in the spa or play croquet.

Our inspector loved: The soothing blend of rustic elegance and spectacular scenery and the fun drive up to the Inn.

Directions: I-40 to exit 20. Exit to state highway 276; 2.8 miles to The Swag sign; right on Grindstone Road; right on Hempill Road. 7 miles to Inn's gate; 2.5 miles up the paved private driveway.

Web: www.johansens.com/swagcountryinn
E-mail: letters@theswag.com
Tel: 1 828 926 0430
Fax: 1 828 926 2036

Price Guide: (incl. all meals)
rooms from $265
suites to $295 - $640

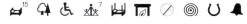

The Verandas

202 NUN STREET, WILMINGTON, NORTH CAROLINA 28401-5020

Directions: From I-40 exit 8, turn left into Market Street. After 4.5 miles turn left into 3rd Street; after four blocks turn right into Nun Street.

Web: www.johansens.com/verandas
E-mail: verandas4@aol.com
Tel: 1 910 251 2212
Fax: 1 910 251 8932

Price Guide:
rooms $150–$200

Close to the Cape Fear River in the picturesque town of Wilmington, The Verandas is a completely refurbished elegant white clapboard mansion with an opulent ambience created by architectural grandeur, many original artworks and period details. Comfortable rockers on four Italianate verandas are perfect for relaxation, and light pours from the tall windows into the parlours with their pale yellow walls, crystal chandeliers and oak floors. Cowhide chairs mixed with antique furniture and a grandfather clock add to the graceful Piano Room and quiet library. The enclosed cupola with panoramic views over the Wilmington skyline is wonderful for sipping a glass of wine while watching the sunset. Spacious, individually decorated bedrooms boast gorgeous fabrics, and quality toiletries ensure luxurious comfort in the marble bathrooms. Breakfast is a delight with exotic fruit compotes, croissants filled with peaches and other delicacies served on a long mahogany table or on the terrace surrounded by intimate back gardens. Guests can visit numerous museums and historical houses, take a carriage tour of historic Wilmington or a river trip on Cape Fear. Activities include golf, fishing and beach trips. The hotel is also AAA 4 Diamond.

Our inspector loved: *This beautiful Inn.*

NORTH CAROLINA - WINSTON SALEM

Augustus T. Zevely Inn

803 SOUTH MAIN STREET, WINSTON-SALEM, NORTH CAROLINA 27101

Located in the centre of Old Salem, the Inn is featured on the National Historic Register and has been meticulously restored to its original mid 19th century appearance. To reflect the warm and inviting atmosphere of the traditional Moravian town, all of the Inn's furnishings have been carefully selected while some of the fixtures, floor coverings and window treatments have been especially produced. A characteristically Moravian corner fireplace burns in the parlour that is used as a gathering place for guests and serves complimentary sherry or brandy. Across the hall is a breakfast room which was once the office of Dr. Augustus T. Zevely, today, it offers a selection of fare every morning, including Moravian baked goods, as well as cheese and wine in the evenings. A mural in the Inn depicts a historically accurate scene of Old Salem in 1844 and a 2 storey porch at the rear is shaded by a beautiful magnolia tree and provides an ideal location for relaxing and spotting the resident guinea fowl. 12 rooms and suites are again decorated to reflect their original uses and each have a private bathroom, television and telephone while some feature whirlpool or steam baths. Old Salem itself is well worth exploring, as are Salem College and the Salem Tavern.

Our inspector loved: The warm, cosy atmosphere.

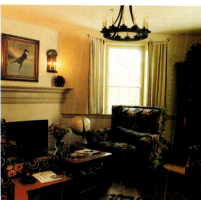

Directions: Directions are available upon request.

Web: www.johansens.com/augustustzevely
E Mail: ctheall@dddcompany.com
Tel: 1 336 748 9299
Fax: 1 336 721 2211

Price Guide:
rooms $115–205

OREGON

Hotel location shown in red with page number

OREGON - GRANTS PASS

Weasku Inn

5560 ROGUE RIVER HIGHWAY, GRANTS PASS, OREGON 97527

Nestling on the banks of the Rogue River this exquisite timber lodge boasts an outstanding natural setting. Owner Carl Johnson has created a warm and welcoming atmosphere throughout the inn that feels more like a family home than a hotel. Since being built in 1924 Weasku Inn has become a legend in Oregon and attracted numerous Hollywood personalities such as Clark Cable, Bing Crosby and Walt Disney. Renovated in 1998 this superbly designed inn exudes a stylish air with subtle warm décor and solid, comfortable furniture. There are five lodge guest rooms, nine river cabins, two river suite cabins and a two-room A-frame cabin. All are spacious and have every modern facility including private bath, direct dial telephone and color cable television; some have whirlpool tubs. All river cabins have beamed ceilings, open fireplaces, Pacific Northwest furnishings and private decks overlooking the river. The magnificent Great Room in the Lodge is highlighted by a huge fireplace, native American rugs and period furniture. Adjoining is an intimate meeting room with French windows which opens onto a deck with garden views. Breakfasts are full continental. Jet boating, rafting, canoeing and fishing are all available and a visit to the Oregon Caves can be arranged.

Our inspector loved: *The river cabins on the banks of the Rugue River at this exquisite family owned Inn, frequented by Hollywood personalities.*

Directions: Exit 48 off I-5, cross bridge, turn right, travel for three miles. The inn is on the right past Savage Rapid's Dam.

Web: www.johansens.com/weaskuinn
E-mail: info@weasku.com
Tel: 1 541 471 8000
Fax: 1 541 471 7038
Toll free: 1 800 4 WEASKU

Price Guide:
rooms $110–$150
suites $195–295

Pennsylvania

Hotel location shown in red with page number

RITTENHOUSE SQUARE EUROPEAN BOUTIQUE HOTEL

1715 RITTENHOUSE SQUARE, PHILADELPHIA, PENNSYLVANIA 19103

This traditional, 19th-century carriage house in the fashionable Rittenhouse Square district of downtown Philadelphia has been sympathetically restored and transformed into a luxury Bed and Breakfast by Innkeeper Harriet Seltzer. It is an intimate, comfortable retreat with style, sophistication, charm and fine furnishings. Ten individually designed guestrooms and suites are delightfully decorated with designer fabrics and furnished with antiques. Each unique scheme creates a different atmosphere, from the wildly romantic to elegant European. Guests can enjoy all the luxury normally associated with five star hotels. All rooms are extremely comfortable, have air conditioning, marble bathrooms, plush robes, triple sheeting with nightly turndown service, computer workstations with Internet access, telephone and 100 channel cable television. A Continental breakfast is served in the charming lower level café which is also available for private functions and meetings. Harriet invites guests to join her and her team each evening for a wine and snack reception in the welcoming and elegant drawing room. A 24-hour Concierge service is available. Rittenhouse Square is within walking distance of many of the city's leading restaurants and cafés, museums, historical attractions and shops.

Our inspector loved: *Sitting in the parlour with a glass of wine, listening to classical music.*

Directions: Between Locust and Spruce Streets, between 17th and 18th Streets.

Web: www.johansens.com/rittenhouse
E-mail: innkeeper@rittenhousebb.com
Tel: 1 215 545 6500
Fax: 1 215 546 8787

Price Guide:
rooms $209
suite $259

PENNSYLVANIA - PHILADELPHIA

THE THOMAS BOND HOUSE
129 SOUTH 2ND STREET, PHILADELPHIA, PENNSYLVANIA 19106

The celebrated physician, Thomas Bond, is best remembered for co-founding Pennsylvania Hospital, the first public hospital in the United States. In 1769 he built this 4 storey house in this fashionable Philadelphia residential area where it remains as an important example of classic revival Georgian-style architecture. Guests are welcomed into an array of unique features such as the ionic modillion cornice at its roof line, the Rumford fireplace in the parlour and a 'borrowed light window' on the garret floor. Rooms have been carefully restored and furnished in-keeping with the customs of the Federal period and include the Dr. Thomas Bond Sr. Room with its queen size rice four poster bed, oriental rugs and period Chippendale furniture and the Robert Fulton Room with its extensive original millwork and view over the Delaware River. A downstairs room is available for meetings and parties and visitors can relax in the parlour and enjoy a game of chess or bridge. Breakfast is served daily and evenings start with complimentary cheese and wine. The Innkeeper is happy to organise dinner or theatre reservations, as well as use of a local health club. The Thomas Bond House is within walking distance of many of the old city's historic sites including Independence Hall.

Directions: Situated between Chestnut and Walnut Streets.

Web: www.johansens.com/thomasbond
E Mail: ctheall@dddcompany.com
Tel: 1 215 923 8523
Fax: 1 215 923 8504

Price Guide:
rooms $115–$175

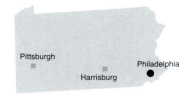

Our inspector loved: This warm fine Inn, especially the parlour.

SOUTH CAROLINA
Hotel location shown in red with page number

SOUTH CAROLINA - AIKEN

Rosemary & Lookaway Inn

804 CAROLINA AVENUE, NORTH AUGUSTA, SOUTH CAROLINA 29841

These 2 antebellum mansions were built at the turn of the century and lie just across the Savannah River from Augusta, home to the prestigious Masters Golf Tournament. Both houses were prominent in the development of North Augusta and are now on the Historic Register. Their stunning period features include 50 foot columns, wide verandas, grand staircases and camellia bushes and all of the rooms are beautifully furnished with antiques and fine reproductions. Each of the 23 spacious bedrooms have en suite bathrooms and some boast jacuzzis and private terraces. Fabrics and décor are individual throughout but four poster and canopy beds ensure a sound night's sleep for all guests. A full, home-cooked breakfast is served in the breakfast room daily and in the evening, hors d'oeuvres are served during cocktail hour. Local activities include golf, apple and berry picking, city tours and balloon rides, while nearby places of interest include Lake Thurmond, Hitchcock Gardens and Preserve and the University of South Carolina. The Innkeeper of Rosemary and Lookaway Hall also has an additional property, the Sandhurst Estate, which offers accommodation in the neighbouring village of Aiken.

Directions: From Augusta, take the 13th street James Jackson Bridge. The street then becomes Georgia Avenue, the Hotel is 1 block up between Georgia & Central Avenues.

Web: www.johansens.com/rosemaryandlookawayinn
Tel: 1 803 278 6222
Fax: 1 803 278 4877

Price Guide:
rooms $125–$250

Our inspector loved: The staircase, which looks like the famous one from Gone with the Wind.

VENDUE INN
19 VENDUE RANGE, CHARLESTON, SOUTH CAROLINA 29401

Built in the 1850s, this converted warehouse is situated near the water's edge within easy strolling distance of Charleston's delightful centre. Its impressive façade and old-fashioned windows give it a graceful appearance, which is complemented by a friendly greeting from the Vendue Inn's uniformed valet. The hotel is traditionally decorated with hardwood floors, oriental rugs and authentic antiques. Bedrooms are lavishly appointed with superb décor and luxurious bathrooms, and the suites offer four-poster beds, marble baths, Jacuzzis and gas fireplaces. All bedrooms have up-to-date facilities including data port, voicemail and extra telephone lines . In the evening wine and hors d'oeuvres are served in the Music Room, and the rooftop bar is the perfect place to enjoy a cocktail and appetisers while watching the sun go down over the waterfront and the city. Dining is a delight in the intimate Library Restaurant, which serves delectable American cuisine and excellent wines. A full Southern breakfast buffet comes with all overnight stays. Guests may use the hotel's complimentary bicycles, explore Charleston's quaint market, the Waterfront Park or the many historic homes and museums in the area.

Our inspector loved: The wonderful rooftop bar.

Directions: From I-26 take Hwy 17 north, exit East Bay Street, then turn right.

Web: www.johansens.com/vendueinn
E-mail: vendueinnresv@aol.com
Tel: 1 843 577 7970
Fax: 1 843 577 2913

Price Guide:
rooms $160
suites $239

SOUTH CAROLINA - PAWLEYS ISLAND

Litchfield Plantation

KINGS RIVER ROAD, BOX 290, PAWLEYS ISLAND, SOUTH CAROLINA 29585

Dramatically situated at the heart of a former rice plantation, Litchfield is a beautifully preserved country inn. Visitors are immediately struck by the magic of the location, as the quarter mile avenue to the main house is flanked by century-old oak trees which form an enchanting tunnel to this languid South Carolina hideaway. Guests can stay in the luxurious suites within the main house, or choose the seclusion of one of the many villas dotted around the 600-acre estate. These gorgeously designed and individually decorated retreats benefit from spacious lounges and huge bathrooms, some with Jacuzzi tubs. The Carriage House, an attractive low country-style building is the venue for excellent continental cuisine complemented by seasonal specialities, prepared by cordon bleu chefs. Tennis courts adorn the estate, whilst the large heated pool has excellent views of the rice fields. Guests can relax at the 3-storey beach house, moor their yachts at the marina, or take trips along the coast. The region attracts golf fanatics and the inn has ten of South Carolina's most celebrated golf courses at its doorstep. Deep sea and sport fishing, trips to historic Charleston and river cruises are also available to visitors

Directions: From Charleston, take Hwy 17 north for about 70 miles. Turn left onto Waverly Road; at stop, turn right onto Kings River Road, after 1 mile entrance is on left.

Web: www.johansens.com/litchrfieldplantation
E-mail: vacation@litchfieldplantation.com
Tel: 1 843 237 9121
US Toll Free: 800 869 1410
Fax: 1 843 237 1041

Price Guide: (incl. full breakfast)
rooms from $215
suites $240–$620

Our inspector loved: *Feeling as if you had been transported in to the 1700's. The drive onto the Plantation will take your breath away.*

La Bastide
10 ROAD OF VINES, TRAVELERS REST, SOUTH CAROLINA 29690

Set in a French winemaking village in the foothills of the magnificent Blue Ridge Mountains, La Bastide is an intimate "French Provençal" country inn offering informal hospitality. Original timbers and old terracotta roof tiles create a charming atmosphere complemented by beautiful, carefully chosen interior decoration. The wrought-iron chandeliers and staircase are covered in vines and grapes, tapestries adorn the walls and delightful fabrics are used throughout. Picture windows in the cathedral ceilinged lounge open onto a walled courtyard where a relaxing game of croquet or petanque is played; entry to the well-stocked library is via a remarkable walk-through fireplace. The spacious bedrooms boast large marble bathrooms, original and French reproduction furniture, beautiful linens and feather beds. Fine French cuisine, for which the chef uses only the freshest local ingredients is complemented by excellent wines and served in the romantic restaurant. It is possible to dine outside on the delightful patio and a lavish breakfast is served in the cheerful breakfast room, where the tables are brightly decorated with print cloths. Fishing, tennis, horse riding, croquet and an exceptional golf course are available for the energetic.

Our inspector loved: *Dreaming of days 'en Provence' with views of vineyards from the shuttered windows.*

Directions: From Greenville take Highway 276 towards Travelers Rest; then take Hwy 25 north; after 10 miles turn into Old Route 25. The inn is on the right.

Web: www.johansens.com/labastde
E-mail: labastide@mindspring.com
Tel: 1 864 836 8463
Fax: 1 864 836 4820

Price Guide:
rooms $260–$310

Tennessee

Hotel location shown in red with page number

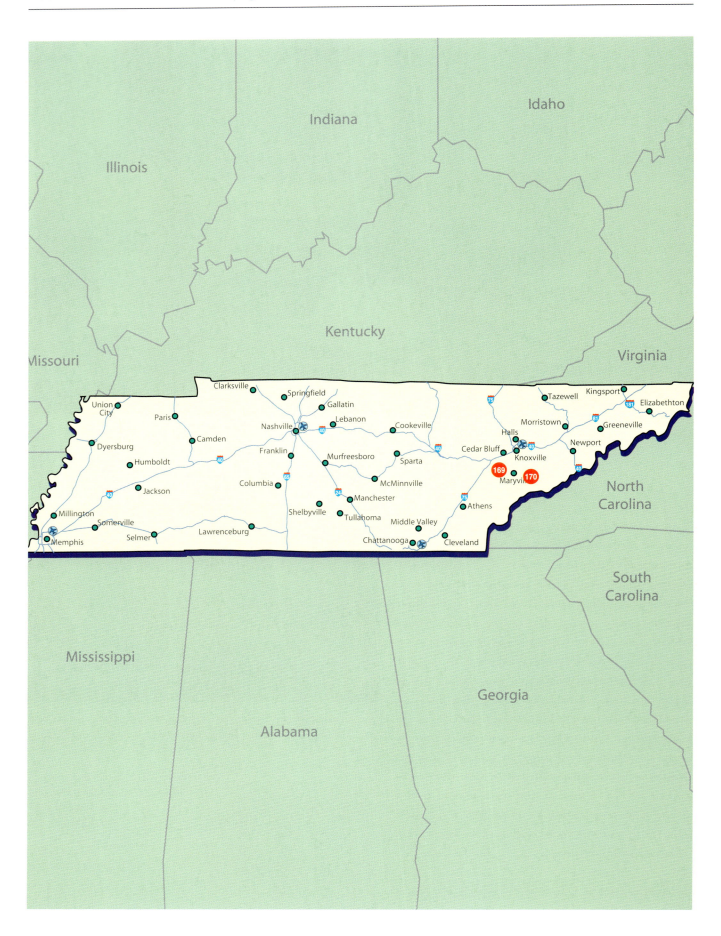

TENNESSEE - KINGSTON

WHITESTONE COUNTRY INN
1200 PAINT ROCK ROAD, KINGSTON, TENNESSEE 37763

Set in 360 acres of the glorious Tennessee countryside, and on the shores of the fantastic Watts Bar Lake, the Whitestone Country Inn is the perfect destination in which to relax, unwind and really enjoy the great outdoors. The atmosphere is one of unpretentious luxury, and the surrounding scenery plays a key part in a stay at Whitestone. Each of the bedrooms is individually crafted in the name of one of the birds from the adjacent Paint Rock Wildlife and Waterfowl Refuge. Unique stained glass artwork of each bird sits above each doorway and the rooms are decorated in corresponding colours. This is fantastic walking territory with 8 miles of hiking trails, and the fabulous Watts Bar Lake, all 39,000 acres of it, is host to a wide range of water pursuits. There is 8,000 feet of shoreline, and the Inn has facilities for kayaking, canoeing, and paddle boats. The Inn is made up of a collection of 6 charming buildings, each one has its own particular purpose. The Lion and Lamb building has conference facilities for up to 50, the Entrance Barn houses 3 luxurious suites, and the old Schoolhouse has 2 suites, office and gift shop. All rooms have whirlpool tubs, fireplaces, whilst 7 of the luxury suites have waterfall spa showers.

Our inspector loved: *The Oasis in pristine beauty where God left his shoes.*

Directions: From I-75 exit 72, take Highway 72 west. Travel for 9 miles then turn right into Paint Rock Road. From I-40 exit 352, take Highway 58 south. Travel for 6 miles then turn left onto Highway 72E, after 5 miles turn left into Paint Rock Road.

Web: www.johansens.com/whitestonecountryinn
E-mail: moreinfo@whitestoneinn.com
Tel: 1 865 376 0113
Fax: 1 865 376 4454
US Toll Free: 1 888 247 2464

Price Guide:
suites $150–$350

TENNESSEE - WALLAND

BLACKBERRY FARM

1471 WEST MILLERS COVE ROAD, WALLAND, GREAT SMOKY MOUNTAINS, TENNESSEE 37886

Directions: From Knoxville Follow Hwy 129S onto Hwy 321N, towards Townsend. Pass the Foothills Parkway and turn right onto W. Millers Cove Rd.

Web: www.johansens.com/blackberryfarm
E-mail: info@blackberryfarm.com
Tel: 1 865 380 2260
Fax: 1 865 681 7753
US Toll Free: 1 888 437 8981

Price Guide:
(including Breakfast, lunch & 5 course dinner)
rooms $395–$795
suites $695–$1950

With an increasing string of accolades, Blackberry Farm really does offer guests an extaordinary experience. Nestled in the foothills of the Great Smoky Mountains, this 1,100 acre property, described as "the loveliest, most luxurious place ever.", constantly ranks amongst the top 10 hotels in North America. The views of the mountains are magnificent whether snow-clad in winter, or golden-hued in autumn and guests have many opportunities to enjoy these beautiful surroundings with outdoor activities such as fly fishing, horseback riding, hiking, mountain biking. or simply relaxing in a rocker on the veranda. Additional year round activities include cooking schools with famous chefs and pampering in the Farmhouse Spa. The welcome inside the Hotel is warm and inviting with idyllic bedrooms draped with English chintz and elegant period furniture. The kitchen at Blackberry Farm is home to Chef John Fleer's highly acclaimed Foothills Cuisine. Guests enjoy breakfast, gourmet picnic lunch and five-course candlelight dinner served in the mountain dining room, offering fabulous views of the Great Smoky Mountains. All this, and the nation's best service (according to the Condé Nast Traveler Gold List), is located 18 miles from Knoxville airport which features direct flights daily from 13 major cities.

Our inspector loved: The peace & clear air that you feel in this oasis at the foot of the Great Smoky Mountains.

Texas

Hotel location shown in red with page number

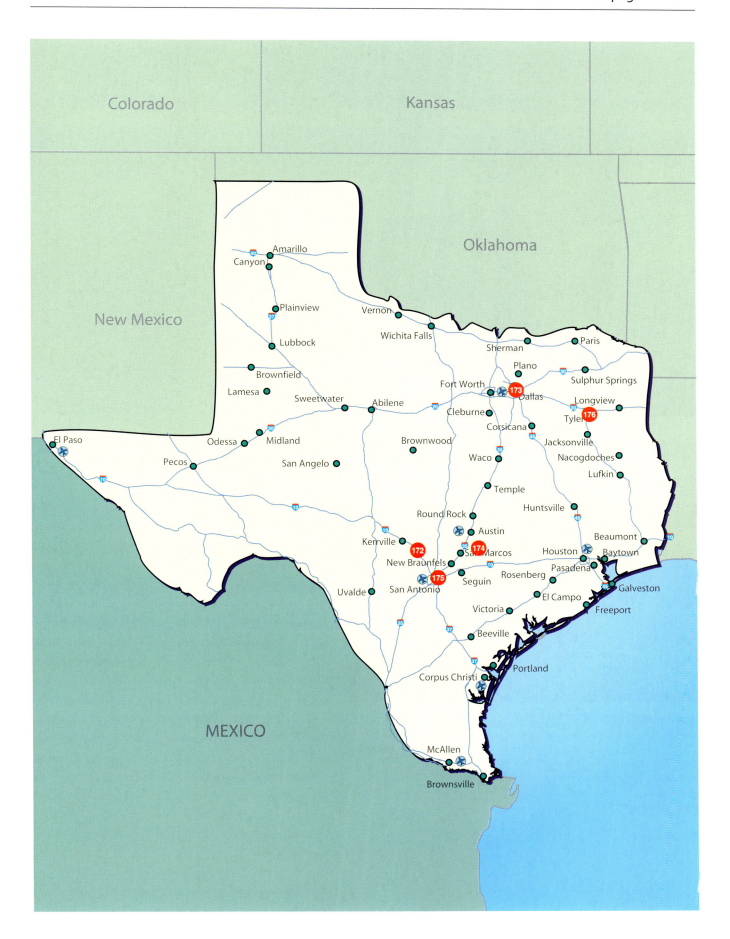

Ye Kendall Inn

128 WEST BLANCO, BOERNE, TEXAS 78006

Directions: 35 minutes from San Antonio, in downtown Boerne on main square.

Web: www.johansens.com/yekendallinn
E-mail: info@yekendallinn.com
Tel: 1 830 249 2138
Fax: 1 830 249 7371

Price Guide:
rooms $109–$139
suites $140–$190

The Inn was established in 1859 as a stagecoach stop for weary travellers and today, as a registered state and national historic landmark, it continues this tradition. Famous guests have included Jefferson Davis, President Dwight D. Eisenhower and Robert E. Lee, and many English and American antiques pay homage to the grandeur of its past. All 17 guest rooms, suites and cabins are well appointed and beautifully restored and furnished. The original main building is constructed of 22 inch thick limestone walls with lovely front and back porches attached. It is thought that a tunnel, once used as a shelter from hostile Native American Indians, runs from the cellar to another building a block away. Located on 5 ½ acres of land the Inn overlooks Cibolo Creek and Boerne's main plaza and a lush courtyard and landscaped gardens feature native plants, fountains and a Koi pond. At the Limestone Grille, Executive Chef Michael McClure creates widely acclaimed 'New American' cuisine and guests can enjoy dinner served on the porch or by the fireplace in the open-air courtyard. Nearby attractions include golf, horse riding and a spa, while the Inn has its own eclectic shops that offer a range of antiques, clothing, gifts and accessories.

Our inspector loved: The excellent food, especially the lamb stew.

TEXAS - DALLAS

THE ADOLPHUS
1321 COMMERCE STREET, DALLAS, TEXAS 75202

With increasing renown for its wonderful mix of art and antiques, The Adolphus is a cultural haven in the heart of Dallas. Ideally situated for the shops, opera and State Fair this is a hotel that offers twenty-first century luxury with a little extra. All the bedrooms are elegant and spacious with marble bathrooms and stylish fabrics, yet it is the clever use of original pieces that gives the hotel a feel of the English manor house, and a distinct sense of bygone charm. Original Flemish tapestries, a Napoleonic mirror and a Steinway grand piano that once belonged to the Guggenheims are all to be found in the lobby living room, creating a sympathetic background to afternoon tea. The French Room is a spectacular setting for a light interpretation of classical French cuisine with crystal chandeliers and gilt sconces reflecting on arched and mural-painted 18 foot ceilings. The executive is equally well-catered for at the Adolphus - the Executive Business Center provides custom typing and desktop publishing as well as computer workstations, while staff pride themselves on their conference services. Each event is assigned a dedicated planner to cover each and every detail, while audio-visual experts are located in house and complemented by award-winning caterers.

Our inspector loved: The grand lounges & dining room where Executive Chef William Koval creates culinary masterpieces.

Directions: Located in the heart of the financial district.

Web: www.johansens.com/hoteladolphus
Tel: 1 214 742 8200
Fax: 1 214 651 3563

Price Guide:
de luxe rooms $285–$315
junior suite $295–$425
suite $500–$3500

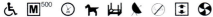

TEXAS - KYLE

THE INN ABOVE ONION CREEK

4444 HIGHWAY 150 WEST, KYLE, TEXAS 78640

Directions: 25 miles south west of Austin. 1 hour from San Antonio airport.

Web: www.johansens.com/onioncreek
E-mail: info@innaboveonioncreek.com
Tel: 1 888 579 7686
Fax: 1 512 268 1090

Price Guide:
rooms $175–$275
suite $275

Stunning views, spectacular sunsets and dazzling stars set the scene at this replica 1800's homestead, whose quiet location in several acres of breathtaking Texas Hill country make it simply perfect for a relaxing getaway. The Inn has a unique homely atmosphere and great lengths are taken by staff to deliver an impeccable service. Inviting public rooms are meticulously designed with comfort as a priority, enhanced by cosy armchairs, large fireplaces, antiques and superb attention to detail. Each of the individually designed luxury bedrooms is named after a historical figure of the region and has a wonderful feather bed, huge bath and whirlpool tub. A magnificent home-cooked breakfast is irresistible and the three course evening meal makes use of the freshest ingredients for fine International fare. The kitchen garden has beautiful seasonal flowers, vegetables, roses and old fashioned vines, whilst nature lovers will enjoy the abundance of deer, blackbuck antelope, wild turkey, fox, racoons and birdlife in the area. Horse riding, golf, cycling, swimming and tubing is available for outdoor enthusiasts and there is a large swimming pool in the grounds with plenty of shade.

Our inspector loved: The location. The beauty of the countryside or the shopping in Wimberley or the sights of Austin.

Havana River Walk Inn

1015 NAVARRO, SAN ANTONIO, TEXAS 78205

This unique Inn was built in 1914 as a residence hotel and today retains its air of vintage-style and elegance. All of the beautiful 27 air conditioned rooms have wooden floors, sisal rugs and down comforters, while some include elaborate four poster beds. The European antiques are wonderful, as are the fresh flowers, thick robes and bottled water, careful finishing touches add that little bit of extra comfort. As well as luxurious surroundings there are up-to-the-minute facilities such as cable television and data ports. Within the charming décor and atmosphere of the Inn, which has been awarded a Condé Nast Gold Reserve, it is easy to feel that you are in another country, an ambience which is enhanced by music in the public areas. Chef, Beau Smith, creates excellent cuisine and there is also a Cigar Bar. The Riverwalk has many shops and restaurants to enjoy and is especially attractive at night. Nearby places of interest include downtown San Antonio, Sea World and the Alamo.

Our inspector loved: *The wonderfully decorated rooms.*

Directions: On the river in downtown San Antonio.

Web: www.johansens.com/havanariverwalkinn
E-mail: info@havanariverwalkinn.com
Tel: 1 210 222 2008
Fax: 1 210 222 2717

Price Guide:
rooms $109–$209
suites $249–$599

TEXAS - TYLER

KIEPERSOL ESTATES

21508 MERLOT LANE, TYLER, TEXAS 75703

Directions: From U.S. Highway 69 take Route 344, the Hotel is 2 miles away.

Web: www.johansens.com/kiepersol
E-mail: bandb@kiepersol.com
Tel: 1 903 894 3300
Fax: 1 903 894 4140

Price Guide:
rooms $130–$200
suites $155–$2000

Kiepersol Estates brings a touch of South Africa to Texas. Owner Pierre de Wet is from that sunshine country and has instilled in Kiepersol the atmosphere, ambience, furnishings, décor and welcomness of his homeland. Even the name of this superb bed and breakfast establishment is taken from a tree grown in South Africa. A group of Boer War British soldiers fleeing from a charging lion rushed to climb this tree shouting, 'Kiepersol, Kiepersol, Kiepersol.' Witnessing Boers named the tree Kiepersol but years later it was realised that the soldiers were actually yelling, 'We hope the tree will keep us all.' Guests have the choice of 5 superb rooms, 3 with private patio and hot tub. Each room has its own personality and every comfort such as king-size bed and plush velvet bedding. The rooms are just steps away from a beautiful, wood-panelled lounge with deep leather sofas, a beamed bar with cane ceiling fans and a sunny restaurant. Diners can enjoy views over a heart-shaped lake while relishing an excellent selection of steaks and seafood complemented by wines from a cellar with approximately 150 selections. Some are from the Estate's vineyard, which visitors can tour by horse-drawn carriage. Weddings are catered for with the ceremony held in a chapel in the grounds.

Our inspector loved: *The feeling of Africa everywhere, especially the Cane fans over the bar and then to have a vineyard as well.*

VIRGINIA
Hotel location shown in red with page number

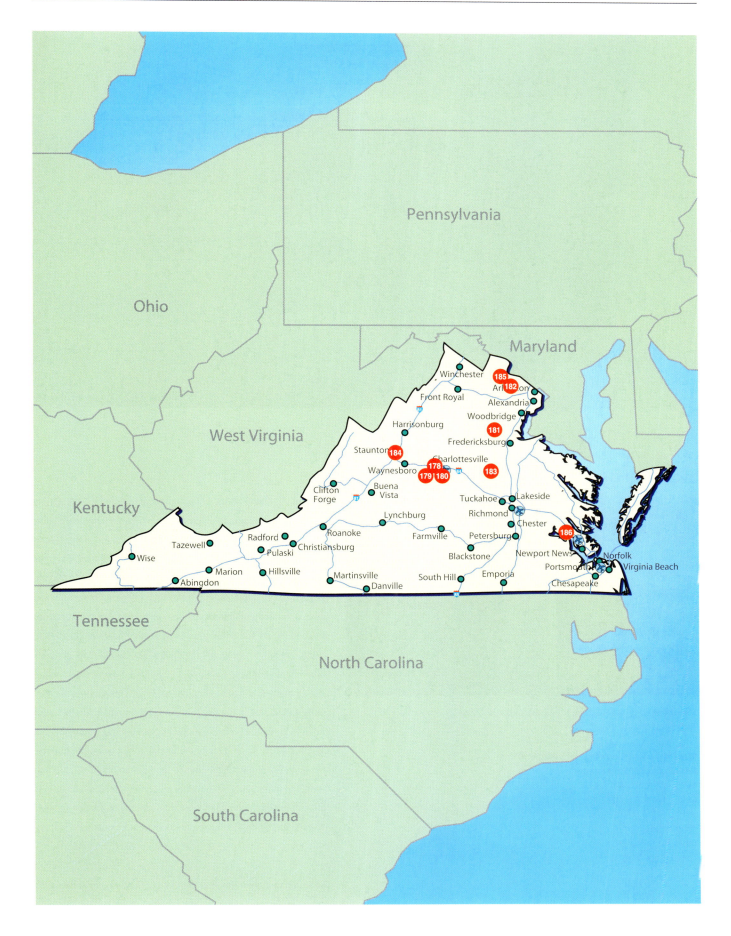

200 South Street Inn

200 SOUTH STREET, CHARLOTTESVILLE, VIRGINIA, 22902

Directions: 2 hours south-west of Washington on route 29. 1 hour west of Richmond on route 64.

Web: www.johansens.com/200southstreetinn
E-mail: southst@cstone.net
Tel: 1 434 979 0200
Fax: 1 434 979 4403

Price Guide:
rooms $125–$210
suites $210–$220

This charming Hotel is the amalgamation of 2 historic 19th century houses, set in the heart of a lively downtown. The first house was built in 1856 for a friend of Thomas Jefferson and the second some 50 years later and careful restoration has ensured that there is still a distinct period feel to the Hotel from the elegant and sweeping banister in the hallways to the wide, cool veranda. Each of the 20 bedrooms and suites is furnished in individual style, (many have canopied or sleigh beds) and every room contains some charming English or Belgian antique pieces. There is a warm Virginia welcome awaiting all guests with wine and cheese on arrival and a relaxed breakfast of home-baked breads and pastries can be taken on the veranda. There is plenty to entice guests away to the nearby historic downtown mall with its collection of antique shops, bookstores and restaurants but there is also a great deal of history in the region too. Thomas Jefferson's house, Monticello, is only 4 miles from the Hotel and Ash Lawn and Montpelier, the homes of James Monroe and James Madison, are also nearby. Skyline Drive and the Blue Ridge Parkway are less than half an hour away and a definite stop for anyone wishing to walk or cycle amongst the spectacular Virginia countryside.

Our inspector loved: The smell of the freshly baked Coffee Cake served each morning on the classic outdoor veranda.

CLIFTON - THE COUNTRY INN & ESTATE

1296 CLIFTON INN DRIVE, CHARLOTTESVILLE, VIRGINIA 22911

Enter an estate steeped in history and secluded in some of the most refreshing and beautiful land imaginable. Clifton - the Country Inn and Estate, an eighteenth century manor house, is an exquisite example of Federal and Colonial style architecture and elegance set against a stunning 100 acre environment. Once inside, this superbly designed inn continues to exude a dignified and stylish air, with simple furniture that is none the less comfortable and a subtle yet warm colour scheme. The rooms are the height of grandeur, decorated exuberantly with plenty of space in which to recline and while away the hours. Each room looks out across Clifton's finely kept lawns, gardens or private lake. Dinner is prepared with the very freshest of ingredients, incorporated to provide a feast for all the senses. With the choice of the historic dining room, or the verandah, a candle lit dinner at Clifton, along with its renowned selection of wine from the private cellar, is a gastronomic experience to remember. Guests can hike and bike, swim play tennis or picnic, or simply let the old world beauty transport you to a charming paradise in modern times.

Our inspector loved: *The complimentary hors d'oeu'vre served in the drawing room each evening.*

Directions: 5 miles East of downtown Charlottesville, Clifton is just off 250 East on State Route 729, Shadwell, Virginia

Web: www.johansens.com/cliftonthecountryinn
Tel: 1 434 971 1800
Fax: 1 434 971 7098
US Toll Free: 1 888 971 1800

Price Guide: (incl. breakfast & afternoon tea):
rooms $125–$345
suites $185–$495

VIRGINIA - CHARLOTTESVILLE

Prospect Hill Plantation Inn

PO BOX 6909, CHARLOTTESVILLE, VIRGINIA 22906

Directions: Located 15 miles east of Charlottesville. Exit I-64 east at 136, and take route 15 south to Zion Crossroads. Turn left on Route 250 east. Go 1 mile to Route 613, turn left and go 3 miles to the inn on left.

Web: www.johansens.com/prospecthill
Tel: 1 540 967 0844
Fax: 1 540 967 0102
US toll free: 1 800 277 0844

Price Guide:
(Breakfast Dinner & Gratuities included)
rooms $295–$395
suites $395–$420

Approached by a 500-ft drive lined with 150-year-old boxwoods, Prospect Hill is a stunning piece of Virginian history that has been lovingly restored and maintained since 1977 by the Sheehan family. The manor house that greets guests is in classic colonial style, dating back to 1732, whilst the outbuildings date back to 1699. The plantation was run as a working estate until the end of the 19th century, and the conversion to luxury hotel has been done with care and style, retaining the authentic atmosphere that lends a degree of romance and nostalgia. Honeymooners may choose to stay in Sanco Pansy's Cottage, located deep within the grounds, whilst other accommodations include the Manor House, Overseer's Cottage and the Carriage House Suite with its exposed beam ceiling, floor-to-ceiling windows and queen-size bed. The 50-acre grounds are a delight in which to enjoy the peace and seclusion, and contain a stunning arboretum with shady pavilion and swimming pool. Dinner is lovingly prepared by hosts The Sheehan Family. A bell calls guests to the dining room, where there is a French-inspired, five-course extravaganza accompanied by recommended wines; any dietary requirements can be accommodated.

Our inspector loved: *The 500 foot driveway, that is lined with 100-year old Boxwood hedges.*

VIRGINIA - CULPEPER

PRINCE MICHEL RESTAURANT & SUITES

PRINCE MICHEL DE VIRGINIA, HCR 4, BOX 77, LEON, VIRGINIA 22725

The founder of Prince Michel Vineyards, Jean Leducq, was following in the steps of Thomas Jefferson and George Washington when he recognised the potential for cultivating fine wines in the rich red Virginia soil. Some 20 years later he now has an award-winning estate where the French traditions of wine-making flourish, now enhanced by the addition of the Prince Michel Vineyards Suites and Restaurant. These were added for those who wished to take longer over their wine-tasting and savour their wines over a delicate menu of classic French dishes followed by a stay in the relaxed elegance of one of the four individually designed suites that overlook the vineyards and farmland, each awarded a 4 diamond rating. King-size beds, vast showers, and jacuzzi baths with neck massager ensure total relaxation and the living areas are spacious and welcoming with separate dining areas and roaring log fires. The views of the underlying valley are wonderful and there is much more of the Virginia countryside to explore. Monticello is nearby and it is easy to hire mountain bikes for the intrepid explorers. Washington DC, Charlottesville and Montpelier are within easy access although the landscape of the estate itself is such that few will wish to venture further afield.

Directions: 30 miles from Charlottesville on route 29 north. Midway between Culpeper and Madison.

Web: www.johansens.com/princemichel
E-mail: info@princemichel.com
Tel: 1 540 547 9720
Fax: 1 540 547 3088

Price Guide:
suites $250–$400

Our inspector loved: Being able to stroll through the Grapevines behind the suites, with the view of the Blue Ridge Mountains in the background.

VIRGINIA - MIDDLEBURG

The Goodstone Inn & Estate

36205 SNAKE HILL ROAD, MIDDLEBURG, VIRGINIA 20117

This superb inn is located in the heart of Virginia's famous hunt and wine region just three miles from the historic town of Middleburg. Steeped in history, Goodstone is situated on 265 acres of picturesque estate grounds with the Blue Ridge Mountains in the distance. 13 individually decorated guest rooms and suites are situated in luxury residences renovated in elegant English and French country styles. The Carriage House, once a stable, now has four rooms converted from its original horse stalls. The Dutch Cottage with its copper roof has two elegant bedrooms. The Spring House with its first and second-floor porches has four guest rooms including two charming attic rooms. The three-bedroom Farm Cottage has fireplaces in its library and Great Room, with high vaulted ceilings and rough hewn beams. Each residence has a sitting room and fully equipped modern kitchen. The heart of the Inn is the Carriage House, where breakfast and Sunday brunch are served. Leisure facilities include a heated pool shaded by the ivy-covered remains of the original mansion, golf, canoeing and mountain biking. Outstanding equestrian centres are located nearby. Seasonal midweek rates and special packages are available.

Directions: From Middleburg take Route 50 west. Turn right at light onto North Madison Street, follow Foxcroft Road and turn left onto Snake Hill Road.

Web: www.johansens.com/goodstoneinn
E-mail: information@goodstone.com
Tel: 1 540 687 4645
Fax: 1 540 687 6115

Price Guide:
rooms $195–$400
suites $250–$495

Our inspector loved: The heated outdoor pool, shaded & hidden by the ivy-covered ruins of the original mansion.

VIRGINIA - ORANGE

WILLOW GROVE INN
14079 PLANTATION WAY, ORANGE, VIRGINIA 22960

Warm, old fashioned hospitality is a trademark of Willow Grove. A designated Virginia Historic Landmark and listed on the National Register of Historic Places, Willow Grove was built as a modest federal house by Joseph Clark in 1778. Throughout the years its expansion included work by those who crafted Montpelier, President James Madison's Orange County Home, and President Thomas Jefferson's Univeristy of Virginia. Today, Willow Grove retains Jefferson's Classical Revival style exterior and simple federal interior. All of the rooms, suites and antebellum cottages provide a showcase for the 30-year collection of antiques and period furnishings that include heirloom linens, hand-hooked rugs and vintage watercolours. Freshly brewed coffee and home-baked pastries are delivered to guests' rooms in the morning. Innovative menus feature traditional Virginia cuisine in the three dining rooms, all adorned with antique china, sparkling crystal and silver. Executive chefs, Ben Miller and Dawn Schilling, incorporate local produce and seasonal delicacies in all their specialities. The 37 acres of grounds boast tree-shaded lawns, ancient stone barns and even a hammock in the Victorian garden. Further afield the Blue Ridge Mountains, historic landmarks and local vineyards can be explored.

Our inspector loved: The carefully preserved architecture of the original 1778 Virginia Plantation.

Directions: Located outside of Orange, close to Route 29, on Route 15.

Web: www.johansens.com/willowgroveinn
Tel: 1 540 672 5982
Fax: 1 540 672 3674

Price Guide:
rooms $295–$395
suites $340–$395

VIRGINIA - STAUNTON

FREDERICK HOUSE
28 NORTH NEW STREET, STAUNTON, VIRGINIA 24401

Directions: Located in historic downtown Staunton near Highway route 64/81

Web: www.johansens.com/frederickhouse
E-mail: stay@frederickhouse.com
Tel: 1 540 885 4220
Fax: 1 540 885 5180
US Toll Free: 1 800 334 5575

Price Guide:
rooms $85–$140
suites $115–$180

Entering these beautifully restored 19th century houses that comprise the Frederick House collection the guest instantly steps back into a bygone age. These adjoining town houses and 2 detached houses lie in the quiet downtown of historic Staunton, which is in itself a great starting point for a tour of Virginia's historic sites, combining the intimacy of a local town with fine architecture and a wide variety of shopping and cultural activities. The earliest of the Frederick houses dates back to 1810 and is the epitome of period elegance with its Federal staircase. Each of the rooms has been painstakingly designed to incorporate period features and charm with modern facilities. Each is uniquely decorated and displays original antiques, books and pictures. Making careful use of the building's hillside setting, the gardens have also become a favourite with guests at Frederick House, featuring pretty terraces, small gardens pots and planters and an abundance of flowering trees and culinary herbs that scent the walkways. The quiet downtown location belies the accessibility to a wealth of historic attractions:– Woodrow Wilson's birthplace; the Frontier Cultural Museum; Mary Baldwin College; and Shakespeare's playhouse, Blackfriars, are all within easy walking distance.

Our inspector loved: *The hand painted wall stencils in many of the rooms*

VIRGINIA - WHITE POST

L'AUBERGE PROVENÇALE

PO BOX 190, WHITE POST, VIRGINIA 22663

Just one hour from Baltimore and deep into Blue Ridge Mountain country lies this wonderful haven of rustic French style. The main house, Mount Airy, dates back to 1753 and has been lovingly restored by its 2 French owners who now pride themselves on their winning mix of glorious food and pretty, provincial style. Each of the bedrooms is decorated with charming fabrics and elegant period pieces of either French or Spanish origin, resulting in a stylish, yet informal ambience. The dining room comprises of 3 interconnecting rooms, which creates a sense of intimacy and it is here that Chef patron Alain Borel produces light and beautifully presented Provençale cuisine using vegetables and herbs from his own garden. The entire villa is decorated in southern Mediterranean style with textured walls and French fabrics and the brick terrace and jacuzzi are breathtaking. The surrounding countryside is a perfect backdrop for all outdoor pursuits and there are many local vineyards offering tastings. Local antique shops are ideal for leisurely browsing and Washington DC and The White House are easily accessible.

Our inspector loved: The overall ambience that the French Innkeepers have created of staying in a very romantic Auberge of Provence in Southern France.

Directions: Take Route 50 south onto Route 340, and L'Auberge is directly on the right.

Web: www.johansens.com/laubergeprovencale
Tel: 1 540 837 1375
Fax: 1 540 837 2004

Price Guide:
rooms $150–$205
suites $225–$275

185

VIRGINIA - WILLIAMSBURG

LEGACY OF WILLIAMSBURG INN
930 JAMES TOWMN ROAD, WILLIAMSBURG, VIRGINIA 23185–3917

Directions: Located off Route 199, 8 miles from Route 64. The Inn is 4 blocks from the historic area of Colonial Williamsburg.

Web: www.johansens.com/legacywilliamsburg
E-mail: legacy@tni.net
Tel: 1 757 220 0524
Fax: 1 757 220 2211

Price Guide:
rooms $135–$145
suites $175–$205

An intimate colonial refuge, this charming and unique Inn is the premier bed and breakfast of historic Williamsburg and was featured in the 'Top 10 Romantic Inns' list, 2002. The interior of each room is pure 18th century and cosy en suite bedrooms are furnished with antiques, overstuffed queen-size beds and plush bath robes. The Nicholson and the Williamsburg suites include sitting rooms with a deck overlooking a treetop gazebo and attached sun porch respectively. Wood-burning fireplaces and candles light the Inn throughout and the living room, known in colonial days as the Keeping Room, features inlaid brick and a display of antique pewter and redware while the library holds many books on American history. In the Tavern Room sits an English built pool table alongside a darts board. A delicious breakfast is served daily by innkeeper Marshall Wile and afterwards, guests can enjoy a stroll in the pretty gardens or simply relax on the sun porch and gazebo. Colonial Williamsburg has many places of interest worth a visit including its working houses and museums, Busch Gardens and James River Plantations and Jamestown settlement.

Our inspector loved: The delightful 'Keeping Room' where a delicious breakfast is served.

WYOMING
Hotel location shown in red with page number

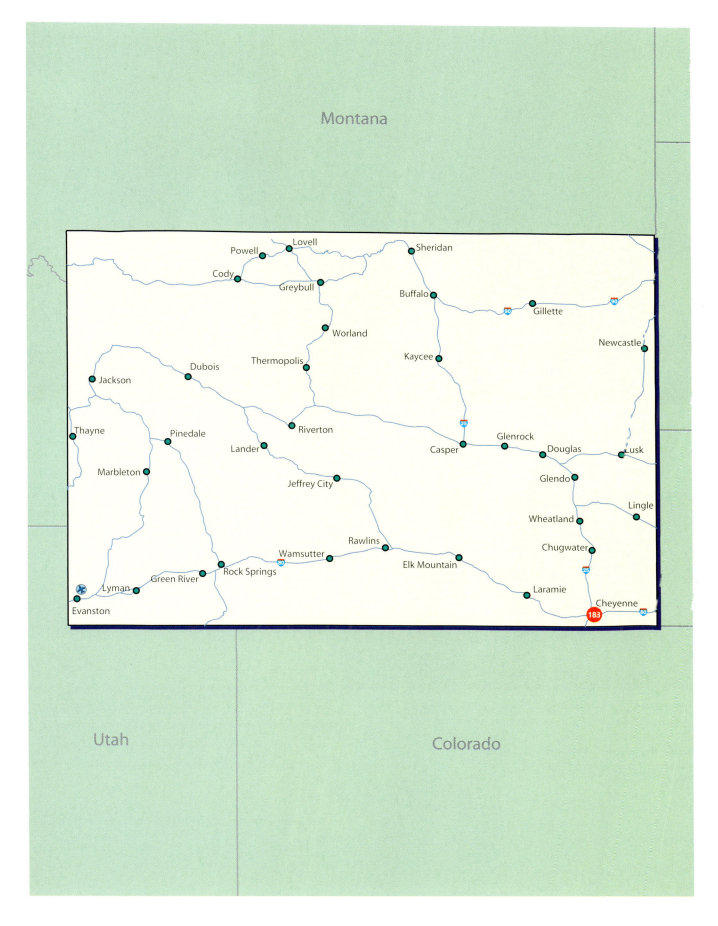

WYOMING - CHEYENNE

NAGLE WARREN MANSION
222 EAST 17TH STREET, CHEYENNE, WYOMING 82001

One of Cheyenne's most stylish residences, the Nagle Warren Mansion is steeped in a rich and interesting history. Built in 1888 by Erasmus Nagle, the mansion was home to Francis E. Warren, Governor and Wyoming Senator. Set on the edge of downtown Cheyenne, the elegant Victorian décor is complemented by the fine craftsmanship of a bygone era. Vestiges of the past are evident as guests walk up the ornate wooden staircases admiring the authentic period touches. Antique furnishings abound throughout the mansion. In the 12 bedrooms, the contemporary guests' needs have been met with each room offering air conditioning, telephone and colour television. The delicious breakfast includes freshly baked muffins, and special recipes by the cook are a daily treat. Guests can spend the day hiking through mountains, and afterwards the outdoor hot tub is most inviting! Set in an enclosed gazebo, it will delight guests regardless of the season. Less strenuous pastimes include shopping or exploring historic Cheyenne.

Directions: From the I-25 proceed to the I-80 east, leave at Exit 362. If you are eastbound turn left on Central, if westbound turn right.

Web: www.johansens.com/naglewarrenmansion
E-mail: jostenfoss@aol.com
Tel: 1 307 637 3333
Fax: 1 307 638 6879
US Toll Free: 1 800 811 2610

Price Guide: (incl. breakfast)
rooms $108–$139
suite $125–$150

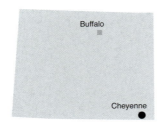

Our inspector loved: The 'English High Tea' served every Friday and Saturday at 3pm.

Mexico

Hotel location shown in red with page number

MEXICO - BAJA CALIFORNIA

Casa Natalia

BLVD MIJARES 4, SAN JOSE DEL CABO, BAJA CALIFORNIA SUR 23400

Directions: From SJD airport take the highway to San José then follow signs to downtown.

Web: www.johansens.com/casanatalia
E-mail: casa.natalia@1cabonet.com.mx
Tel: 52 624 14 251 00
Fax: 52 624 14251 10
US Toll Free: 1 888 277 3814

Price Guide:
rooms $180–$220
suite $345

A European-style boutique hotel, the Casa Natalia nestles amongst palm trees and tropical bougainvillea in the heart of historic San José del Cabo. Owners, Nathalie and Loic Tenoux, were inspired by the natural beauty of the region and worked with a famed Mexican architect to create an environment that reflected the spectacular deserts, mountains, seas and skies in its hand-plastered walls, wood-beams, tropical flowers and waterfalls. Each of the guest rooms are individually named and decorated, combining local artwork, striking contemporary furnishings and earthy colours. The overall ambience is one of comfortable elegance, with extra special touches of luxury added, such as the in-room spa service. Sliding glass doors open onto private balconies which feature hammocks and views across the courtyard, pool or neighbouring tropical estuary. At night, open flame braziers light up the outdoors and guests can enjoy dinner and cocktails al fresco. The Mi Cocina restaurant serves a nouvelle Mexican-Euro cuisine, accompanied by fine wines and tequilas. Outside the Hotel, the charming town of San José del Cabo awaits discovery along with the stunning local beaches. Activities such as golf, fishing, horse riding, sailing and safaris can also be organised.

Our inspector loved: *This elegant jewel tucked away in sleepy San José.*

MEXICO - CANCUN

Villas Tacul

BOULEVARD KUKULKAN, KM 5.5, CANCUN, QUINTANA ROO, 77500 MEXICO

This pretty and unexpected oasis situated right on the beach offers privacy and comfort for guests wishing to escape to a more intimate environment. Twenty three individually designed villas, of which nine are on the beach and the others only a few steps away, feature up to five bedrooms decorated in Mexican Colonial style. Private dining can be enjoyed by guests where a kitchen is provided as an option from the two restaurants. This twelve acre tropical estate on the edge of the clear turquoise waters of the Caribbean, is shaded by a grove of palms in well manicured and colourful gardens surrounding a large free form swimming pool. Two tennis courts, basketball and volleyball courts plus most water sports including windsurf, sail boats, wave runners and hobie cats are available for those guests with more athletic intentions. Breakfast and lunch is available near the pool at 'La Pergola' restaurant and in the evening dinner is served under the unique thatch of the romantic 'El Encanto' restaurant where International and Mexican cuisine is featured on the menu.

Our inspector loved: *Having a private villa next to the Mexican Caribbean.*

Directions: Villas Tacul is only twenty minutes by taxi from Cancun International Airport and the hotel will arrange transport in advance.

Web: www.johansens.com/villastacul
E-mail: vtacul@cancun.com.mx
Tel: 52 998 883 00 00
Fax: 52 998 849 70 70

Price Guide:
rooms $120–$300
5 bedroom villa $850–$1275

191

MEXICO - ISLA MUJERES

La Casa De Los Sueños

CARRETERA GARRAFON, S/N ISLA MUJERES, QUINTANA ROO, MEXICO 77400

Directions: Located at the Southern Tip of Isla Mujeres, approximately one hour from Cancun International Airport.

Web: www.johansens.com/lossuenos
E-mail: info@lossuenos.com
Tel: 52 99887 70651
Fax: 52 99887 70708

Price Guide:
rooms $215–$425

Six miles offshore from Cancun about thirty minutes by boat, is the enchanting Isla Mujeres (Island of Women) where privacy and tranquillity are assured, no more so, than within the stylish and stunning surroundings of this contemporary Mexican residence 'La Casa de los Sueños' This small luxurious retreat with private beach and boat dock, offers all ocean front, air conditioned deluxe rooms and suites with balconies. Mexican art and sculpture and a wonderfully uplifting sense of vivid solid colour and light create a visual feast and an adults only experience. An unusual and comfortable open-air sunken sitting room gives an uninterrupted floor level view of the Caribbean, the perfect place for a light lunch or an evening sundowner. Breakfast is included and coffee and juice served to each room before breakfast. Dinner is available on some evenings during high season. Massage, facial, manicure, pedicure, Yoga and Reiki can be arranged as guest services. Bicycles are provided for guests as the most enjoyable way to explore the island. Other activities include snorkelling, kayaking, scuba diving and the opportunity to visit a turtle farm and swim with dolphins.

Our inspector loved: The juxtaposition of colour, light and complete privacy.

MEXICO - RIVIERA MAYA

Maroma

HIGHWAY 307 KM 51, RIVIERA MAYA, QUINTANA ROO, 77710 MEXICO

At the far end of a mile long jungle track, set in the loveliest of dazzling coral beach bays, shaded by a forest of coconut palms, lies the cool paradise of Maroma. Created by owners Jose Luis and Sally Moreno, to share with visitors from around the world, Maroma is both wonderfully hospitable and very private. This beautiful house is built in the tradition of a spacious Mexican hacienda of brilliant whitewash and thatch. Featuring 58 luxurious accommodations with terracotta floors and teak and mahogany furniture, each room has a king sized bed, Roman style tiled shower, private verandah and an inviting hammock offering views of the lush tropical gardens and the glittering turquoise of the Caribbean ocean. Soft blue, illuminated footpaths guide guests to the pretty candle lit restaurant for dinner where fresh fish, seafood or locally caught lobster highlight the imaginative menu. 'Anfitrionas' are available to help plan your day including visits to the archaeological sites of Chichen Itza and Tulum. There is a wide range of spa treatments including the ultimate 'Temazcal', an energising and cleansing steam bath combined with a mud bath.

Our inspector loved: *A sense of being utterly spoilt in luxurious surroundings.*

Directions: 30 minutes from Cancun International Airport on route 307 towards Tulum. Airport transportation can be arranged.

Web: www.johansens.com/maroma
E-mail: reservations@maromahotel.com
Tel: 52 998 872 8200
Fax: 52 998 872 8220

Price Guide:
rooms $225–$640
suite $650–$3100

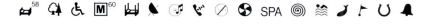

MEXICO - ZIHUATANEJO

Hotel Villa Del Sol

PLAYA LA ROPA S/N, PO BOX 84, ZIHUATANEJO 40880, MEXICO

Directions: The hotel is 15 minutes from Ixtapa-Zihuatanejo International Airport. The airport has direct services from Los Angeles, Phoenix, New York and Mexico City.

Web: www.johansens.com/villadelsol
E-mail: hotel@villasol.com.mx
Tel: 52 755 4 2239/3239
Fax: 52 7554 2758/4066
US Toll Free: 888 398 2645

Price Guide:
rooms $170–$435
suite $400–$1170

Cross a bit of Hispanic charm and an incredible amount of natural beauty and the result is the Villa del Sol. Set like a pearl on the Pacific shoreline of Mexico at Ixtapa-Zihuatanejo, the Hotel Villa del Sol lives up to its name with dazzling sunshine, idyllic beaches and magnificent groves of flourishing palm trees that simply blanket the area in a haze of green. The rooms are expansive and stunning using designs and colours that hark back to the days of the ancient civilisations that populate the area. Those wishing to indulge in an afternoon siesta must choose one of the numerous little nooks and crannies where you can doze in comfort on a swinging chair or hanging hammock. Dinner is a mélange of flavours, with dishes drawing on irresistible Mexican tastes and using fresh seafood straight out of the Pacific. There are innumerable leisure activities at the Villa del Sol, with watersports widely available and including everything from sailing to snorkelling. For something a little more cultural, take to the cobblestone streets of Zihuatanejo and explore the fascinating surrounds with its art gallery and interesting shops

Our inspector loved: Dozing in a hammock after lunch.

Bermuda

Hotel location shown in red with page number

BERMUDA - DEVONSHIRE

ARIEL SANDS
34 SOUTH SHORE ROAD, DEVONSHIRE, BERMUDA

Directions: Centrally located, only 20 minutes from the airport.

Web: www.johansens.com/arielsands
E-mail: reservations@arielsands.com
Tel: 1 441 236 1010
Fax: 1 441 236 0087

Price Guide:
rooms $260–$620

Nestling in 14 acres of glorious countryside on Bermuda's beautiful South Shore this Hotel is surrounded by gorgeous colours under a brilliant blue sky. Ariel Sands is an idyllic waterside retreat that combines privacy, peace and casual elegance with quality service, warmth and convenience. The deep greens of surrounding lawns and foliage with the terracotta pink and white paintwork of its cosy encircling cottages blend superbly with the pastel interior décor. It is a tranquil sanctuary of luxury where every guest can feel pampered. There are 47 deluxe rooms, suites and cottages, all delightfully appointed with every amenity: air-conditioning; bathroom; direct dial telephone with modem/fax capabilities; radio and colour cable television; refrigerator; personal safe and coffee maker. Shaded private patios offer lovely garden and sea views. Superb food is served in an enchanting restaurant which offers elegant dining on 4 ocean front terraces. Ariel Sands can be as lively or as restful as guests require; a variety of island tours can be arranged and there is a fully-equipped spa and exercise room, two seawater pools, one heated freshwater pool, two tennis courts, snorkeling, sailing and golf nearby. All watched over by the locally famed statue of Ariel standing just off the brilliant white sanded beach up to its ankles in water at high tide.

Our inspector loved: The statue of Ariel just off the beach.

ROSEDON HOTEL

PO BOX HM 290, HAMILTON HMAX, BERMUDA

Originally built in 1903 by an expatriate English family, this stunningly refurbished colonial hotel provides a quiet, friendly and relaxed atmosphere in sensational surroundings. Enclosed by bountiful tropical gardens the Rosedon Hotel is a tranquil sanctuary only minutes from the bustling town of Hamilton. Suffused with the atmosphere of colonial splendour, the main house is beautifully decorated in a traditional style and is festooned with antique furniture. The Bermudian-style rooms are all spacious and well-appointed, and have balconies overlooking the swimming pool. Breakfast and lunch are served on the poolside patio, while light dinners are available on request. With Hamilton just a short stroll away, visitors can enjoy the many shops and department stores that the capital boasts, as well as its sociable nightlife. Undoubtedly Bermuda's chief asset is its beautiful coastline and visitors do not forget the peerless beaches and the crystal clear ocean, into which the nearby aquarium gives an invaluable insight. The Rosedon Hotel also organises introductions to all the island's championship golf courses and provides transportation to a South Shore Beach and Tennis Club. Conveniently located for the business traveller, the hotel has placed a data port in each room and does not charge for local calls.

Our inspector loved: The secluded beautiful gardens.

Directions: A short walk from Hamilton.

Web: www.johansens.com/rosedonhotel
E-mail: rosedon@ibl.bm
Tel: 1 441 295 1640
Fax: 1 441 295 5904

Price Guide: (incl. breakfast)
rooms $214–$298

BERMUDA - PAGET

Fourways Inn

PO BOX PG 294, PAGET PG BX, BERMUDA

Directions: Fourways is in the centre of the island, a ten minutes taxi ride or ferry crossing from Hamilton.

Web: www.johansens.com/fourwaysinn
E-mail: info@fourways.com
Tel: 1 441 236 6517
Fax: 1 441 236 5528

Price Guide:
rooms $150–$250
suites $190–$350

Fourways is a glorious, relaxing hideaway nestling in the centre of this sunshine island. It combines privacy, elegance and warmth with convenience and excellent value for money. Every guest can feel pampered. Ten intimate cottages with shady terraces are scattered over hillside gardens which are emblazoned with brightly coloured hibiscus blossoms, tropical flowers, tall palms and manicured lawns. They are well-appointed and have every amenity from air conditioning, a kitchenette, spacious bathroom, mini bar and cable television to a safety deposit box. The cottages, each named after a ship, surround a magnificent fresh water heated swimming pool where cool drinks can be enjoyed in the shade of overhanging palms and matching green coloured umbrellas. Fourways is renowned for its gastronomic dining. Its award winning restaurant, housed in a luxurious 18th century residence refurbished for elegant dining, is one of Bermuda's best. Every dish is served with gourmet perfection and enhanced by a list of over 700 fine wines. There is also a fresh pastry and bread shop on site. Guests can enjoy free facilities at nearby Stonington Beach and tee times can be arranged at all of the islands championship golf courses which are no further than a 20 minutes drive away.

Our inspector loved: The breads and pastries prepared by the french chef.

NEWSTEAD HOTEL
27 HARBOUR ROAD, PAGET PG02, BERMUDA

Sunshine yellow under a sparkling white roof the gracious, classical colonial style Newstead Hotel stands regally on a gently terraced hillside overlooking Hamilton Harbour and the beautiful outer islands of Bermuda. It is an enchanting manor house incorporating the traditional and modern in an exquisitely manicured garden setting of quiet tranquillity. Most of the bedrooms have been recently refurbished with cheerful prints and the finest fabrics and furniture. Most rooms have private terraces or balconies and enjoy panoramic views over the harbour, the garden or the freshwater swimming pool surrounded by chaises longues and sun umbrellas. Hotel guests can enjoy seafood and flames seared steaks in our Award Winning Rockfish Grill, overlooking the city lights of Hamilton and the harbour. Relax in our Tropical Spa, or visit our salon. There are two Har Tru tennis courts and water sports facilities on the property. Major golf courses are within easy reach. Sightseeing tours can also be arranged.

Our inspector loved: *The wonderful gardens full of brightly coloured hibiscus, a great place to enjoy pre dinner drinks.*

Directions: Overlooking Hamilton Harbour a ten minute ferry ride from the centre of Hamilton.

Web: www.johansens.com/newsteadhotel
E-mail: reservations@newsteadhotel.com
Tel: 1 441 236 6060
Fax: 1 441 236 7454

Price Guide:
rooms double $250–$375
suites $285–$465

Cambridge Beaches

KINGS POINT, SOMERSET, MA02 BERMUDA

Directions: A taxi will deliver you from Bermuda's international airport.

Web: www.johansens.com/cambridgebeaches
E-mail: cambeach@ibl.bm
Tel: 1 441 234 0331
Fax: 1 441 234 3352

Price Guide:
rooms $260–$700
suite $425–$1600

Cambridge Beaches is a glorious, relaxing hideaway situated on its own 25 acre peninsula on the tranquil western tip of this sunshine island. This exclusive cottage colony offers luxury and privacy to an international clientele seeking renewal and romance. Mind body and spirit are restored in the Ocean Spa, an award winning, multi-faceted facility offers 100 different health and beauty treatments, bath, steam and sauna rooms, Roman style solarium with retractable sunroof, full-length swimming pool, whirlpool and gymnasium. An extensive range of water and land sports is available, from sailing and scuba diving to tennis and golf. There are 5 magnificent, pink sanded beaches offering privacy and numerous coves to explore. The 94 cottage-style, air conditioned rooms and suites are individually decorated with every amenity and comfort, including a spacious terrace or patio on which to relax and enjoy stunning sea views. The cottages surround a centralized, 275 year old Club House which contains lounge, library, reading and games rooms and bars. It also features the formal indoor Tamarisk Room for gourmet dining and the charming outdoor Bay Terrace for smart casual dining and dancing beneath the stars.

Our inspector loved: The 5 beaches, one for every time of day and direction of breeze.

The Reefs
56 SOUTH SHORE ROAD, SOUTHAMPTON, SN02 BERMUDA

This is one of Bermuda's most picturesque resorts. Nestling in coral cliffs above a private beach reached by walkways and soft sand strolls from shore and hilltop cottage suites provide relaxing family accommodation and romantic retreats. Each cottage, with pastel walls and snowy-white roof, has a garden and patio and all enjoy magnificent views. They have everything for everyone, combining privacy and tasteful décor with elegant furnishings and thoughtful attention to detail. The services and amenities are those of a first-class hotel. Dining is a pleasure, guests can choose from the tropical setting of a superb domed conservatory to the charm of an elegant dining room to the relaxed ocean-side ambience of the Coconuts restaurant, or the Sand Bar for light refreshments and cooling drinks. The cuisine is of the highest standard served with gourmet perfection and complemented by an extensive wine list. A barbecue dinner on the spacious terrace overlooking the Atlantic is a popular speciality. Guests are encouraged to kick off their shoes and dance island style at cocktail hour. Another favourite rendezvous is the Club House lounge where traditional English tea can be enjoyed. Tennis courts and a fitness centre are available. Golf, sailing and riding can be arranged.

Our inspector loved: The 'dining on the beach' option - very romantic.

Directions: Taxi's available from the airport.

Web: www.johansens.com/thereefs
E-mail: reefsbda@ibl.bm
Tel: 1 441 238 0222
Fax: 1 441 238 8372

Price Guide: per person
rooms $530–$638
suites $760–$848

BERMUDA - WARWICK

Surf Side Beach Club
90 SOUTH SHORE ROAD, WARWICK, BERMUDA

Directions: Three miles west of Hamilton.

Web: www.johansens.com/surfside
E-mail: surf@ibl.bm
Tel: 1 441 236 7100
Fax: 1 441 236 9765

Price Guide: (until March 2003)
Deluxe units $250
superior suite $300
Penthouse accommodation for
4 persons $500

Surf Side is a sunny hideaway overlooking Bermuda's unique South Shore, surrounded by five acres of landscaped hillside terraces and walkways above beautiful, white-sanded beaches and coves. Scattered among the colourful hibiscus blossoms, tall palms and manicured lawns are 37 newly renovated cottages, apartment-style units and penthouses, and another three bedroom units on an adjoining lot. Each room has its own sea view and is designed for privacy. Guests are provided with every home comfort, from tastefully furnished bedrooms and lounges to fully-fitted kitchens and either a secluded garden patio or a wide, plant-bedecked balcony where the only sound is that of breaking waves. With a natural ambience created by the moon, soft tropical breezes and delicate scent of flowers, the Palms Restaurant and Bar serves outstanding cuisine and cocktails beside the pool. The relaxed and unpretentious atmosphere is ideal for those who love to be self-sufficient and free to discover the delights of the island. Apart from sauna and Jacuzzi, Surf Side Beach Club features a new beauty salon and mini-spa. Guests can also enjoy complimentary tennis nearby, and golf and riding can be arranged.

Our inspector loved: *The Bird's Nests, secluded sunbathing and viewing areas cut into the cliffside, overlooking the Blue - Green Atlantic Coast.*

ANGUILLA
Hotel location shown in red with page number

CARIBBEAN - ANGUILLA

FRANGIPANI BEACH CLUB

PO BOX 1378, MEADS BAY, ANGUILLA, WEST INDIES

Directions: Available upon request.

Web: www.johansens.com/frangipanibeachclub
E-mail: frangipani@anguillanet.com
Tel: 1 264 497 6442/6444
Fax: 1 264 497 6440

Price Guide:
rooms $185–$265
suites $270–$1020

The pink stucco villas of the Frangipani Beach Club open directly onto Meads Bay Beach, ensuring that its guests are fully able to appreciate Anguilla's white sands, blue seas and amazing sunsets. Each Spanish Mediterranean style suite is beautifully furnished with king sized beds, marble baths and Cable TV. Light and airy, they also provide the option of independent catering with well-equipped kitchens. Those who prefer to take a break from kitchen duty can sit back and indulge at the popular beachside restaurant and bar which serves wonderful food and sports an impressive wine list. One of the best kept secrets of the Caribbean, the island of Anguilla remains largely unspoilt and undiscovered, so is worthy of exploration. Its easy accessibility means that nothing on the island seems far away, and the lack of commercialism offers visitors a welcome breath of fresh air. Snorkelling and fishing equipment are complimentary to Club guests, while the more active can swim in the pool on the Complex, or seek out various watersports, available at extra cost. Relaxation is truly the name of the game here. From the shady umbrellas on the terrace, to the comfortable surroundings and fantastic ocean views, the serenity of Frangipani Beach Club is the perfect environment in which to unwind.

Our inspector loved: The villas opening directly onto the beach.

ANTIGUA
Hotel location shown in red with page number

CARIBBEAN - ANTIGUA

BLUE WATERS

PO BOX 256, ST JOHNS, ANTIGUA, WEST INDIES

Directions: Four miles from the capital of St John's.

Web: www.johansens.com/bluewaters
E-mail: res@bluewaters.net
Tel: 1 268 462 0290
Fax: 1 268 462 0293

Price Guide:
rooms $200–$1610

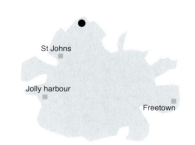

This is one of Antigua's longest established and exclusive resorts, nestling among 14 superb acres of cascading bougainvillaea, flowering hibiscus and shady palm trees on the shore of historic Soldiers Bay, and edged with two magnificent, white sandy beaches. Peace and tranquillity abound in a luxurious tropical atmosphere. The 77 recently refurbished en suite guest rooms are beautifully decorated and exceptionally appointed. Each is air-conditioned, has cool terracotta tile floors and breathtaking sea views. Just a two-minute walk away there is even more luxury in the newly developed and very private Rock Cottage. Guests at the villa enjoy their own plunge pool, Jacuzzi, landing stage, five bedrooms furnished to the highest standards, a kitchen, lounge and dining room, as well as all facilities available at the resort. Excellent gourmet cuisine is beautifully presented in the friendly, fully air-conditioned and comfortable Vyviens Restaurant. For those who prefer a more outdoor dining experience the open-sided Palm Restaurant is not to be missed. Pre-dinner drinks and afternoon 'coolers' can be savoured in a choice of two attractive bars. An extensive range of sports and leisure facilities include sea and pool swimming, tennis, snorkelling, windsurfing, sailing, aerobics and golf at a nearby 18-hole championship course.

Our inspector loved: The master suite at Rock Cottage.

CURTAIN BLUFF
PO BOX 288, ANTIGUA, WEST INDIES

Howard W Hulford opened Curtain Bluff in 1962, and is planning its 40th anniversary in 2002. The setting is unique with smooth, lagoon-fed beach on one side and blustery windward surf on the other. This is a remarkable achievement by any standards, and is perfect testimony to the superb service, ability to provide only the best accommodation and a wine cellar that boasts 25,000 bottles. Attention to detail is obvious here, from the immaculately tended tropical gardens to the spacious rattan-styled bedrooms that provide an abundance of cooling fans, telephones and all other modern amenities. Style and culinary excellence are in the capable hands of French-born chef Christophe Blatz. Guests may dine in the garden pavilion, where the finest food is served with a view out over the lawns and dance floor. Those seeking greater informality will love the beach bar with its weekly beachfront barbecue, or total privacy can be provided by taking dinner on your balcony. Curtain Bluff is one the sportiest hotels in the region offering five-star tennis facilities, squash and putting green; and with its private peninsula, the water sports facilities are unrivalled. There is even the opportunity of a sail on Tamarind, Curtain Bluff's 47-ft Wellington ketch. Jan 10-Mar 10 no kids under 12.

Our inspector loved: *The wine cellar, a wonderful selection.*

Directions: Approximately a 35-minute drive from the airport.

Web: www.johansens.com/curtainbluff

Tel: 1 268 462 8400
Fax: 1 268 462 8409

Price Guide:
rooms from $725 fully inclusive

GALLEY BAY

FIVE ISLANDS, PO BOX 305, ST JOHN'S, ANTIGUA, WEST INDIES

Situated on a pristine 3/4-mile stretch of white sandy beach, just 10 minutes from Antigua's capital, St John's, Galley Bay is a vibrant and quintessentially Caribbean hideaway. The endless sunshine and unspoilt beauty of Antigua make this an ideal holiday destination. Thatch roofed bungalows and beachfront rooms are positioned amidst 40 acres of lush gardens and majestic coconut palms with a lagoon and bird sanctuary. Simple and stylish rattan and bamboo furniture adorns the 70 spacious rooms. Succulent tropical flavours of Creole and Euro-Caribbean dishes are served in the Sea Grape Restaurant, or guests can choose a traditional grill whilst sipping sundowners and watching the sunset in the beachside Gauguin Restaurant. Cascading waterfalls are a feature of the freeform swimming pool and there is a well-equipped, air-conditioned fitness centre overlooking the lagoon. The hotel also offers a beauty salon, resort boutique, library and games room. Leisure pursuits include most non-motorised watersports such as sailing, snorkelling and windsurfing. There is golf, tennis, bird walks and an opportunity to explore the lagoon as well as day trips to the surrounding islands. Places of interest include St John's Harbour, Nelson's Dockyard and many ruined fortresses on the surrounding hilltops.

Directions: 8 miles from V.C. Bird Int'l Airport. Five Islands signposted from St John's.

Web: www.johansens.com/galleybay
Tel: 1 268 462 0302
Fax: 1 268 462 4551

Price Guide:
rooms $450–1045
suites $630–1025

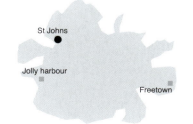

Our inspector loved: The suites right on the beach.

The Inn at English Harbour

PO BOX 187, ST JOHNS, ANTIGUA, WEST INDIES

On the southern coast of Antigua's national park, in 10 acres of wooded headland and with its own white sandy beach, this charming Inn with its magnificent views over Nelson's Dockyard and historic English Harbour is one of the Caribbean's favourite hideaways. The Addari family owners are committed to making it the leading hotel on the island and are sparing no expense in reconstructing and refurbishing it throughout. In December 2001, 24 new, high standard suites were opened close to the beach. Between the hotel and soft sands lies superb landscaped gardens, a swimming pool with refreshment service, fitness centre and tennis court. The rooms are built in 3 blocks, each in a two-storey courtyard style, all are spacious and individually decorated and furnished with comfortable chairs and sofas. Special features include: dark local wood ceilings; canopied and voile-draped four-poster beds and bathrooms with luxury double showers. Each has either a terrace or a verandah from where guests can sip cool drinks while enjoying the panoramic vista. Excellent candlelight dinners are served in the popular Terrace Restaurant in the main part of the Inn. Complimentary activities include sunfish-sailing, windsurfing, rowing, kayaking and snorkelling. Water-skiing, scuba-diving and deep-sea fishing can be arranged.

Directions: 16 miles from airport and 12 miles from the capital, St Johns.

Web: www.johansens.com/innatenglishharbour
E-mail: theinn@candw.ag
Tel: 1 268 460 1014
Fax: 1 268 460 1603

Price Guide:
rooms $175–$640

Our inspector loved: The large cool suites.

BARBADOS

Hotel location shown in red with page number

Coral Reef Club
ST. JAMES, BARBADOS, WEST INDIES

Quietly nestled in 12 acres of lush tropical gardens on Barbados' famed west coast, Coral Reef Club has been family owned and managed for the last 40 years. The O'Hara family is dedicated to providing excellence and no stone is left unturned to ensure guests' every comfort. The Hotel is situated on a white sandy beach and offers a full range of complimentary watersports including waterskiing. A gymnasium is also available to guests . A quiet stroll along the coast is a relaxing way to explore the surroundings before sampling some of the excellent seafood suggestions available at the elegant oceanfront restaurant. There are just 88 rooms, cottages and junior suites named after the flowers, fruit and trees found in the grounds. All rooms are spacious and well appointed and the new luxury cottages feature a separate living room and private plunge pool. For the utmost luxury however, the 5 Plantation Suites, with their own plunge pools are simply stunning and are the epitome of 21st century elegance and style.

Our inspector loved: The cocktail party for guests, hosted at the owners' family house on the property.

Directions: Situated on the west coast of Barbados, the Hotel is 18 miles from Grantley Adams Airport and 1 mile north of Holetown.

Web: www.johansens.com/coralreefclub
E-mail: coral@caribsurf.com
Tel: 1 246 422 2372
Fax: 1 246 422 1776

Price Guide:
rooms $185–750
suites $320–2,185

THE SANDPIPER

HOLETOWN, ST. JAMES, BARBADOS, WEST INDIES

Directions: Situated on the west coast of Barbados, the Hotel is 18 miles from Grantley Adams Airport and ¼ mile north of Holetown.

Web: www.johansens.com/sandpiper
E-mail: coral@caribsurf.com
Tel: 1 246 422 2251
Fax: 1 246 422 0900

Price Guide:
rooms $210–725
suites $315–1,590

With just 45 rooms and suites The Sandpiper is a real little gem of a hotel and a true vacation hideaway on the desirable west coast of Barbados. Both discreet and elegant it has quickly become a favourite retreat for those discerning guests looking for that winning combination of intimacy, informality and privacy. Lush tropical gardens lead down to a large bay with white sands overlooking crystal blue waters, where the swimming is wonderful and the range of complimentary watersports is excellent while golf and tennis are available for land lovers. The Sandpiper also has its own gymnasium. Each of the bedrooms and suites has its own private terrace and all are carefully appointed to be light, spacious and airy, with a touch of Caribbean colour and flair. The restaurant, set in a lush garden surrounded by tranquil koi ponds, has gained a fine reputation and offers an eclectic menu with a Caribbean undertone. The attentive staff have a strong eye for detail and ensure that guests are looked after without sacrificing the relaxed atmosphere that is such a unique part of the Caribbean.

Our inspector loved: The 'South Seas" atmosphere of the Hotel at night, with the flaming torches subtly lighting up the waterfalls.

CURAÇAO
Hotel location shown in red with page number

CARIBBEAN - CURAÇAO

AVILA BEACH HOTEL

PENSTRAAT 130, WILLEMSTAD, CURAÇAO, NETHERLANDS ANTILLES, WEST INDIES

Originally the governor's residence, the Avila Beach Hotel is a stunning testament to Dutch-Caribbean style architecture. Situated in Willemstad on the Dutch Antilles island of Curaçao, this tastefully refined hotel is an ideal escape from the pressures of a hectic lifestyle. Inside, the hotel is simply breathtaking. The 'Blues Wing' consists of rooms with vaulted ceilings, which are held in white and soft pastel colours and feature Caribbean wicker and cane furniture. The furniture is stylish and comfortable, and almost every room offers a panoramic vista across the ocean as well as having a private balcony or terrace. Each is well appointed providing maximum comfort and offers every necessary convenience. Avila is renowned for its fine cuisine and diners are truly spoilt for choice with the convivial Avila Café, the elegant Belle Terrace and the informal Blues Jazz Club and Seafood Restaurant with its fantastic view of the beach. Wherever guests dine, the food is superbly prepared and exquisite to taste whilst making use of the fresh ingredients that abound both on and off shore. Guests may relax on the private beach or wander around the tropical gardens, with palm trees framing the walk ways. For the more active there is tennis, squash, golf or any number of watersports to choose from on Curaçao.

Directions: There are regular direct flights from Miami. Local car hire companies will provide directions or taxis are readily available.

Web: www.johansens.com/avilabeach
E-mail: info@avilahotel.com
Tel: 599 9 461 4377
Fax: 599 9 461 1493

Price Guide:
rooms $180–$242
suite $415–$500

Our inspector loved: *The spectacular ocean views from most rooms.*

Grenada
Hotel location shown in red with page number

CARIBBEAN - GRENADA

SPICE ISLAND BEACH RESORT

GRAND ANSE BEACH, BOX 6, ST. GEORGE'S, GRENADA, WEST INDIES

Powder white sands, the sound of a crystal clear sea and the cool shade of palm trees creates the backdrop for a Spice Island Beach Resort, located just steps away from the picturesque Grand Anse Beach. Unsurpassed comfort and tranquillity are the essence of this magnificent Caribbean paradise, which offers a personal welcome and warm service. Sunny courtyards and terraces are filled with beautiful flowers and the cool lounges are elegantly furnished and perfect for relaxation. Air conditioned bedrooms have breathtaking views of the sea or the gardens and are decorated in colourful tropical style. Some of the suites have a private swimming pool, marble bathrooms and even a sauna for two, honeymooners and returning guests are greeted with fresh flowers, tropical fruit and chilled sparkling wine. At the seafront restaurant, exciting authentic Creole and International specialities are served to the enticing rhythms of the very best of Grenada's calypso, reggae and steel bands. Dishes include freshly caught seafood cooked with island grown spices and there are plenty of vegetarian options. Janissa's Spa offers a range of health and beauty treatments to pamper the body and relax the mind. Tennis, scuba diving, snorkelling and sailing are available and the hotel has a well-equipped fitness centre and swimming pool.

Directions: The Resort is a 10 minute drive from the airport.

Web: www.johansens.com/spiceisland
E-mail: spiceisl@caribsurf.com
Tel: 1 473 444 4423
Fax: 1 473 444 4807

Price Guide:
single $380–$880
double $470–$990

Our inspector loved: The Royal Private Pool suites.

Jamaica

Hotel location shown in red with page number

BLUE LAGOON VILLAS
FAIRY HILL, PORT ANTONIO, JAMAICA, WEST INDIES

Blue Lagoon Villas, are approached down a shady unmade lane that dives invitingly off to the left as the coast road climbs to the right. These beautiful, individually designed 1 to 4 bedroom villas, sit right on the flawless ocean with a vast canopy of rain forest stretching away behind. Each property has a private deck and most have first floor bedroom balconies, affording an unobstructed private panorama. The most overwhelming sensation on arrival is that you are entering a most stylishly decorated and luxuriously furnished family home in a location close to paradise. Blue Lagoon Villas offer the most attentive service, provided by experienced and helpful local permanent staff. Guests can choose to do as little or as much as they wish, the temptation here is to do absolutely nothing, apart from a stroll or a gentle swim to the mystical azure waters of the famous 'Blue Lagoon'. 'Frenchman's Cove' is a short distance away or, river rafting can be arranged for the more adventurous. Nearby Port Antonio is also fun to explore. There are ten villas whose only similarity is the quality of accommodation and service they provide, some are in the hills.

Directions: Accessible by air via connecting inter-island service from either Kingston or Montego Bay international airports, or a 2 hour drive from Kingston.

Web: www.johansens.com/bluelagoonvillas
E-mail: reservations@bluelagoonvillas.com
Tel: 1 876 993 7701
Fax: 1 876 993 8492

Price Guide:
rooms $571–$1700

Our inspector loved: *The temptation to do absolutely nothing*

GRAND LIDO SANS SOUCI
PO BOX 103, OCHO RIOS, ST ANN, JAMAICA, WEST INDIES

Situated on a steep wooded bluff on the northern coast of Jamaica, this all inclusive award winning resort with historical links, has earned a place amongst the older more traditional hotels in the Caribbean. The amenities include every kind of water activity plus a secluded beach, where you can sunbathe 'au naturel'. It is however the mineral water pool and European style spa facilities that deserve special attention. Several outdoor massage gazebos have been constructed high on hidden bluffs, with only the sounds of the Caribbean Sea below, to soothe the body and mind. Spa treatments also include; half hour massage, reflexology, manicure, pedicure, body scrub, facial and sauna. There is also a fully equipped fitness centre, four swimming pools, two flood lit tennis courts, and complimentary green fees and transportation to the Super Clubs Golf Course at Runaway Bay. French gourmet, Italian and authentic Jamaican dishes can be appreciated at the three principal restaurants and there is a beach grill for more informal dining. Entertainment is arranged each evening and once each week guests can enjoy a Jamaican Night on the beach and a Gala Night on the lawns.

Our inspector loved: *This super inclusive, all suites beach resort with 24 hour room dining.*

Directions: Courtesy coach from Sangster Int. Airport, Montego Bay.

Web: www.johansens.com/grandlidosanssouci
Tel: 1 876 994 1206
Fax: 1 876 994 1544

Price Guide: (all inclusive per person)
suites $300
penthouses $650

CARIBBEAN - JAMAICA

HALF MOON GOLF, TENNIS & BEACH CLUB
MONTEGO BAY, JAMAICA, WEST INDIES

Directions: A 15-minute drive from Montego Bay airport.

Web: www.johansens.com/halfmoongolf
E-mail: reservations@halfmoonclub.com
Tel: 1 876 953 2211
Fax: 1 876 953 2731

Price Guide:
rooms $240
suites $350–$1190

Set in 400 acres of beautiful tropical gardens edged by a crescent-shaped bay fringed with a 2.5km-long white sandy beach the multi-award-winning Half Moon is ranked among the finest resorts in the world. This elegant and luxurious resort provides everything the discerning traveller requires. Service and facilities are impeccable. A fact borne out by Royal, celebrity and business tycoon guests who have returned again and again. These include Her Majesty Queen Elizabeth, George Bush, Joan Collins, Paul Newman and Fidel Castro. A wide variety of first-class accommodation suits every need. There is a choice of rooms, suites and villas, all with picturesque views, air conditioning and supreme home-from-home comforts. The 32 Royal Villas offer between five and seven luxury bedrooms, private porch and pool, plus the services of a butler, maid and cook. The 12 Imperial Suites are the most opulent on the property while 59 Royal Suites ensure continuous pampering. Guests have a choice of seven restaurants, ranging from the contemporary open-air Seagrape Terrace to the romantic Il Giardino and the enchanting Sugar Mill with its gourmet dinners. Sporting and leisure facilities include 13 tennis courts, four squash courts and an 18-hole championship golf course with the only David Leadbetter Golf Academy in the Caribbean.

Our inspector loved: The wonderful amenities and exceptional service.

MOCKING BIRD HILL
PO BOX 254, PORT ANTONIO, JAMAICA

Up in the breezes, with a panoramic view of the sea, across a lush canopy of trees, sits this aptly named little gem of a hotel. The crisp blue and white exterior conceals large, comfortable spaces and bedrooms decorated boldly with locally printed fabrics that complement original art and bamboo furnishings. Mocking Bird Hill is eco friendly, gently reminding guests of the fragility of our environment and providing thoughtful bedroom gifts from handmade paper to chocolate balls. This perfect hilltop retreat renews the spirit and tempts the senses with delicious Nouvelle Caribbean Cuisine at Mille Fleurs, the gourmet restaurant with an uninterrupted view of the ocean. The white sands of 'Frenchman's Cove' private beach are minutes away and for the more athletic, hiking through the Rio Grande Valley under misty forested canopies can easily be arranged. Mocking Bird Hill is the creation of well-known Jamaican artist Barbara Walker and Shireen Aga, who take genuine pleasure in attending to your needs or leaving you undisturbed in your hammock to dream of hummingbirds or distant sailing ships.

Our inspector loved: This private paradise for honeymooners.

Directions: The hotel is located approximately 15 minutes from the centre of Port Antonio. Take the road (east) from Port Antonio towards Boston and look out for the sign board on the right before Frenchman's Cove.

Web: www.johansens.com/mockingbirdhill
E-mail: mockbrd@cwjamaica.com
Tel: 1 876 993 7134
Fax: 1 876 993 7133

Price Guide:
rooms $125–$230

Nevis & St Kitts

Hotel location shown in red with page number

The Hermitage
NEVIS, WEST INDIES

In a unique position 800 feet above sea level, the Hermitage can boast one of the most favourable climatic locations, for here the combination of mountain air and sea breezes ensures that the temperature remains between 75-80 degrees, day and night. Guests are assured of a true Caribbean welcome and a special atmosphere throughout their stay. The hotel is surrounded by lush rain forest and the hotel gardens are a delight to the senses, packed with hibiscus, mango trees and bougainvillea. There are just fifteen rooms and suites, six of which are within private cottages, and the style is one of period Colonial elegance, with cool canopy-draped beds and authentic 18th-century furnishings. The cottages have private balconies for romantic starlit dining, and the verandah of the 330-year-old great house is a delightful setting in which to enjoy the home-prepared cooking of host Maureen Lupinacci. Many of the ingredients are produced on the plantation, amongst them home-reared pork and lamb, fruit and herbs, whilst fish is caught from the waters below. Total relaxation is the order of the day here, but the activity-conscious are catered for with nature walks, diving and special Equestrian breaks; whilst a picnic down at the stunning water's edge is idyllic.

Our inspector loved: *The rooms with verandas where you can sit and watch the monkeys playing in the trees.*

Directions: The hotel can arrange air charter to meet flights at St Kitts, Antigua & St Maarten.

Web: www.johansens.com/hermitagenevis
E-mail: nevherm@caribsurf.com
Tel: 1 869 469 3477
Fax: 1 869 469 2481

Price Guide:
rooms $170–$325
Cottages $205–$450
Manor House Villa $650–$790

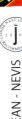

Montpelier Plantation Inn

MONTPELIER ESTATE, PO BOX 474, NEVIS, WEST INDIES

Directions: 12 miles from the airport.

Web: www.johansens.com/montpelierplantation
E-mail: info@montpeliernevis.com
Tel: 1 869 469 3462
Fax: 1 869 469 2932

Price Guide:
rooms $200–$350
suites $275–$425

Located 750 feet above the sea on the slopes of Mount Nevis, the completely refurbished Inn was once a sugar estate dating back to the early 1700's and in 1787 it hosted the wedding of Horatio Nelson and Fanny Nisbet. Today a beautiful old sugar mill stands as testament to its past and owners The Hoffman Family aim to create a country house hotel ambience with an informal style and tranquillity. Each of the 17 newly refurbished rooms are designed to catch the breeze and have private verandas which offer stunning views of the sea, mountains and the lights of Nevis and St. Kitts at night. A large freshwater pool sits in tropical gardens and during the day a complimentary bus service travels to the Inn's private 2 acre beach, situated at the prettiest part of Pinneys. The Inn's Nevisian and European chefs create classic cuisine with a contemporary twist using fresh local produce such as lobster, fish and organically reared pork. Home-made breads and pastries feature at breakfast, as do jams and marmalades made from the Inn's fruits. Dinner is served outside on the Western Verandah after cocktails in The Great Room. Activities available nearby include golf, horse riding, eco-rambles and sailing. The Montpelier has its own tennis court and provides snorkelling equipment on free loan.

Our inspector loved: The old sugar mill which the owners plan to turn into a gourmet dining room.

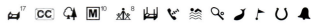

NISBET PLANTATION BEACH CLUB
ST JAMES PARISH, NEVIS, WEST INDIES

A tropical oasis awaits guests arriving at the Nisbet Plantation, with its mile-long stretch of white sandy beach and coral protected reef. Originally built as a sugar plantation in 1778, the main focus of the club is the elegant Great House, which now accommodates the formal dining room as an elegant gathering place for pre-dinner drinks or even English afternoon tea. The bedrooms are found in a collection of plantation style cottages that are carefully dispersed throughout the grounds for maximum privacy and are charmingly furnished with crisp linens and cheerful prints. Each has private patio and wonderful beachfront views as well as ceiling fans for a relaxing breeze. This is a paradise for snorkelling and scuba diving, there is also a freshwater swimming pool and tennis court as well as sailing and sport fishing nearby. The Robert Trent Jones Jr. golf course is also just minutes' away. The beachside bar is hard to leave – serving delightful light snacks and drinks, it makes a great place to relax and spend informal evenings. The dining room at the Great House however, has a more dramatic atmosphere and is often host to local entertainment, after which, the beach beckons for a romantic bedtime stroll.

Our inspector loved: *The avenue of palms stretching from the guest cottages to the ocean.*

Directions: Taxi from Airport

Web: www.johansens.com/nisbetplantation
E-mail: nisbetbc@caribsurf.com
Tel: +1 869 469 9325
Fax: +1 869 469 9864

Price Guide:
rooms $290–$670

THE GOLDEN LEMON

DIEPPE BAY, ST KITTS, WEST INDIES

Directions: The Golden Lemon is located at Dieppe Bay.

Web: www.johansens.com/goldenlemon
E-mail: info@goldenlemon.com
Tel: 1 869 465 7260
Fax: 1 869 465 4019

Price Guide:
rooms $300–$465
villas $465

Welcoming, charming and peaceful, the Golden Lemon is a luxurious hideaway situated in an idyllic location – an ideal escape from the pressures of a busy lifestyle. This tastefully refined and grand-style Caribbean gem stands on a densely palm-fringed beach of black and gold-flecked sand. Behind rises the majestic, wooded Mount Liamuiga. Guests have a choice of staying in the 17th-century Great House or in one of 15 contemporary one and two bedroom seaside villas, each with private plunge pool. Guest rooms and villas are light and airy with stylish furniture, delightful furnishings and cool white and soft pastel colour décor. They have every comfort, facility and necessary convenience for the discerning traveller, and the Golden Lemon's staff take great pride in making a stay a welcoming and unforgettable experience. All rooms offer a panoramic vista across the ocean. The food, which benefits from the superb quality of local produce, reflects the excellence of the surroundings. Guests can enjoy starting the day with a tasty breakfast en suite and follow with lunch and beautifully presented dinner on the front gallery, in the garden by the side of a 40-foot swimming pool or in the elegant dining room. Guests can snorkel over one of the best reefs of the island. There are no televisions at this hotel.

Our inspector loved: *This wonderful location overlooking Eustations and the decor of the rooms - some with their own plunge pools.*

Ottley's Plantation Inn
PO BOX 345, BASSETERRE, ST KITTS, WEST INDIES

This beautiful former sugar plantation, which dates back to the 17th century, is set in 35 acres of lawns and gardens at the foot of the majestic Mount Liamuiga. Restored to provide exceptional accommodation, this friendly, family-run 4-star hotel transports guests back to an era of gracious living and elegance. The rooms in the plantation's acclaimed Great House and cottages are beautifully decorated in English colonial style with floral chintzes and wicker and carved mahogany furniture; all display local artworks and crafts. All rooms have verandah or patio, private bathroom, ceiling fan and air conditioning, whilst some cottage rooms offer Jacuzzis and private plunge pools on ocean view sundecks. For a family or group of friends there is the extraordinary three-bedroom Grand Villa, which offers a fully equipped kitchen, two plunge pools and Jacuzzis and a grand outdoor patio with view of the ocean. Dining at the hotel's restaurant, The Royal Palm, is an experience not to be missed. Chef Pamela Yahn uses fresh island ingredients for her innovative, creative 'New Island' cuisine, served al fresco by the 66-ft spring-fed pool. The Royal Palm is also renowned for its Sunday champagne brunch. Guests can explore the extensive grounds and nearby beaches, walk along rainforest trails or go shopping in Basseterre. Golf enthusiasts will enjoy the acclaimed 18-hole Frigate Bay golf course.

Directions: St. Kitts

Web: www.johansens.com/ottleys
E-mail: ottleys@caribsurf.com
Tel: 1 869 465 7234
Fax: 1 869 465 4760

Price Guide:
rooms $195–$475

Our inspector loved: The early morning walks along the forest trail.

CARIBBEAN - ST KITTS

Rawlins Plantation Inn

PO BOX 340, ST KITTS, WEST INDIES

Directions: Rawlins is situated in the quiet, rural northern end of the island, 15 miles from the airport and the capital Basseterre.

Web: www.johansens.com/Rawlins plantation
E-mail: rawplant@caribsurf.com
Tel: 1 869 465 6221
Fax: 1 869 465 4954

Price Guide:
rooms $220–$450 (Half Board)

The approach to Rawlins Plantation Inn along an undulating track cutting through cane fields does not prepare you for the exquisite neatness of the buildings and colourful gardens that constitute your destination. This initial and delightful image is enhanced by the interiors of dark wooden floors, whitewashed or exposed stone walls, bright cotton fabrics, antiques and an atmosphere of tranquillity stirred only by the paddle fans and a cool breeze. Bedrooms are situated around the main building, offering comfortable accommodation in old stables, stonehouses and, for the really romantic, a lava rock windmill. The grounds are carefully landscaped featuring lush, tropical plants of hibiscus, chenille, bougainvillaea, mango, gardenia and breadfruit and are situated 350 feet above sea level on the slopes of Mount Liamuiga. The kitchen garden provides fresh ingredients to complement the contributions provided by neighbouring farmers and local fishermen to the menu. Owners and hosts Paul and Claire Rawson are committed to the comfort and well-being of their guests, who may enjoy convivial conversation each evening on the spacious verandah and wish to stroll around the beautiful grounds. Visits to the rainforest or beach are easily arranged.

Our inspector loved: *The tiny Bananaquit birds fluttering about the colourful Hibiscus and trying to steal from the sugar bowls.*

St Lucia
Hotel location shown in red with page number

ANSE CHASTANET

PO BOX 7000, SOUFRIERE, ST. LUCIA, WEST INDIES

Directions: 1½ miles north of Soufriére.

Web: www.johansens.com/ansechastanet
E-mail: ansechastanet@candw.lc
Tel: 1 758 459 7000
Fax: 1 758 459 7700
Toll free: 1 800 223 1108

Price Guide:
rooms $245–$365
suites $485–605

This romantic hideaway is beautifully situated amongst its own 600 acre estate that has two stunning natural beaches, two natural valleys with lush rolling hillsides, capped off by some of the most spectacular mountains in the Caribbean. This unique setting has been carefully enhanced by the owner to produce a luxurious hotel that is in total harmony with its surroundings. Each of the 49 individually designed bedrooms incorporate locally crafted furniture and feature art from both local and International artists depicting the eclectic style of the Resort. These rooms are scattered over the flower-decked hillside and many have breathtaking views of the famous Piton Mountains and the Caribbean Sea. A further 12 rooms are found at beach level and are just a few steps from the water's edge. The award winning Piton Restaurant serves Tropical World Cuisine with spectacular mountain views whilst the more informal beachside restaurant offers a combination of Creole and traditional favourites. Located in the heart of the marine reserves, the resort operates its own professional scuba facility. The truly active can enjoy mountain biking on 12 miles of resort trails. The newly opened spa, Kai Belte, offers both traditional and Ayurvedic treatments from professional therapists.

Our inspector loved: The open air rooms that let you connect with mother nature instantly.

MAGO ESTATE HOTEL
PO BOX 247, SOUFRIÈRE, ST LUCIA, WEST INDIES

Set amidst some of the Caribbean's most luscious and awe-inspiring vegetation, the Mago Estate is a secluded and unique hotel with breathtaking views of the "Piton", the landmark most often associated with St. Lucia. This tropical hideaway genuinely reanimates the soul. The surrounding lush forest boasts a plethora of indigenous trees, and visitors can bask in the mélange of colours and scents emanating from the mango, mahogany and papaya trees, as well as the unique bougainvillaea and hibiscus plants. The Mago Estate is the perfect place to imbibe the relaxed atmosphere of St. Lucia. An austere rock formation and two stunning mango trees frame the bar area, while the shangrila units all afford stunning views of the ocean and natural habitat. Individually designed with furniture imported from India, the rooms also exude the ambience of antiquity. Indeed the entire hotel is lavishly decorated, with the dining room positively festooned with Persian rugs, handcrafted furniture and antique art. The beautifully presented food, a blend of Creole and French, is simply divine. Activities at the hotel's health club include body massage and daily tai chi and yoga classes.

Our inspector loved: *The uniqueness of the 'tree house' feeling which is truly a one of a kind location.*

Directions: Signed off the island's main road near to Soufrière Town.

Web: www.johansens.com/magoestate
E-mail: info@magohotel.com
Tel: 1 758 459 5880
Fax: 1 758 459 7352

Price Guide:
(including breakfast)
Shangrila units $100–$450

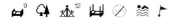

St Vincent & The Grenadines

Hotel location shown in red with page number

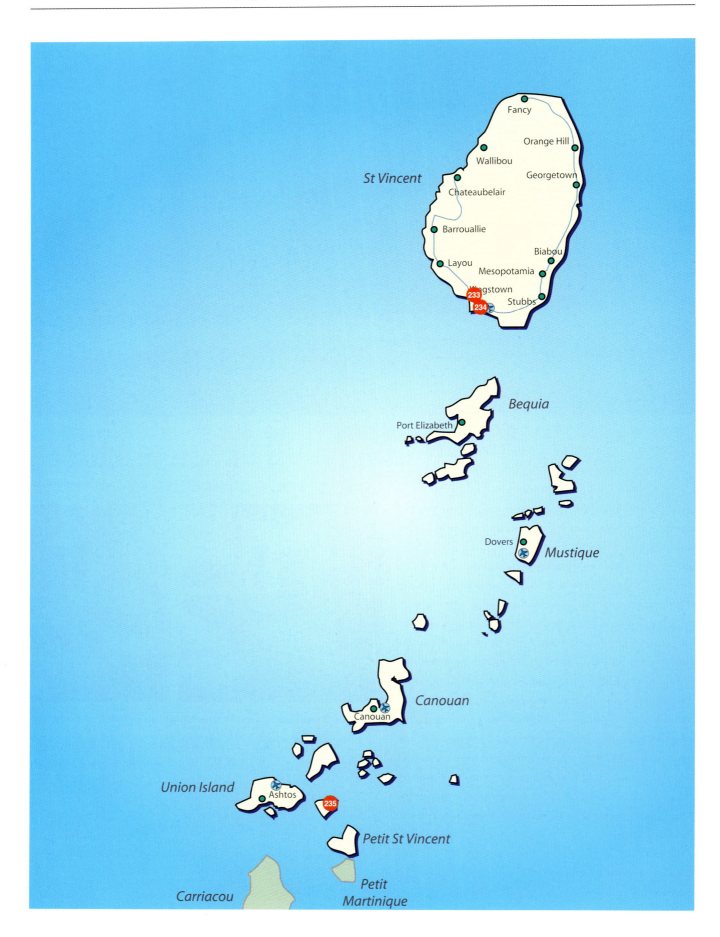

Camelot Inn - A Boutique Hotel

PO BOX 787, KINGSTOWN, THE GRENADINES, ST VINCENT, WEST INDIES

Once the residence of the French governor of St Vincent, this plantation-style historic boutique hotel offers the visitor professional and friendly service in an ambience of regal splendour. Set amongst a garden of mango trees, as well as a vast array of tropical flowers, Camelot Inn, International Platinum Star Award Winner 1999/2000 for excellence in quality and service, has awe-inspiring views of Kingstown and the Grenadine Islands. The 22 rooms are lavishly designed, many with balconies commanding views of the harbour below. The inn has preserved its 200 year-old cobblestone dining room, making meals there a truly singular experience. The atmosphere of being part of the island's rich history is only surpassed by the fare, an eclectic mix of native and international, served with impeccable grace by the excellent staff and accompanied by finest wines. Clearly the Camelot Inn is purpose-made for aficionados of watersports, and a free coach is provided to shuttle visitors to the beach. Snorkelling, scuba diving, sailing and deep-sea fishing can also be arranged. A mere five minutes from Kingstown, visitors can also enjoy the vibrant nightlife of St Vincent's capital. The famous Botanical Gardens are also close at hand.

Our inspector loved: The balcony views of the harbour below.

Directions: 10 minutes from E.T. Joshua airport and 5 minutes from Kingstown

Web: www.johansens.com/camelotinn
E-mail: caminn@caribsurf.com
Tel: 1 784 456 2100
Fax: 1 784 456 2233

Price Guide: (incl. breakfast)
rooms from $135–$195
suites from $350

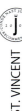

CARIBBEAN - ST. VINCENT

GRAND VIEW BEACH HOTEL

VILLA POINT, BOX 173, ST VINCENT, WEST INDIES

Set in eight luscious acres of tropical garden with imperious views of the Grenadine Islands, the Grand View Beach Hotel has to be ranked amongst the finest hotels in the Caribbean. Befitting a small family-run hotel, the hospitality is warm and friendly and guests are guaranteed privacy and seclusion in majestic surroundings. The colonial style house is lavishly decorated, adorned throughout with antiques and pictures reflecting its aristocratic past. The rooms, all quiet and comfortable, are bathed in soothing pastel shades, while the two Honeymoon Suites have whirlpool tubs, air-conditioning and large balconies with wonderful views of the ocean. The Grand View specialises in freshly-caught fish and lobsters and the imaginatively crafted meals are served in a sumptuous dining room with breathtaking vistas over the Great Head Bay and the forested mountains beyond. The property also offers an impressive range of amenities for a small hotel, including tennis and squash courts, a superb gym, a secluded beach for diving and snorkelling and a swimming pool complete with swim-up bar. Trips to the Grenadine Islands and Botanical Gardens can also be arranged.

Directions: Grand View is located at Villa Point, on the South Coast of St. Vincent, five minutes from the airport, and ten minutes from Kingstown

Web: www.johansens.com/grandviewbeach
E-mail: grandview@caribsurf.com
Tel: 1 784 458 4811
Fax: 1 784 457 4174

Price Guide:
rooms $104–$215
suite $125–$265

Our inspector loved: *The modern art, the work of the owners daughter, displayed around the hotel.*

234

Palm Island
ST VINCENT & THE GRENADINES, WEST INDIES

This is a tranquil paradise of dazzling white sand beaches fringed with palms, breathtaking seascapes and exotic tropical landscapes. Situated in the island chain of St Vincent and The Grenadines, Palm Island is a 135-acre hideaway at the end of the Windward Island group of the Eastern Caribbean. There are five beaches, a freshwater swimming pool with cascading waterfalls, two bars, two restaurants, a vast range of watersports, walking and jogging trails, fitness centre and, at an additional charge, boat trips to the nearby Tobago Cays. Accommodation is simple but stylish, reflecting an escape from the demands and stress of contemporary life. All the delightfully designed guest rooms feature air conditioning, rattan and bamboo furniture, original artwork, a balcony or patio and an excellent range of amenities. The Palm View and Beachfront bungalows nestle among shady trees and colourful gardens just a few yards from the sand with views of distant islands. Plantation House has two rooms upstairs and two down that are ideal for the small family. Each includes two Queen-size beds with a pull-out couch in an extended living area. Dining is relaxed, with gourmet meals being enjoyed in the Royal Palm and casual, grill-type fare served in the Sunset Beach Restaurant with its own bar.

Our inspector loved: Playing Robinson Crusoe in paradise.

Directions: Daily air flights from Barbados to Union Island, then a 10-minute launch ride to Palm Beach.

Web: www.johansens.com/palmisland
E-mail: res@classicislands.com
Tel: 1 800 345 0271
Fax: 1 954 481 1661

Price Guide:
rooms from $595
suite from $730

Turks & Caicos

Hotel location shown in red with page number

POINT GRACE

PO BOX 700, PROVIDENCIALES, TURKS AND CAICOS ISLANDS, BRITISH WEST INDIES

An exceptional hideaway, the recently opened Point Grace Hotel is beautifully designed with spectacular views of the pristine 12-mile beach of Grace Bay (rated No 1 by Condé Nast). Attention to detail is inspiring in this stunning hotel with cool colours and stylish fabrics. The elegant and tastefully decorated suites are filled with exquisite Indonesian teak furniture and have expansive living areas and luxurious bathrooms. All offer refrigerators, CD and DVD players, cable television, air conditioning and ceiling fans. The breathtaking penthouse is complete with library, study and massage suite. Grace's Cottage, an elegant gourmet restaurant, is open for dinner, whilst a breakfast as well as lunch are served on the terrace. Bar service is available throughout the day. Guests can experience true refinement in the unspoilt and virtually undiscovered tropical paradise of Providenciales, one of the 49 islands that are the British Crown Colony of Turks and Caicos. Outdoor pursuits include non-motorised watersports such as diving, snorkelling, sailing and fishing in the cool, clear waters and coral reefs. For golf enthusiasts there is a championship golf course nearby, and the marine parks and wildlife reserves in the area are exciting to explore. A complimentary half-hour de-stress massage is available upon arrival.

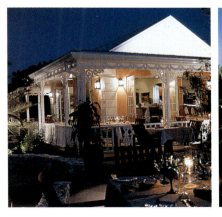

Directions: Daily flights from Miami, Charlotte, Boston. Also frequent flights from New York and London.

Web: www.johansens.com/pointgrace
E-mail: reservations@pointgrace.com
Tel: 1 649 946 5096
Fax: 1 649 946 5097

Price Guide
suites $395–$1765
Penthouse $4000–$6800

Our inspector loved: Dinner at Grace's Cottage.

CARIBBEAN - TURKS & CAICOS

THE SANDS AT GRACE BAY

PO BOX 681, PROVIDENCIALES, TURKS & CAICOS ISLANDS, BRITISH WEST INDIES

This first-class condominium resort enjoys a beautiful landscaped setting with exotic flowers, streams, three swimming pools and a Jacuzzi. The view of fabulously clear turquoise sea and white sands stretching for 12 miles is breathtaking, and indeed the Grace Bay beach was voted number one in the world by a Condé Nast reader's poll. Suites are spacious and comfortable with tasteful furnishings, full kitchens, air conditioning and large balconies. The atmosphere is one of 'barefoot elegance'; staff are friendly, and the beach-side restaurant relaxed and casual. The glorious weather of the islands lends itself to an outdoor lifestyle, and activities available include watersports such as diving, snorkelling, sailing and kayaking as well as world-class deep sea fishing, championship golf and tennis on the resort's flood lit court. Many attractions exist within the surrounding area, and guests can enjoy visits to marine parks, conch farms, wildlife reserves and excursions to other islands. With its excellent facilities and tranquil location The Sands is a superb resort for families, or simply for those who wish to get away from it all and escape to an idyllic, unspoilt corner of the Caribbean.

Directions: Complimentary transfer from and to the airport, which is 15 minutes away. Direct flights from Miami, Boston, Charlotte, New York and London.

Web: www.johansens.com/sandsgracebay
E-mail: vacations@thesandsresort.com
Tel: 1 649 946 5199
Fax: 1 649 946 5198

Price Guide: (plus 20% tax and facility fee)
Garden Viewsuites $175–$625
Ocean Viewsuites $200–$725
Ocean Frontsuites $230–$995

Our inspector loved: The bell for sighting Jojo the dolphin.

Fiji Islands

Hotel location shown in red with page number

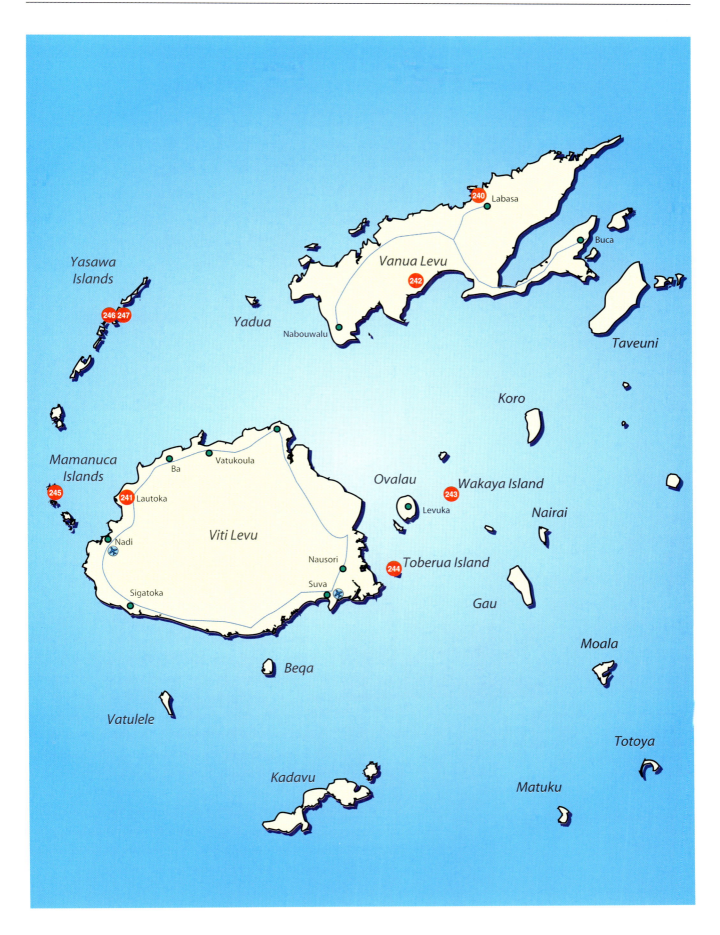

FIJI ISLANDS - LABASA

NUKUBATI ISLAND

PO BOX 1928, LABASA, FIJI ISLANDS

Directions: Transfer by plane from Nadi

Web: www.johansens.com/www.nukubati.com
E-mail: nukubatihq@msn.com.au
Tel: 61 2 93888 196
Fax: 61 2 93888 204

Price Guide: (fully inclusive)
rooms US$750
suites US$860

This really is a truly idyllic hideaway – arriving by sea plane and stepping onto white sands, one is instantly free from working day stresses or even the concept of time. The alternative route via Labasa airport is no less dramatic, driving through lush farmland, past sugar cane and rice crops and stopping to pick fresh guava and other fruits in season. The delightfully friendly staff wait on the shores to greet guests and attend to their every need, each one treated as though they were the first. The airy pavilion is a stunning place to relax and sip an evening cocktail watching the sunset, although it is a hard choice to choose this or the intimate privacy of one's own verandah. Three new bure have been added and the existing bure extended in a recent refurbishment. The layout is open plan and beautifully appointed with comfortable lounges and quiet writing tables; whilst the bathrooms are luxuriously large – the honeymoon bure even has two shower heads in the large open shower! The food is all taken from chef's island garden or the local waters and could not be fresher – lobster, crab and prawns are all abundant, and the fruit from the "Fijian Garden" is unrivalled. Nukubati is located in the great sea reef – one of the world's largest reefs, and the hotel offers an excellent shop with the very latest equipment, enabling guests to be just as active, or inactive, as they please!

Our inspector loved: *The magnificent and welcoming central pavillion.*

BLUE LAGOON CRUISES
183 VITOGO PARADE, LAUTOKA, FIJI ISLANDS

Annually surveyed by Lloyds of London and recently fully refurbished, the elegant 56 metre Mystique Princess gleams like a new pin. Truly a millionaire's yacht, guest reports to date have been excellent, and the Blue Lagoon Cruise is not to be missed as part of a Fijian holiday experience. On this floating palace guests can relax in the lap of luxury, pampered by the wonderfully attentive and friendly crew. Early morning 'wake up' swims in warm azure waters are followed by strolls along white sandy beaches. Delicious food is always available, from the sumptuous breakfast to morning and afternoon tea, barbecue picnic lunches and candlelit dinners. From Fiji's most pristine islands visitors can go snorkelling, scuba-diving and glass-bottom boat viewing with visibility to coral reefs up to 90 feet below the surface. Aboard, the brand new Biodroga Spa offers wonderful indulgent treatments, including a 'Couples in Love' package. The deluxe en suite staterooms are spacious, beautifully appointed and fitted with every comfort from king sized bed to TV, video and personal safe. Most have large panoramic windows; all have sea views.

Our inspector loved: The complete Fijian experience.

Directions: Blue Lagoon Cruises headquarters and passenger lounge are situated in Lautoka, a 30 minute drive from Nadi International Airport.

Web: www.johansens.com/bluelagooncruises
E-mail: blc@is.com.fj
Tel: 1 679 6661 622
Fax: 1 679 6664 098

Price Guide:
rooms US$1099–US$1675
suites US$1599–$2100

FIJI ISLANDS - SAVU SAVU

Namale

SAVU SAVU, FIJI ISLANDS

Directions: Resort arranges transfers from Nadi International Airport.

Web: www.johansens.com/namale
E-mail: namalefiji@aol.com
Tel: 1 858 535 6380
Fax: 1 858 535 6385

Price Guide:
rooms US$575–US$900
suites US$1350–US$1800

As soon as one passes through the gates of the magnificent Namale resort, there is a sense that maybe one has entered paradise. The meandering tropical gardens seem as endless as the ocean with its outstanding reef, framed by rain forest-clad hills. The resort has 13 exclusive bures and 2 deluxe houses, and all epitomise luxury. The décor is truly opulent with magnificent interiors and private decks, right down to the oversized pillows that lie on oversized beds. The main bure "Vale Levu" offers magnificence on an unrivalled scale and is the ultimate in relaxation with sumptuous sofas and elegant chairs. The staff are gentle and unobtrusive, granting each guest their privacy yet seemingly anticipating their every need. Mealtimes are a delight with mouthwatering combinations of local and International cuisine – the dilemma being to choose between dining on one of the private decks overlooking the ocean, or amongst the magnificent trees. A holiday at Namale offers total relaxation – soaking up the sun and taking leisurely walks through the delightful gardens. Namale excels in the variety of activities offered from jacuzzi's, tennis, bowling, horseback riding, scuba diving, virtual golf and so much more you could stay a month and not get to it all. The newest addition is a full-service Spa with a panoramic view overlooking their magical natural blowhole.

Our inspector loved: This garden of eden called Namale.

THE WAKAYA CLUB

WAKAYA ISLAND, FIJI ISLANDS

Wakaya was first sighted by Captain Bligh in 1789 and is steeped in history, myth and legend. It is an ultimate, exotic tropical hideaway. Lush forests, soaring cliffs, glittering waterfalls, swaying palms, and powder-soft beaches cover its five square miles. The Wakaya Club was designed for privacy and only 18 guests are accepted at one time in only nine Bures, authentic Fijian thatched roof cottages with their own private beachfront. They are outstanding, with airy, high-pitched ceiling, fanciful hand-woven bamboo wallcovering, gleaming yaka plank flooring and a superb four-poster king-size bamboo bed in an elegantly appointed bedroom. The owner's home "Vale O" (a 12,000 sq. ft. villa), is also available for up to three couples. The Fijian native service is enchanting and excellent. Four chefs and two pastry chefs flex their creative muscles for guests with delectable local, Indian, Chinese and Continental delicacies featuring Fijian game, seafood and fruits and vegetables from Wakaya's own organic gardens. Unique salads and soups, sumptuous main dishes and desserts are presented with flair. Guests can do as much or as little as they wish. They can relax and marvel at the club's private art collection, take a quiet nature walk through woodland alive with deer, feral pigs, fascinating birds and colourful flora, play golf or tennis, scuba dive or snorkel.

Directions: Private plane transfers from Nadi or Suva International Airports.

Web: www.johansens.com/wakaya
E-mail: info@wakaya.com
Tel: 1 970 927 2044
Fax: 1 970 927 2048
US Toll Free: 1 800 828 3454

Price Guide:
suites $1600–$2100
villa $3500–$6500

Our inspector loved: The private art collection at Wakaya is superb.

Toberua Island Resort

PO BOX 3332, NAUSORI, FIJI ISLANDS

Directions: Seaplane from Nadi then covered boat to Toberua.

Web: www.johansens.com/toberuaisland
E-mail: toberua@connect.com.fj
Tel: 679 347 2777
Fax: 679 347 2888

Price Guide:
rooms FJ$490–FJ$790
suites FJ$580–FJ$790

This is a paradise island frequently called the jewel of Fiji. Privately owned and situated off the eastern tip of Viti Levu. Toberua is 4 acres of pure white sand and unspoilt natural beauty when the tide is in and around 20 acres when it retires twice a day. It offers intimacy, privacy and peace where guests can be as active or as inactive as they wish. On arrival they are escorted by cheerful house girls through lush botanical gardens to one of 14 thatched en suite 'bures' (Fijian cottages) that nestle on the water's edge. Each is the essence of comfort, boasting all modern facilities from refrigerator and hot water to mini bar and indoor/outdoor bathroom. Ceilings soar a traditional 28 feet upwards. Dining is a delight. Excellent meals are enjoyed under the stars or in the comfortable dining room. Daily changing menus are International with a choice of fantastic Fijian specialities such as crayfish and prawns. The bar/library is a popular meeting place for pre-dinner drinks. There is good snorkelling, scuba-diving, windsurfing, sailing and coral viewing. Excursions include visits to neighbouring Bird Island, boat trips to a mangrove plantation and visits to the local village of Varani.

Our inspector loved: *Playing reef golf, only at Toberua.*

VOMO ISLAND
PO BOX 5650, LAUTOKA, FIJI ISLANDS

Vomo Island resort is an unspoilt, exotic paradise nestled into Vomo's majestic mountainside and surrounded by spectacular coral reefs and white sandy beaches. 80 acres of manicured grounds and lush tropical gardens have a golf course at one end and spectacular plunging cliffs at the other. Air-conditioned villas are the ultimate in luxury with an enclosed lanai, hardwood floors, comfortable furnishings and en suite bathroom with Jacuzzi. Exquisite cuisine and fine wines are served in each of the resort's restaurants. The Rocks Restaurant is situated high on the promontory overlooking Vomo Lai Lai and is perfect for enjoying the sunset whilst sipping cocktails or feasting on lobster from the sizzling grill. Vomo Island has plenty to offer. At the beauty therapy clinic experienced staff is waiting to pamper you with a massage, facial or manicure, or for the more energetic the hotel has a superb swimming pool, tennis, golf, volleyball, badminton, pentanque, croquet and table tennis. Other outdoor pursuits include fishing, non-motorised water sports, snorkelling, scuba diving, mountain biking, trekking and bush walking. The locals give interesting demonstrations on coconut weaving, coconut tree climbing and flower stringing and there are excellent sunset cruises and helicopter scenic tours.

Directions: 19 miles west of Nadi International Airport. Transfer by plane or helicopter.

Vanu Levi

Yasawa Islands

Viti Levu

Web: www.johansens.com/vomoisland
E-mail: sales@vomo.com.fj
Tel: 679 6668 122
Fax: 679 6668 500

Price Guide: Upon Request

Our inspector loved: Having a whole tropical island to yourself.

FIJI ISLANDS - YASAWA ISLANDS

Turtle Island

YASAWA ISLANDS, PO BOX 9317, NADI AIRPORT, NADI, FIJI ISLANDS

Directions: Guests are met at Nadi International Airport and are advised of seaplane departure times.

Web: www.johansens.com/turtleisland
E-mail: info@turtlefiji.com.au
Tel: 61 3 9823 8300
Fax: 61 3 9823 8383
UK Toll Free: 0800 028 5938

Price Guide:
From US$573 per person

Turtle Island has won many international awards and was voted top five-star resort in the Pacific region in the publication World's Best Awards by Travel & Leisure readers. This idyllic and endearing 500-acre unspoilt private island is situated alongside the famous Blue Lagoon. Catering for 14 couples only and with 14 separate beaches, it is restful and romantic with acres of rainforest, stunning coral reefs and a horizon of sapphire coloured water. The unique magnificent Fijian-style, two-room beachfront cottages (bures) are complete with hand-crafted furniture, four-poster king-size bed, Jacuzzi, fully stocked refrigerator, double and outdoor shower, verandah with queen-size day bed, double hammock, deck chairs on the beach and two paddle craft. The tariff includes accommodation, all activities such as deep sea fishing, diving, horse riding, all meals and beverages, laundry and use of entire island. Turtle Island is a life experience, a place where you bathe in the delights that have been lost to modern society. The warm Fijian staff, the beauty of an island untouched by industry, where ecology, cultural integrity, environmental responsibility and partnership with the local Fijian community is a primary concern, and where people understand that your holiday is a very special event.

Our inspector loved: *The very special Turtle atmosphere.*

Yasawa Island Resort
PO BOX 10128, NADI AIRPORT, NADI, FIJI ISLANDS

Virtually untouched and remote from the mainland, the Yasawa Islands have just 12,000 native inhabitants and are surrounded by azure blue waters, reefs and corals of all varieties. The Resort is secluded and exclusive, nestling on 1km of white sandy beach with a backdrop of palm trees and grass hut villages. Already established as one of the island escapes, it has recently been blessed with a $2 million upgrade and owner Garth Downey believes it combines beauty and tranquillity with the modern and romantic to offer the ultimate in luxury and pampering. Each of the air-conditioned en suite bures are beautifully decorated and furnished with its own separate living room and Bose system. The ultra secluded Lomalagi is recognised as the most exclusive bure in Fiji and comprises of a private patio and beach with an impressive split-level room. Fresh seafood is caught and served daily, with lobster available for lunch, dinner and even breakfast. With some real treasures in its cellar the Resort boasts the best wine list in the Pacific. Leisure facilities include swimming in the pool or from the beach, snorkelling, deep sea fishing, gourmet picnics, diving, visiting traditional villages and exploring the nearby Blue Lagoon Caves which featured in the film starring Brooke Shields.

Our inspector loved: *The stunning wine-list; some real treasures for the connoisseur.*

Directions: There are daily flights from Nadi to an airstrip adjacent to the resort.

Web: www.johansens.com/yasawaisland
E-mail: yasawa@is.com.fj
Tel: 679 772 2266
Fax: 579 772 4456

Price Guide:
single US$500–US$600
double US$625–US$950

Samoa

Hotel location shown in red with page number

AGGIE GREY'S HOTEL

PO BOX 67, APIA, SAMOA

Founded by Aggie Grey in 1933, the Hotel originally grew a reputation amongst World War II servicemen stationed in Samoa as a lively place to meet and whilst buildings and décor have changed, the atmosphere is still much the same. The famous and not-so-famous have flocked to its gates for 70 years, for its unpretentious and lively style. Some of the rooms today bear the names of previous incumbents: Marlon Brando; Raymond Burr; and William Holden for example. The main Hotel is still very reflective of the colonial style, whilst accommodation varies from spacious and airy poolside rooms, to exotic island bungalows known as Fales, which are typical of the local style and craftsmanship. Guests must experience the Fiafia, which begins with the cultural performance, this is followed by a gastronomic delight in the main dining room of the house and moves slowly out to the poolside for an exciting fire dancing finale. At other times, the main dining room offers a traditional à la carte menu with local specialities or the casual Island Restaurant has a more relaxed atmosphere with a familiar range of cuisine accompanied by a few local delicacies.

Our inspector loved: The sense of history that makes Aggies one of the world's legendary places.

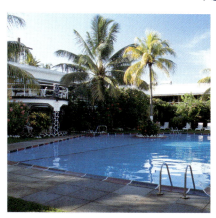

Directions: 45 minutes from International airport.

Web: www.johansens.com/aggiegreys
E-mail: aggiegreys@aggiegreys.com
Tel: 685 228 80
Fax: 685 236 26 or 685 23203

Price Guide:
rooms US$95–US$150
suites US$190–US$225

Mini Listings Great Britain & Ireland

Condé Nast Johansens are delighted to recommend over 720 properties across Great Britain and Ireland. These properties can be found in *Recommended Hotels - GB & Ireland 2003* and *Recommended Country Houses, Small Hotels & Inns - GB & Ireland 2003*. Call 1-800-564-7518 or see the order forms on page 285 to order guides.

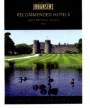 

Recommended Hotels
Great Britain & Ireland 2003

England

The Bath Priory Hotel And Restaurant	Bath & NE Somerset	+44 (0)1225 331922
The Bath Spa Hotel	Bath & NE Somerset	+44 (0)870 400 8222
Combe Grove Manor Hotel & Country Club	Bath & NE Somerset	+44 (0)1225 834644
Homewood Park	Bath & NE Somerset	+44 (0)1225 723731
Hunstrete House	Bath & NE Somerset	+44 (0)1761 490490
The Queensberry	Bath & NE Somerset	+44 (0)1225 447928
The Royal Crescent Hotel	Bath & NE Somerset	+44 (0)1225 823333
The Windsor Hotel	Bath & NE Somerset	+44 (0)1225 422100
Flitwick Manor	Bedfordshire	+44 (0)1525 712242
Moore Place Hotel	Bedfordshire	+44 (0)1908 282000
The Berystede	Berkshire	+44 (0)870 400 8111
The Castle Hotel	Berkshire	+44 (0)870 400 8300
Cliveden	Berkshire	+44 (0)1628 668561
Donnington Valley Hotel & Golf Club	Berkshire	+44 (0)1635 551199
Fredrick's Hotel & Restaurant	Berkshire	+44 (0)1628 581000
The French Horn	Berkshire	+44 (0)1189 692204
Monkey Island Hotel	Berkshire	+44 (0)1628 623400
The Regency Park Hotel	Berkshire	+44 (0)1635 871555
Sir Christopher Wren's House Hotel	Berkshire	+44 (0)1753 861354
The Swan At Streatley	Berkshire	+44 (0)1491 878800
The Vineyard At Stockcross	Berkshire	+44 (0)1635 528770
The Burlington Hotel	Birmingham	+44 (0)121 643 9191
Hotel Du Vin & Bistro	Birmingham	+44 (0)121 200 0600
Hotel Du Vin & Bistro	Birmingham	+44 (0)121 200 0600
Hotel Du Vin & Bistro	Birmingham	+44 (0)121 200 0600
Hotel Du Vin & Bistro	Birmingham	+44 (0)121 200 0600
Hotel Du Vin & Bistro	Birmingham	+44 (0)121 200 0600
New Hall	Birmingham	+44 (0)121 378 2442
Taplow House Hotel	Buckinghamshire	+44 (0)1628 670056
Danesfield House Hotel And Spa	Buckinghamshire	+44 (0)1628 891010
Hartwell House	Buckinghamshire	+44 (0)1296 747444
Stoke Park Club	Buckinghamshire	+44 (0)1753 717171
The Haycock	Cambridgeshire	+44 (0)1780 782223
Hotel Felix	Cambridgeshire	+44 (0)1223 277977
The Alderley Edge Hotel	Cheshire	+44 (0)1625 583033
The Chester Crabwall Manor	Cheshire	+44 (0)1244 851666
Crewe Hall	Cheshire	+44 (0)1270 253333
Mere Court Hotel	Cheshire	+44 (0)1565 831000
Nunsmere Hall	Cheshire	+44 (0)1606 889100
Rookery Hall	Cheshire	+44 (0)1270 610016
Rowton Hall Hotel	Cheshire	+44 (0)1244 335262
The Stanneylands Hotel	Cheshire	+44 (0)1625 525225
Budock Vean - The Hotel On The River	Cornwall	+44 (0)1326 252100
Fowey Hall Hotel & Restaurant	Cornwall	+44 (0)1726 833866
The Garrack Hotel & Restaurant	Cornwall	+44 (0)1736 796199
The Greenbank Hotel	Cornwall	+44 (0)1326 312440
Hustyns Hotel & Leisure Club	Cornwall	+44 (0)1208 893700
The Lugger Hotel	Cornwall	+44 (0)1872 501322
Meudon Hotel	Cornwall	+44 (0)1326 250541
The Nare Hotel	Cornwall	+44 (0)1872 501111
Penmere Manor	Cornwall	+44 (0)1326 211411
Rose-In-Vale Country House Hotel	Cornwall	+44 (0)1872 552202
The Rosevine Hotel	Cornwall	+44 (0)1872 580206
St Martin's On The Isle	Cornwall	+44 (0)1720 422090
Talland Bay Hotel	Cornwall	+44 (0)1503 272667
Treglos Hotel	Cornwall	+44 (0)1841 520727
The Well House	Cornwall	+44 (0)1579 342001
Appleby Manor Country House Hotel	Cumbria	+44 (0)17683 51571
The Borrowdale Gates Country House Hotel	Cumbria	+44 (0)17687 77204
The Derwentwater Hotel	Cumbria	+44 (0)17687 72538
Farlam Hall Hotel	Cumbria	+44 (0)16977 46234
Gilpin Lodge	Cumbria	+44 (0)15394 88818
Graythwaite Manor	Cumbria	+44 (0)15395 32001
Holbeck Ghyll Country House Hotel	Cumbria	+44 (0)15394 32375
The Inn on the Lake	Cumbria	+44 (0)17684 82444
Lakeside Hotel On Lake Windermere	Cumbria	+44 (0)8701 541586
Langdale Chase	Cumbria	+44 (0)15394 32201
Lovelady Shield Country House Hotel	Cumbria	+44 (0)1434 381203
Miller Howe	Cumbria	+44 (0)15394 42536
Rampsbeck Country House Hotel	Cumbria	+44 (0)17684 86442
Rothay Manor	Cumbria	+44 (0)15394 33605
The Samling	Cumbria	+44 (0)15394 31922
Sharrow Bay Country House Hotel	Cumbria	+44 (0)17684 86301
Storrs Hall	Cumbria	+44 (0)15394 47111
Tufton Arms Hotel	Cumbria	+44 (0)17683 51593
The Wordsworth Hotel	Cumbria	+44 (0)15394 35592
Callow Hall	Derbyshire	+44 (0)1335 300900
Cavendish Hotel	Derbyshire	+44 (0)1246 582311
East Lodge Country House Hotel	Derbyshire	+44 (0)1629 734474
Fischer's	Derbyshire	+44 (0)1246 583259
The George At Hathersage	Derbyshire	+44 (0)1433 650436
Hassop Hall	Derbyshire	+44 (0)1629 640488
The Izaak Walton Hotel	Derbyshire	+44 (0)1335 350555
The Lee Wood Hotel & Restaurant	Derbyshire	+44 (0)1298 23002
Riber Hall	Derbyshire	+44 (0)1629 582795
Ringwood Hall Hotel	Derbyshire	+44 (0)1246 280077
Risley Hall Country House Hotel	Derbyshire	+44 (0)115 939 9000
Riverside House	Derbyshire	+44 (0)1629 814275
The Arundell Arms	Devon	+44 (0)1566 784666
Buckland-Tout-Saints	Devon	+44 (0)1548 853055
Fairwater Head Country House Hotel	Devon	+44 (0)1297 678349
Gidleigh Park	Devon	+44 (0)1647 432367
Hotel Barcelona	Devon	+44 (0)1392 281000
Hotel Riviera	Devon	+44 (0)1395 515201
Mill End	Devon	+44 (0)1647 432282
Northcote Manor Country House Hotel	Devon	01769 560501
Orestone Manor Hotel & Restaurant	Devon	+44 (0)1803 328098
The Osborne Hotel & Langtry's Restaurant	Devon	+44 (0)1803 213311
The Palace Hotel	Devon	+44 (0)1803 200200
Plantation House Hotel & Matisse Restaurant	Devon	+44 (0)1548 831100
Soar Mill Cove Hotel	Devon	+44 (0)1548 561566
The Tides Reach Hotel	Devon	+44 (0)1548 843466
Watersmeet Hotel	Devon	+44 (0)1271 870333
Woolacombe Bay Hotel	Devon	+44 (0)1271 870388
Bridge House Hotel	Dorset	+44 (0)1308 862200
The Dormy	Dorset	+44 (0)1202 872121
Langtry Manor - Lovenest Of A King	Dorset	+44 (0)1202 553887
Menzies East Cliff Court	Dorset	+44 (0)1202 554545
Moonfleet Manor	Dorset	+44 (0)1305 786948
Norfolk Royale Hotel	Dorset	+44 (0)1202 551521
Plumber Manor	Dorset	+44 (0)1258 472507
The Priory Hotel	Dorset	+44 (0)1929 551666
The Priory Hotel	Dorset	+44 (0)1929 551666
Summer Lodge	Dorset	+44 (0)1935 83424
Headlam Hall	Durham	+44 (0)1325 730238
Seaham Hall Hotel & Oriental Spa	Durham	+44 (0)191 516 1400
Willerby Manor Hotel	East Riding Of Yorkshire	+44 (0)1482 652616
Ashdown Park Hotel And Country Club	East Sussex	+44 (0)1342 824988
Buxted Park Country House Hotel	East Sussex	+44 (0)1825 732711
Dale Hill	East Sussex	+44 (0)1580 200112
The Grand Hotel	East Sussex	+44 (0)1323 412345
Horsted Place Country House Hotel	East Sussex	+44 (0)1825 750581
Newick Park	East Sussex	+44 (0)1825 723633
Powdermills Hotel	East Sussex	+44 (0)1424 775511
White Lodge Country House Hotel	East Sussex	+44 (0)1323 870265
Five Lakes Hotel, Golf, Country Club & Spa	Essex	+44 (0)1621 868888
Greenwoods Estate	Essex	+44 (0)1277 829990
Maison Talbooth	Essex	+44 (0)1206 322367
The Pier At Harwich	Essex	+44 (0)1255 241212

250

MINI LISTINGS GREAT BRITAIN & IRELAND

Condé Nast Johansens are delighted to recommend over 720 properties across Great Britain and Ireland. These properties can be found in *Recommended Hotels - GB & Ireland 2003* and *Recommended Country Houses, Small Hotels & Inns - GB & Ireland 2003*.
Call 1-800-564-7518 or see the order forms on page 285 to order guides.

The Bear Of Rodborough	Gloucestershire	+44 (0)1453 878522
Calcot Manor	Gloucestershire	+44 (0)1666 890391
Charingworth Manor	Gloucestershire	+44 (0)1386 593555
The Close Hotel	Gloucestershire	+44 (0)1666 502272
Corse Lawn House Hotel	Gloucestershire	+44 (0)1452 780479
Cotswold House	Gloucestershire	+44 (0)1386 840330
The Grapevine Hotel	Gloucestershire	+44 (0)1451 830344
The Greenway	Gloucestershire	+44 (0)1242 862352
Hotel Kandinsky	Gloucestershire	+44 (0)1242 527788
Hotel On The Park	Gloucestershire	+44 (0)1242 518898
Lords Of The Manor Hotel	Gloucestershire	+44 (0)1451 820243
Lower Slaughter Manor	Gloucestershire	+44 (0)1451 820456
The Manor House Hotel	Gloucestershire	+44 (0)1608 650501
The Noel Arms Hotel	Gloucestershire	+44 (0)1386 840317
The Painswick Hotel	Gloucestershire	+44 (0)1452 812160

▼

The Swan Hotel At Bibury	**Gloucestershire**	**+44 (0)1285 740695**
The Unicorn Hotel	Gloucestershire	+44 (0)1451 830257
Washbourne Court Hotel	Gloucestershire	+44 (0)1451 822143
Wyck Hill House	Gloucestershire	+44 (0)1451 831936
Didsbury House	Greater Manchester	+44 (0)161 448 2200
Etrop Grange	Greater Manchester	+44 (0)161 499 0500
Careys Manor Hotel	Hampshire	+44 (0)1590 623551
Chewton Glen	Hampshire	+44 (0)1425 275341
Esseborne Manor	Hampshire	+44 (0)1264 736444
Fifehead Manor	Hampshire	+44 (0)1264 781565
Lainston House Hotel	Hampshire	+44 (0)1962 863588
Le Poussin At Parkhill	Hampshire	+44 (0)23 8028 2944
The Master Builder's House	Hampshire	+44 (0)1590 616253
The Montagu Arms Hotel	Hampshire	+44 (0)1590 612324
Old Thorns Hotel, Golf & Country Club	Hampshire	+44 (0)1428 724555
Passford House Hotel	Hampshire	+44 (0)1590 682398
Rhinefield House Hotel	Hampshire	+44 (0)1590 622922
Stanwell House	Hampshire	+44 (0)1590 677123
Tylney Hall	Hampshire	+44 (0)1256 764881
Allt-Yr-Ynys Hotel	Herefordshire	+44 (0)1873 890307
The Chase Hotel	Herefordshire	+44 (0)1989 763161
Down Hall Country House Hotel	Hertfordshire	+44 (0)1279 731441
Hanbury Manor	Hertfordshire	+44 (0)1920 487722
Pendley Manor Hotel & Conference Centre	Hertfordshire	+44 (0)1442 891891
Sopwell House Hotel, Country Club & Spa	Hertfordshire	+44 (0)1727 864477
St Michael's Manor	Hertfordshire	+44 (0)1727 864444
The Priory Bay Hotel	Isle Of Wight	+44 (0)1983 613146
Chilston Park	Kent	+44 (0)1622 859803
Eastwell Manor	Kent	+44 (0)1233 213000
Rowhill Grange Hotel And Spa	Kent	+44 (0)1322 615136
The Spa Hotel	Kent	+44 (0)1892 520331
Astley Bank Hotel & Conference Centre	Lancashire	+44 (0)1254 777700
The Gibbon Bridge Hotel	Lancashire	+44 (0)1995 61456
Northcote Manor	Lancashire	+44 (0)1254 240555
Quorn Country Hotel	Leicestershire	+44 (0)1509 415050
Stapleford Park Hotel, Spa, Golf & Sporting Estate	Leicestershire	+44 (0)1572 787 522
The George Of Stamford	Lincolnshire	+44 (0)1780 750750
The Olde Barn Hotel	Lincolnshire	+44 (0)1400 250909

The Petersham	London	+44 (0)20 8940 7471
41	London	+44 (0)20 7300 0041
51 Buckingham Gate	London	+44 (0)20 7769 7766
The Academy, The Bloomsbury Town House	London	+44 (0)20 7631 4115
The Ascott Mayfair	London	+44 (0)20 7659 4321
The Athenaeum Hotel & Apartments	London	+44 (0)20 7499 3464
Basil Street Hotel	London	+44 (0)20 7581 3311
The Beaufort	London	+44 (0)20 7584 5252
Beaufort House	London	+44 (0)20 7584 2600
The Cadogan	London	+44 (0)20 7235 7141
Cannizaro House	London	+44 (0)870 333 9124
The Capital Hotel & Apartments	London	+44 (0)20 7589 5171
The Chesterfield Mayfair	London	+44 (0)20 7491 2622
Circus Apartments	London	+44 (0)20 7719 7000
The Cliveden Town House	London	+44 (0)20 7730 6466
The Colonnade, The Little Venice Town House	London	+44 (0)20 7286 1052
The Cranley	London	+44 (0)20 7373 0123
Dolphin Square Hotel	London	+44 (0)20 7834 3800
The Dorchester	London	+44 (0)20 7629 8888
Dorset Square Hotel	London	+44 (0)20 7723 7874
Draycott House Apartments	London	+44 (0)20 7584 4659
The Gallery	London	+44 (0)20 7915 0000
Great Eastern Hotel	London	+44 (0)20 7618 5000
The Halkin	London	+44 (0)20 7333 1000
Harrington Hall	London	+44 (0)20 7396 9696
Kensington House Hotel	London	+44 (0)20 7937 2345
Kingsway Hall	London	+44 (0)20 7309 0909
The Leonard	London	+44 (0)20 7935 2010
The Lexham Apartments	London	+44 (0)20 7559 4444
London Bridge Hotel & Apartments	London	+44 (0)20 7855 2200
The Milestone Hotel & Apartments	London	+44 (0)20 7917 1000
Number Eleven Cadogan Gardens	London	+44 (0)20 7730 7000
Number Sixteen	London	+44 (0)20 7589 5232
One Aldwych	London	+44 (0)20 7300 1000
The Pelham Hotel	London	+44 (0)20 7589 8288
Pembridge Court Hotel	London	+44 (0)20 7229 9977
The Queensgate	London	+44 (0)20 7761 4000
The Richmond Gate Hotel And Restaurant	London	+44 (0)20 8940 0061
The Rubens At The Palace	London	+44 (0)20 7834 6600
Twenty Nevern Square	London	+44 (0)20 7565 9555
Warren House	London	+44 (0)20 8547 1777
West Lodge Park Country House Hotel	London	+44 (0)20 8216 3900
The Westbourne	London	+44 (0)20 7243 6008
Barnham Broom	Norfolk	+44 (0)1603 759393
Park Farm Country Hotel & Leisure	Norfolk	+44 (0)1603 810264
Ambassador Hotel	North Yorkshire	+44 (0)1904 641316
The Balmoral Hotel	North Yorkshire	+44 (0)1423 508208
Crathorne Hall	North Yorkshire	+44 (0)1642 700398
The Devonshire Arms Country House Hotel	North Yorkshire	+44 (0)1756 718111
Grants Hotel	North Yorkshire	+44 (0)1423 560666
Hackness Grange	North Yorkshire	+44 (0)1723 882345
Hazlewood Castle Hotel	North Yorkshire	+44 (0)1937 535353
Middlethorpe Hall	North Yorkshire	+44 (0)1904 641241
Monk Fryston Hall Hotel	North Yorkshire	+44 (0)1977 682369
Mount Royale Hotel	North Yorkshire	+44 (0)1904 628856
Rudding Park Hotel & Golf	North Yorkshire	+44 (0)1423 871350
Simonstone Hall	North Yorkshire	+44 (0)1969 667255
Swinton Park	North Yorkshire	+44 (0)1765 680900
The Worsley Arms Hotel	North Yorkshire	+44 (0)1653 628234
Wrea Head Country Hotel	North Yorkshire	+44 (0)1723 378211
Fawsley Hall	Northamptonshire	+44 (0)1327 892000
Whittlebury Hall	Northamptonshire	+44 (0)1327 857857
Linden Hall	Northumberland	+44 (0)1670 500000
Marshall Meadows Country House Hotel	Northumberland	+44 (0)1289 331133
Matfen Hall	Northumberland	+44 (0)1661 836500
Tillmouth Park	Northumberland	+44 (0)1890 882255
Hotel Des Clos	Nottinghamshire	+44 (0)1159 866566
The Bay Tree Hotel	Oxfordshire	+44 (0)1993 322791

251

Mini Listings Great Britain & Ireland

Condé Nast Johansens are delighted to recommend over 720 properties across Great Britain and Ireland.
These properties can be found in *Recommended Hotels - GB & Ireland 2003* and *Recommended Country Houses, Small Hotels & Inns - GB & Ireland 2003*.
Call 1-800-564-7518 or see the order forms on page 285 to order guides.

Bignell Park Hotel & Restaurant	Oxfordshire	+44 (0)1869 362550
The Cotswold Lodge Hotel	Oxfordshire	+44 (0)1865 512121
Le Manoir Aux Quat' Saisons	Oxfordshire	+44 (0)1844 278881
Phyllis Court Club	Oxfordshire	+44 (0)1491 570500
The Plough At Clanfield	Oxfordshire	+44 (0)1367 810222
The Spread Eagle Hotel	Oxfordshire	+44 (0)1844 213661
The Springs Hotel & Golf Club	Oxfordshire	+44 (0)1491 836687
Studley Priory	Oxfordshire	+44 (0)1865 351203
Weston Manor	Oxfordshire	+44 (0)1869 350621
Westwood Country Hotel	Oxfordshire	+44 (0)1865 735 408
Hambleton Hall	Rutland	+44 (0)1572 756991
The Lake Isle	Rutland	+44 (0)1572 822951
Dinham Hall	Shropshire	+44 (0)1584 876464
Madeley Court	Shropshire	+44 (0)1952 680068
The Old Vicarage Hotel	Shropshire	+44 (0)1746 716497
Prince Rupert Hotel	Shropshire	+44 (0)1743 499955
Bindon Country House Hotel	Somerset	+44 (0)1823 400070
Charlton House And The Mulberry Restaurant	Somerset	+44 (0)1749 342008
Mount Somerset Country House Hotel	Somerset	+44 (0)1823 442500
Ston Easton Park	Somerset	+44 (0)1761 241631
The Swan Hotel	Somerset	+44 (0)1749 836300
The Swan Hotel	Somerset	+44 (0)1749 836300
Thornbury Castle	South Gloucestershire	+44 (0)1454 281182
Charnwood Hotel	South Yorkshire	+44 (0)114 258 9411
Hellaby Hall Hotel	South Yorkshire	+44 (0)1709 702701
Whitley Hall Hotel	South Yorkshire	+44 (0)114 245 4444
Hoar Cross Hall Health Spa Resort	Staffordshire	+44 (0)1283 575671
Swinfen Hall Hotel	Staffordshire	+44 (0)1543 481494
Angel Hotel	Suffolk	+44 (0)1284 714000
Bedford Lodge Hotel	Suffolk	+44 (0)1638 663175
Belstead Brook Hotel	Suffolk	+44 (0)1473 684241
Black Lion Hotel & Restaurant	Suffolk	+44 (0)1787 312356
Hintlesham Hall	Suffolk	+44 (0)1473 652334
The Ickworth Hotel	Suffolk	+44 (0)1284 735350
The Marlborough Hotel	Suffolk	+44 (0)1473 226789
Ravenwood Hall Country Hotel & Restaurant	Suffolk	+44 (0)1359 270345
Seckford Hall	Suffolk	+44 (0)1394 385678
Swynford Paddocks Hotel And Restaurant	Suffolk	+44 (0)1638 570234
Wentworth Hotel	Suffolk	+44 (0)1728 452312
The Angel Posting House And Livery	Surrey	+44 (0)1483 564555
Foxhills	Surrey	+44 (0)1932 704500
Great Fosters	Surrey	+44 (0)1784 433822
Langshott Manor	Surrey	+44 (0)1293 786680
Lythe Hill Hotel & Spa	Surrey	+44 (0)1428 651251
Nutfield Priory	Surrey	+44 (0)1737 824400
Oatlands Park Hotel	Surrey	+44 (0)1932 847242
Pennyhill Park Hotel	Surrey	+44 (0)1276 471774
Woodlands Park Hotel	Surrey	+44 (0)1372 843933
The Vermont Hotel	Tyne & Wear	+44 (0)191 233 1010
Alveston Manor	Warwickshire	+44 (0)870 400 8181
Ardencote Manor Hotel and Country Club	Warwickshire	+44 (0)1926 843111
Billesley Manor	Warwickshire	+44 (0)1789 279955
Ettington Park	Warwickshire	+44 (0)1789 450123
The Glebe At Barford	Warwickshire	+44 (0)1926 624218
Mallory Court	Warwickshire	+44 (0)1926 330214
Nailcote Hall	Warwickshire	+44 (0)2476 466174
Nuthurst Grange	Warwickshire	+44 (0)1564 783972
The Welcombe Hotel And Golf Course	Warwickshire	+44 (0)1789 295252
Wroxall Abbey Estate - Wroxall Court	Warwickshire	+44 (0)1926 484470
Alexander House Hotel	West Sussex	+44 (0)1342 714914
Amberley Castle	West Sussex	+44 (0)1798 831992
The Angel Hotel	West Sussex	+44 (0)1730 812421
Bailiffscourt	West Sussex	+44 (0)1903 723511
Gravetye Manor	West Sussex	+44 (0)1342 810567
The Millstream Hotel	West Sussex	+44 (0)1243 573234
Ockenden Manor	West Sussex	+44 (0)1444 416111
South Lodge Hotel	West Sussex	+44 (0)1403 891711
The Spread Eagle Hotel & Health Spa	West Sussex	+44 (0)1730 816911

Chevin Country Park Hotel	West Yorkshire	+44 (0)1943 467818
Haley's Hotel & Restaurant	West Yorkshire	+44 (0)113 278 4446
Holdsworth House	West Yorkshire	+44 (0)1422 240024
Quebecs	West Yorkshire	+44 (0)113 244 8989
Wood Hall	West Yorkshire	+44 (0)1937 587271
Bishopstrow House	Wiltshire	+44 (0)1985 212312
Howard's House	Wiltshire	+44 (0)1722 716392
Lucknam Park, Bath	Wiltshire	+44 (0)1225 742777
The Manor House Hotel & Golf Club	Wiltshire	+44 (0)1249 782206
The Pear Tree At Purton	Wiltshire	+44 (0)1793 772100
Woolley Grange	Wiltshire	+44 (0)1225 864705
The Broadway Hotel	Worcestershire	+44 (0)1386 852401

▼

Brockencote Hall	**Worcestershire**	**+44 (0)1562 777876**
Colwall Park	Worcestershire	+44 (0)1684 540000
The Cottage In The Wood	Worcestershire	+44 (0)1684 575859
Dormy House	Worcestershire	+44 (0)1386 852711
The Evesham Hotel	Worcestershire	+44 (0)1386 765566
Salford Hall Hotel	Worcestershire	+44 (0)1386 871300

Channel Islands

The Atlantic Hotel	Channel Islands	+44 (0)1534 744101
Château La Chaire	Channel Islands	+44 (0)1534 863354
Hotel L'Horizon	Channel Islands	+44 (0)1534 743101
Longueville Manor	Channel Islands	+44 (0)1534 725501

Ireland

Dromoland Castle	Clare	+353 61 368144
Hayfield Manor Hotel	Cork	+353 21 4845900
The Davenport Hotel	Dublin	+353 1 607 3500
Merrion Hall	Dublin	+353 1 668 1426
The Merrion Hotel	Dublin	+353 1 603 0600
The Mill Park Hotel	Dublin	+353 73 22880
Stephen's Green Hotel	Dublin	+353 1 607 3600
Killarney Park Hotel	Kerry	+353 64 35555
Parknasilla Hotel	Kerry	+353 64 45122
Sheen Falls Lodge	Kerry	+353 64 41600
Killashee House Hotel	Kildare	+353 45 879277
Mount Juliet	Kilkenny	+353 56 73000
Ashford Castle	Mayo	+353 92 46003
Knockranny House Hotel	Mayo	+353 982 8600
Nuremore Hotel And Country Club	Monaghan	+353 42 9661438
Dunbrody Country House & Restaurant	Wexford	+353 51 389 600
Kelly's Resort Hotel	Wexford	+353 53 32114
Marlfield House	Wexford	+353 55 21124
Hunter's Hotel	Wicklow	+353 404 40106

252

MINI LISTINGS GREAT BRITAIN & IRELAND

Condé Nast Johansens are delighted to recommend over 720 properties across Great Britain and Ireland.
These properties can be found in *Recommended Hotels - GB & Ireland 2003* and *Recommended Country Houses, Small Hotels & Inns - GB & Ireland 2003*.
Call 1-800-564-7518 or see the order forms on page 285 to order guides.

Scotland

Ardoe House Hotel And Restaurant	Aberdeenshire	+44 (0)1224 860600
Darroch Learg Hotel	Aberdeenshire	+44 (0)13397 55443
Ardanaiseig	Argyll & Bute	+44 (0)1866 833333
Enmore Hotel	Argyll & Bute	+44 (0)1369 702230
Isle of Eriska	Argyll & Bute	+44 (0)1631 720371
Stonefield Castle	Argyll & Bute	+44 (0)1880 820836
Balcary Bay Hotel	Dumfries & Galloway	+44 (0)1556 640217
Cally Palace Hotel	Dumfries & Galloway	+44 (0)1557 814341
The Dryfesdale Hotel	Dumfries & Galloway	+44 (0)1576 202427
Kirroughtree House	Dumfries & Galloway	+44 (0)1671 402141
The Bonham	Edinburgh	+44 (0)131 623 6060
Bruntsfield Hotel	Edinburgh	+44 (0)131 229 1393
Channings	Edinburgh	+44 (0)131 332 3232
The Howard	Edinburgh	+44 (0)131 315 2220
Prestonfield House	Edinburgh	+44 (0)131 668 3346
The Roxburghe	Edinburgh	+44 (0)131 240 5500
The Scotsman	Edinburgh	+44 (0)131 556 5565
The Rusacks	Fife	+44 (0)1334 474321
Strathblane Country House Hotel	Glasgow	+44 (0)1360 770491
Bunchrew House Hotel	Highland	+44 (0)1463 234917
Glenmorangie House At Cadboll	Highland	+44 (0)1862 871671
The Glenmoriston Town House Hotel	Highland	+44 (0)1463 223777
Muckrach Lodge Hotel & Restaurant	Highland	+44 (0)1479 851257
Cuillin Hills Hotel	Highlands	+44 (0)1478 612003
Borthwick Castle	Midlothian	+44 (0)1875 820514
Dalhousie Castle And Spa	Midlothian	+44 (0)1875 820153
Knockomie Hotel	Moray	+44 (0)1309 673146
Ballathie House Hotel	Perth & Kinross	+44 (0)1250 883268
Cromlix House	Perth & Kinross	+44 (0)1786 822125
Dalmunzie House	Perth & Kinross	+44 (0)1250 885224
Gleneagles	Perth & Kinross	+44 (0)1764 662231
Kinfauns Castle	Perth & Kinross	+44 (0)1738 620777
Kinloch House Hotel	Perth & Kinross	+44 (0)1250 884237
The Royal Hotel	Perth & Kinross	+44 (0)1764 679200
Gleddoch House	Renfrewshire	+44 (0)1475 540711
Castle Venlaw	Scottish Borders	+44 (0)1721 720384
Ednam House Hotel	Scottish Borders	+44 (0)1573 224168
The Roxburghe Hotel & Golf Course	Scottish Borders	+44 (0)1573 450331
Enterkine House	South Ayrshire	+44 (0)1292 521608
Glenapp Castle	South Ayrshire	+44 (0)1465 831212
Macdonald Crutherland House Hotel	South Lanarkshire	+44 (0)1355 577000
Forest Hills Hotel	Stirling	+44 (0)1877 387277
Houstoun House	West Lothian	+44 (0)1506 853831
The Norton House Hotel	West Lothian	+44 (0)131 333 1275

Wales

Ynyshir Hall	Ceredigion	+44 (0)1654 781209
Bodysgallen Hall	Conwy	+44 (0)1492 584466
St Tudno Hotel	Conwy	+44 (0)1492 874411
Palé Hall	Gwynedd	+44 (0)1678 530285
Penmaenuchaf Hall	Gwynedd	+44 (0)1341 422129
Portmeirion And Castell Deudraeth	Gwynedd	+44 (0)1766 770000
The Trearddur Bay Hotel	Isle of Anglesey	+44 (0)1407 860301
Llansantffraed Court Hotel	Monmouthshire	+44 (0)1873 840678
Lamphey Court Hotel	Pembrokeshire	+44 (0)1646 672273
Penally Abbey	Pembrokeshire	+44 (0)1834 843033
Warpool Court Hotel	Pembrokeshire	+44 (0)1437 720300
Gliffaes Country House Hotel	Powys	+44 (0)1874 730371
The Lake Country House	Powys	+44 (0)1591 620202
Lake Vyrnwy Hotel	Powys	+44 (0)1691 870 692
Llangoed Hall	Powys	+44 (0)1874 754525
Nant Ddu Lodge Hotel	Powys	+44 (0)1685 379111
Miskin Manor Country House Hotel	Rhondda Cynon Taff	+44 (0)1443 224204

RECOMMENDED COUNTRY HOUSES, SMALL HOTELS & INNS GREAT BRITAIN & IRELAND 2003

England

Apsley House	Bath & NE Somerset	+44 (0)1225 336966
Bath Lodge Hotel	Bath & NE Somerset	+44 (0)1225 723040
The Carpenters Arms	Bath & NE Somerset	+44 (0)1761 490202
The County Hotel	Bath & NE Somerset	+44 (0)1225 425003
Oldfields	Bath & NE Somerset	+44 (0)1225 317934
Tasburgh House	Bath & NE Somerset	+44 (0)1225 425096
Villa Magdala	Bath & NE Somerset	+44 (0)1225 466329
The Inn on the Green	Berkshire	+44 (0)1628 482638
The Leatherne Bottel Riverside Inn & Restaurant	Berkshire	+44 (0)1491 872667
Crown Lodge Hotel	Cambridgeshire	+44 (0)1945 773391
Melbourn Bury	Cambridgeshire	+44 (0)1763 261151
Brook Meadow Hotel	Cheshire	+44 (0)151 339 9350
Broxton Hall Country House Hotel	Cheshire	+44 (0)1829 782321
Frogg Manor Hotel & Restaurant	Cheshire	+44 (0)1829 782629
Willington Hall Hotel	Cheshire	+44 (0)1829 752321
Boscundle Manor	Cornwall	+44 (0)1726 813557
Cormorant On The River, Hotel	Cornwall	+44 (0)1726 833426
The Countryman At Trink Hotel	Cornwall	+44 (0)1736 797571
Hell Bay Hotel	Cornwall	+44 (0)1720 422947
Higher Faugan Country House Hotel	Cornwall	+44 (0)1736 362076
Jubilee Inn	Cornwall	+44 (0)1503 220312
The Old Quay House Hotel	Cornwall	+44 (0)1726 833302
The Port William	Cornwall	+44 (0)1840 770230
Tredethy House	Cornwall	+44 (0)1208 841262
Trehaven Manor Hotel	Cornwall	+44 (0)1503 262028
Trehellas House Hotel & Restaurant	Cornwall	+44 (0)1208 72700
Trelawne Hotel – The Hutches Restaurant	Cornwall	+44 (0)1326 250226
Trevalsa Court Hotel	Cornwall	+44 (0)1726 842468
Broadoaks Country House	Cumbria	+44 (0)1539 445566
Crosby Lodge Country House Hotel	Cumbria	+44 (0)1228 573618
Dale Head Hall Lakeside Hotel	Cumbria	+44 (0)17687 72478
Fayrer Garden House Hotel	Cumbria	+44 (0)15394 88195
Grey Friar Lodge	Cumbria	+44 (0)15394 33158
Hipping Hall	Cumbria	+44 (0)15242 71187
The Leathes Head	Cumbria	+44 (0)17687 77247
Linthwaite House Hotel	Cumbria	+44 (0)15394 88600
Linthwaite House Hotel	Cumbria	+44 (0)15394 88600
Nanny Brow Country House Hotel & Restaurant	Cumbria	+44 (0)15394 32036
The Queen's Head Hotel	Cumbria	+44 (0)15394 36271
Sawrey House Country Hotel & Restaurant	Cumbria	+44 (0)15394 36387
Swinside Lodge Hotel	Cumbria	+44 (0)17687 72948
The Tarn End House Hotel	Cumbria	+44 (0)16977 2340
Temple Sowerby House Hotel	Cumbria	+44 (0)17683 61578
Underwood	Cumbria	+44 (0)1229 771116
White Moss House	Cumbria	+44 (0)15394 35295
Biggin Hall	Derbyshire	+44 (0)1298 84451
Boar's Head Hotel	Derbyshire	+44 (0)1283 820344
Buckingham's Hotel & Restaurant With One Table	Derbyshire	+44 (0)1246 201041
The Chequers Inn	Derbyshire	+44 (0)1433 630231
Dannah Farm Country House	Derbyshire	+44 (0)1773 550273
Littleover Lodge Hotel	Derbyshire	+44 (0)1332 51016
The Maynard Arms	Derbyshire	+44 (0)1433 630321
The Peacock Inn	Derbyshire	+44 (0)1629 733518
The Plough Inn	Derbyshire	+44 (0)1433 650319
Santo's Higham Farm	Derbyshire	+44 (0)1773 833812
The Wind In The Willows	Derbyshire	+44 (0)1457 868001
Browns Hotel, Wine Bar & Brasserie	Devon	+44 (0)1822 618686
Combe House Hotel & Restaurant	Devon	+44 (0)1404 540400
Combe House Hotel & Restaurant	Devon	+44 (0)1404 540400

253

MINI LISTINGS GREAT BRITAIN & IRELAND

Condé Nast Johansens are delighted to recommend over 720 properties across Great Britain and Ireland.

These properties can be found in *Recommended Hotels - GB & Ireland 2003* and *Recommended Country Houses, Small Hotels & Inns - GB & Ireland 2003*.

Call 1-800-564-7518 or see the order forms on page 285 to order guides.

Coulsworthy House	Devon	+44 (0)1271 882813
The Edgemoor	Devon	+44 (0)1626 832466
Hewitt's - Villa Spaldi	Devon	+44 (0)1598 752293
Home Farm Hotel	Devon	+44 (0)1404 831278
Ilsington Country House Hotel	Devon	+44 (0)1364 661452
Ilsington Country House Hotel	Devon	+44 (0)1364 661452
Kingston House	Devon	+44 (0)1803 762 235
Kitley House Hotel & Restaurant	Devon	+44 (0)1752 881555
Kitley House Hotel & Restaurant	Devon	+44 (0)1752 881555
The Lord Haldon Country Hotel	Devon	+44 (0)1392 832483
The New Inn	Devon	+44 (0)1363 84242
Percy's Country Hotel & Restaurant	Devon	+44 (0)1409 211236
Percy's Country Hotel & Restaurant	Devon	+44 (0)1409 211236
Preston House & Little's Restaurant	Devon	+44 (0)1271 890472
The Rising Sun	Devon	+44 (0)1598 753223
The Sea Trout Inn	Devon	+44 (0)1803 762274
Yeoldon House Hotel	Devon	+44 (0)1237 474400
Acorn Inn	Dorset	+44 (0)1935 83228
The Eastbury Hotel	Dorset	+44 (0)1935 813131
Kemps Country House Hotel & Restaurant	Dorset	+44 (0)1929 462563
The Manor Hotel	Dorset	+44 (0)1308 897616
Yalbury Cottage Hotel	Dorset	+44 (0)1305 262382
Grove House	Durham	+44 (0)1388 488203
Horsley Hall	Durham	+44 (0)1388 517239
The Granville	East Sussex	+44 (0)1273 326302
Hooke Hall	East Sussex	+44 (0)1825 761578
The Hope Anchor Hotel	East Sussex	+44 (0)1797 222216
The Cricketers	Essex	+44 (0)1799 550442
The Crown House	Essex	+44 (0)1799 530515
The Pump House Apartment	Essex	+44 (0)1277 656579
Bibury Court	Gloucestershire	+44 (0)1285 740337
Charlton Kings Hotel	Gloucestershire	+44 (0)1242 231061
The Green Dragon Inn	Gloucestershire	+44 (0)1242 870271
The Malt House	Gloucestershire	+44 (0)1386 840295
The New Inn At Coln	Gloucestershire	+44 (0)1285 750651
Three Choirs Vineyards Estate	Gloucestershire	+44 (0)1531 890223
The White Hart Inn	Gloucestershire	+44 (0)1242 602359
The Wild Duck Inn	Gloucestershire	+44 (0)1285 770310
The White Hart Inn	Greater Manchester	+44 (0)1457 872566
Gordleton Mill Inn	Hampshire	+44 (0)1590 682219
Langrish House	Hampshire	+44 (0)1730 266941
New Mill Restaurant	Hampshire	+44 (0)118 973 2277
New Park Manor	Hampshire	+44 (0)1590 623467
New Park Manor	Hampshire	+44 (0)1590 623467
The Nurse's Cottage	Hampshire	+44 (0)1590 683402
Thatched Cottage Hotel & Restaurant	Hampshire	+44 (0)1590 623090
Westover Hall	Hampshire	+44 (0)1590 643044
Whitley Ridge Country House Hotel	Hampshire	+44 (0)1590 622354
The Feathers Hotel	Herefordshire	+44 (0)1531 635266
The Feathers Hotel	Herefordshire	+44 (0)1531 635266
Glewstone Court	Herefordshire	+44 (0)1989 770367
The Steppes	Herefordshire	+44 (0)1432 820424
Wilton Court Hotel	Herefordshire	+44 (0)1989 562569
Redcoats Farmhouse Hotel And Restaurant	Hertfordshire	+44 (0)1438 729500
Rylstone Manor	Isle Of Wight	+44 (0)1983 862806
The Abbot's Fireside Hotel	Kent	+44 (0)1303 840265
The George Hotel	Kent	+44 (0)1580 713348
The George Hotel	Kent	+44 (0)1580 713348
Howfield Manor	Kent	+44 (0)1227 738294
Ringlestone Inn and Farmhouse Hotel	Kent	+44 (0)1622 859900
Romney Bay House	Kent	+44 (0)1797 364747
Wallett's Court	Kent	+44 (0)1304 852424
The Inn At Whitewell	Lancashire	+44 (0)1200 448222
Tree Tops Country House Restaurant & Hotel	Lancashire	+44 (0)1704 572430
Ye Horn's Inn	Lancashire	+44 (0)1772 865230
Abbots Oak	Leicestershire	+44 (0)1530 832 328
Barnsdale Lodge	Leicestershire	+44 (0)1572 724678
Barnsdale Lodge	Leicestershire	+44 (0)1572 724678

The Old Manor Hotel	Leicestershire	+44 (0)1509 211228
Sutton Bonington Hall	Leicestershire	+44 (0)1509 672355
The Crown Hotel	Lincolnshire	+44 (0)1780 763136
The Lea Gate Inn	Lincolnshire	+44 (0)1526 342370
Washingborough Hall	Lincolnshire	+44 (0)1522 790340
Oak Lodge Hotel	London	+44 (0)20 8360 7082
The Beresford	Mersyside	+44 (0)151 651 0004
The Beeches Hotel And Victorian Gardens	Norfolk	+44 (0)1603 621167
Beechwood Hotel	Norfolk	+44 (0)1692 403231
Broom Hall Country Hotel	Norfolk	+44 (0)1953 882125
Brovey Lair	Norfolk	+44 (0)1953 882706
Caldecott Hall	Norfolk	+44 (0)1493 488488
Congham Hall	Norfolk	+44 (0)1485 600250
Congham Hall	Norfolk	+44 (0)1485 600250
Elderton Lodge Hotel & Langtry Restaurant	Norfolk	+44 (0)1263 833547
Felbrigg Lodge	Norfolk	+44 (0)1263 837588
The Great Escape Holiday Company	Norfolk	+44 (0)1485 518717
J.D. Young	Norfolk	+44 (0)1379 852822
The Manor House	Norfolk	+44 (0)1328 820597
The Norfolk Mead Hotel	Norfolk	+44 (0)1603 737531
The Old Rectory	Norfolk	+44 (0)1603 700772
Petersfield House Hotel	Norfolk	+44 (0)1692 630741
The Roman Camp Inn	Norfolk	+44 (0)1263 838291
The Stower Grange	Norfolk	+44 (0)1603 860210
Vere Lodge	Norfolk	+44 (0)1328 838261
The Victoria At Holkham	Norfolk	+44 (0)1328 711008
The White Horse	Norfolk	+44 (0)1485 210262
The Austwick Country House Hotel	North Yorkshire	+44 (0)15242 51224
The Blue Lion	North Yorkshire	+44 (0)1969 624273
The Boar's Head Hotel	North Yorkshire	+44 (0)1423 771888
The Boar's Head Hotel	North Yorkshire	+44 (0)1423 771888
Dunsley Hall	North Yorkshire	+44 (0)1947 893437
Hob Green Hotel And Restaurant	North Yorkshire	+44 (0)1423 770031
Hob Green Hotel And Restaurant	North Yorkshire	+44 (0)1423 770031
The Red Lion	North Yorkshire	+44 (0)1756 720204
Rookhurst Country House Hotel	North Yorkshire	+44 (0)1969 667454
Stow House Hotel	North Yorkshire	+44 (0)1969 663635
The White Swan	North Yorkshire	+44 (0)1751 472288
The Falcon Hotel	Northamptonshire	+44 (0)1604 696200
The Windmill At Badby	Northamptonshire	+44 (0)1327 702363
The Blue Bell Hotel	Northumberland	+44 (0)1668 213543
The Otterburn Tower	Northumberland	+44 (0)1830 520620
Waren House Hotel	Northumberland	+44 (0)1668 214581
Cockliffe Country House Hotel	Nottinghamshire	+44 (0)1159 680179
The Cottage Country House Hotel	Nottinghamshire	+44 (0)1159 846882
Fallowfields	Oxfordshire	+44 (0)1865 820416
The George Hotel	Oxfordshire	+44 (0)1865 340404
Holcombe Hotel	Oxfordshire	+44 (0)1869 338274
The Jersey Arms	Oxfordshire	+44 (0)1869 343234
The Kings Head Inn & Restaurant	Oxfordshire	+44 (0)1608 658365
The Lamb Inn	Oxfordshire	+44 (0)1993 823155
The Lamb Inn	Oxfordshire	+44 (0)1993 830465
The Mill & Old Swan	Oxfordshire	+44 (0)1993 774441
The Shaven Crown Hotel	Oxfordshire	+44 (0)1993 830330
The Hundred House Hotel	Shropshire	+44 (0)1952 730353
Pen-Y-Dyffryn Hall Hotel	Shropshire	+44 (0)1691 653700
Soulton Hall	Shropshire	+44 (0)1939 232786
Stretton Hall	Shropshire	+44 (0)1694 723224
Andrew's On The Weir	Somerset	+44 (0)1643 863300
Ashwick Country House Hotel	Somerset	+44 (0)1398 323868
Beryl	Somerset	+44 (0)1749 678738
Chestnut House	Somerset	+44 (0)1278 683658
Compton House	Somerset	+44 (0)1934 733944
The Crown Hotel	Somerset	+44 (0)1643 831554
Farthings Hotel & Restaurant	Somerset	+44 (0)1823 480664
Glencot House	Somerset	+44 (0)1749 677160
Langley House	Somerset	+44 (0)1984 623318
Mount Somerset Country House Hotel	Somerset	+44 (0)1823 442500

254

Mini Listings Great Britain & Ireland

Condé Nast Johansens are delighted to recommend over 720 properties across Great Britain and Ireland. These properties can be found in *Recommended Hotels - GB & Ireland 2003* and *Recommended Country Houses, Small Hotels & Inns - GB & Ireland 2003*. Call 1-800-564-7518 or see the order forms on page 285 to order guides.

The Old Rectory	Somerset	+44 (0)1460 54364
The Old Rectory	Somerset	+44 (0)1460 54364
Porlock Vale House	Somerset	+44 (0)1643 862338
The Royal Oak Inn	Somerset	+44 (0)1643 851455
The Woodborough Inn	Somerset	+44 (0)1934 844167
Woolverton House	Somerset	+44 (0)1373 830415
Oak Tree Farm	Staffordshire	+44 (0)1827 56807
Ye Olde Dog & Partridge	Staffordshire	+44 (0)1283 813030
Clarice House	Suffolk	+44 (0)1284 705550
The George	Suffolk	+44 (0)1787 280248
The Plough Inn	Suffolk	+44 (0)1440 786789
The Suffolk Golf & Country Club	Suffolk	+44 (0)1284 706777
Thornham Hall & Restaurant	Suffolk	+44 (0)1379 783314
The White Horse Inn	Suffolk	+44 (0)1440 706081
Chase Lodge	Surrey	+44 (0)20 8943 1862

Stanhill Court Hotel	Surrey	+44 (0)1293 862166
Horton Grange Country House Hotel	Tyne & Wear	+44 (0)1661 860686
Clarendon House	Warwickshire	+44 (0)1926 857668
Glebe Farm House	Warwickshire	+44 (0)1789 842501
Burpham Country House Hotel	West Sussex	+44 (0)1903 882160
The Chequers At Slaugham	West Sussex	+44 (0)1444 400239
Crouchers Country Hotel & Restaurant	West Sussex	+44 (0)1243 784995
Forge Hotel	West Sussex	+44 (0)1243 535333
The Half Moon Inn	West Sussex	+44 (0)1403 820223
The Mill House Hotel	West Sussex	+44 (0)1903 892426
The Old Tollgate Restaurant And Hotel	West Sussex	+44 (0)1903 879494
The Rock Inn Hotel	West Yorkshire	+44 (0)1422 379721
The Shibden Mill Inn	West Yorkshire	+44 (0)1422 365840
The Weavers Shed Restaurant With Rooms	West Yorkshire	+44 (0)1484 654284
The George Inn	Wiltshire	+44 (0)1985 840396
Hinton Grange	Wiltshire	+44 (0)117 937 2916
The Old Manor Hotel	Wiltshire	+44 (0)1225 777393
Rudloe Hall	Wiltshire	+44 (0)1225 810555
Stanton Manor	Wiltshire	+44 (0)1666 837552
Widbrook Grange	Wiltshire	+44 (0)1225 864750
The Mill at Harvington	Worcestershire	+44 (0)1386 870688
The Mount Pleasant Hotel	Worcestershire	+44 (0)1684 561837
The White Lion Hotel	Worcestershire	+44 (0)1684 592551

Channel Islands

Bella Luce Hotel & Restaurant	Channel Islands	+44 (0)1481 238764
Eulah Country House	Channel Islands	+44 (0)1534 626626
La Favorita Hotel	Channel Islands	+44 (0)1481 235666
La Sablonnerie	Channel Islands	+44 (0)1481 832061
Les Douvres Hotel & Restaurant	Channel Islands	+44 (0)1481 238731
The White House	Channel Islands	+44 (0)1481 722159
Les Rocquettes Hotel	Guernsey	+44 (0)1481 722146

Ireland

Hyland's Burren Hotel	Clare	+353 65 7077037
Aberdeen Lodge	Dublin	+353 1 283 8155
Ross Lake House Hotel	Galway	+353 91 550109
Caragh Lodge	Kerry	+353 66 9769115
Emlagh House	Kerry	+353 66 915 2345
Gorman's Clifftop House & Restaurant	Kerry	+353 66 9155162
Killarney Royal Hotel	Kerry	+353 64 31853
Coopershill House	Sligo	+353 71 65108
Cashel Palace Hotel	Tipperary	+353 62 62707
Kilmokea Country Manor & Gardens	Wexford	+353 51 388109

Scotland

Maryculter House Hotel	Abderdeenshire	+44 (0)1224 732124
Balgonie Country House	Aberdeenshire	+44 (0)13397 55482
Castleton House Hotel	Angus	+44 (0)1307 840340
Ballachulish House	Argyll & Bute	+44 (0)1855 811266
Barcaldine House	Argyll & Bute	+44 (0)1631 720219
The Frog At Port Dunstaffnage	Argyll & Bute	+44 (0)1631 567005
Kirkton House	Argyll & Bute	+44 (0)1389 841951
Loch Melfort Hotel & Restaurant	Argyll & Bute	+44 (0)1852 200233
Royal Hotel	Argyll & Bute	+44 (0)1700 811239
Western Isles Hotel	Argylls & Bute	+44 (0)1688 302012
Fernhill Hotel	Dumfries & Galloway	+44 (0)1776 810220
Corriegour Lodge Hotel	Highland	+44 (0)1397 712685
Culduthel Lodge	Highland	+44 (0)1463 240089
Hotel Eilean Iarmain	Highland	+44 (0)1471 833332
The Lodge On The Loch	Highland	+44 (0)1855 821237
Portland Arms Hotel	Highland	+44 (0)1593 721721
Ardeonaig	Perth & Kinross	+44 (0)1567 820400
The Four Seasons Hotel	Perth & Kinross	+44 (0)1764 685333
Knockendarroch House	Perth & Kinross	+44 (0)1796 473473
The Lake Hotel	Perth & Kinross	+44 (0)1877 385258
Parklands Hotel & Acanthus Restaurant	Perth & Kinross	+44 (0)1738 622451
The Pend	Perth & Kinross	+44 (0)1350 727586
Bowfield Hotel & Country Club	Renfrewshire	+44 (0)1505 705225
Culzean Castle – The Eisenhower Apartment	South Ayrshire	+44 (0)1655 884455

Wales

The Great House	Bridgend	+44 (0)1656 657644
Inn At The Elm Tree	Cardiff	+44 (0)1633 680225
Conrah Country House Hotel	Ceredigion	+44 (0)1970 617941
Castle Hotel	Conwy	+44 (0)1492 582 800
The Old Rectory Country House	Conwy	+44 (0)1492 580611
Sychnant Pass House	Conwy	+44 (0)1492 596868
Tan-Y-Foel	Conwy	+44 (0)1690 710507
The West Arms Hotel	Denbighshire	+44 (0)1691 600665
Bae Abermaw	Gwynedd	+44 (0)1341 280550
Bontddu Hall	Gwynedd	+44 (0)1341 430661
Bryn Tegid Country House	Gwynedd	+44 (0)1678 521645
Plas Dolmelynllyn	Gwynedd	+44 (0)1341 440273
Porth Tocyn Country House Hotel	Gwynedd	+44 (0)1758 713303
Ye Olde Bull's Head	Isle Of Anglesey	+44 (0)1248 810329
The Bell At Skenfrith	Monmouthshire	+44 (0)1600 750235
Parva Farmhouse And Restaurant	Monmouthshire	+44 (0)1291 689411
Stone Hall Hotel & Restaurant	Pembrokeshire	+44 (0)1348 840212
Glangrwyney Court	Powys	+44 (0)1873 811288
Peterstone Court	Powys	+44 (0)1874 665387
Norton House Hotel And Restaurant	Swansea	+44 (0)1792 404891
Egerton Grey	Vale Of Glamorgan	+44 (0)1446 711666

HISTORIC HOUSES, CASTLES & GARDENS
Incorporating Museums & Galleries.
We are pleased to feature over 200 places to visit during your stay at a Condé Nast Johansens recommended hotel.

England

Bedfordshire

Cecil Higgins Art Gallery – Castle Lane, Bedford, Bedfordshire MK40 4AF. Tel: 01234 211222

John Bunyan Museum – Bunyan Meeting Free Church, Mill Street, Bedford, Bedfordshire MK40 3EU. Tel: 01234 213722

Woburn Abbey – Woburn, Bedfordshire MK17 9WA. Tel: 01525 290666

Berkshire

Savill Garden – Windsor Great Park, Berkshire. Tel: 01753 847518

Taplow Court – Berry Hill, Taplow, Nr Maidenhead, Berkshire SL6 0ER. Tel: 01628 591209

Buckinghamshire

Hughenden Manor – High Wycombe, Buckinghamshire HP14 4LA. Tel: 01494 755573

Stowe Landscape Gardens – Stowe, Buckingham, Buckinghamshire MK18 5EH. Tel: 01280 818809

Waddesdon Manor – Waddesdon, Nr Aylesbury, Buckinghamshire HP18 0JH. Tel: 01296 653211

Cambridgeshire

Ely Cathedral – The Chapter House, The College, Ely, Cambridgeshire CB7 4DL. Tel: 01353 667735

King's College – Cambridge, Cambridgeshire CB2 1ST. Tel: 01223 331212

Cheshire

Adlington Hall – Nr Macclesfield, Cheshire SK10 4LF. Tel: 01625 820201

Dorfold Hall – Nantwich, Cheshire CW5 8LD. Tel: 01270 625245

▼
Dunham Massey Hall, Park & Garden – Dunham, Altrincham, Cheshire WA14 4SJ. Tel: 0161 941 1025

Ness Botanic Gardens – Ness, Neston, South Wirral, Cheshire CH64 4AY. Tel: 0151 353 0123

Norton Priory Museum & Gardens – Tudor Road, Manor Park, Cheshire WA7 1SX. Tel: 01928 569895

Tabley House Stately Home – Tabley House, Knutsford, Cheshire WA16 0HB. Tel: 01565 750151

County Durham

Raby Castle – Staindrop, Darlington, County Durham DL2 3AH. Tel: 01833 660207 / 660202

Cornwall

Jamaica Inn Museums – Jamaica Inn Courtyard, Bolventor, Launceston, Cornwall PL15 7TS. Tel: 0156 68 68 38

Cumbria

Holker Hall and Gardens – Cark-in-Cartmel, Nr Grange-over-Sands, Cumbria LA11 7PL. Tel: 01539 558328

Isel Hall – Cockermouth, Cumbria CA13 0QG.

Levens Hall & Gardens – Kendal, Cumbria LA8 0PD. Tel: 01539 560321

Mirehouse & Keswick – Mirehouse, Keswick, Cumbria CA12 4QE. Tel: 01768 772287

Windermere Steamboat Centre – Rayrigg Road, Windermere, Cumbria LA23 1BN. Tel: 01539 445565

Wordsworth House – Main Street, Cockermouth, Cumbria CA13 9RX. Tel: 01900 824805

Derbyshire

Haddon Hall – Bakewell, Derbyshire DE45 1LA. Tel: 01629 812855

Hardwick Hall – Doe Lea, Chesterfield, Derbyshire S44 5QJ. Tel: 01246 850430

Melbourne Hall & Gardens – Melbourne, Derbyshire DE73 1EN. Tel: 01332 862502

Tissington Hall – Tissington, Ashbourne, Derbyshire DE6 1RA. Tel: 01335 352200

Devon

Cadhay – Ottery St Mary, Devon EX11 1QT. Tel: 01404 812432

The Royal Horticultural Society, Garden Rosemoor – Great Torrington, North Devon EX38 8PH. Tel: 01805 624067

Dorset

Abbotsbury Sub Tropical Gardens – Bullers Way, Abbotsbury, Nr Weymouth, Dorset DT3 4LA. Tel: 01305 871387

Chiffchaffs – Chaffeymoor, Bourton, Gillingham, Dorset SP8 5BY. Tel: 01747 840841

Compton Acres – 164 Canford Cliffs Road, Canford Cliffs, Poole, Dorset BH13 7ES. Tel: 01202 700778

Cranborne Manor Garden – Cranborne, Wimborne, Dorset BH21 5PP. Tel: 01725 517248

Deans Court Garden – Deans Court, Wimborne, Dorset BH21 1EE. Tel: 01202 886116

Mapperton – Mapperton, Beaminster, Dorset DT8 3NR. Tel: 01308 862645

Minterne Gardens – Minterne Magna, Dorchester, Dorset DT2 7AU. Tel: 01300 341370

Sherborne Castle – New Road, Sherborne, Dorset DT9 5NR. Tel: 01935 813182

Tolpuddle Museum – Tolpuddle, Dorset DT2 7EH. Tel: 01305 848237

East Riding of Yorkshire

Burton Agnes Hall & Gardens – Burton Agnes, Driffield, East Riding of Yorkshire YO25 4NB. Tel: 01262 490324

East Sussex

Bentley Wildfowl & Motor Museum – Halland, Nr Lewes, East Sussex BN8 5AF. Tel: 01825 840573

Charleston – Firle, East Sussex BN8 6LL. Tel: 01323 811626

Firle Place – The Estate Office, Lewes, East Sussex BN8 6NS. Tel: 01273 858043

Garden and Grounds of Herstmonceux Castle – Herstmonceux Castle, Hailsham, East Sussex BN27 1RN. Tel: 01323 833816

Merriments Gardens – Hurst Green, East Sussex TN19 7RA. Tel: 01580 860666

Pashley Manor Gardens – Ticehurst, East Sussex TN5 7HE. Tel: 01580 200888

Wilmington Priory – Wilmington, Nr Eastbourne, East Sussex BN26 5SW. Tel: 01628 825920

Essex

▼
Hedingham Castle – Bayley Street, Castle Hedingham, Halstead, Essex CO9 3DJ. Tel: 01787 460261

Ingatestone Hall – Hall Lane, Ingatestone, Essex CM4 9NR. Tel: 01277 353010

The Gardens of Easton – Warwick House, Easton Lodge, Essex CM6 2BB. Tel: 01371 876979

The Sir Alfred Munnings Art Museum – Castle House, Dedham, Essex CO7 6AZ. Tel: 01206 322127

Gloucestershire

Chavenage House – Chavenage, Tetbury, Gloucestershire GL8 8XP. Tel: 01666 502329

Cheltenham Art Gallery & Museum – Clarence Street, Cheltenham, Gloucestershire GL50 3JT. Tel: 01242 237431

Frampton Court – Frampton-on-Severn, Gloucestershire GL2 7DY. Tel: 01452 740267

Hardwicke Court – Gloucester, Gloucestershire GL2 4RS. Tel: 01452 720212

Sezincote – Moreton-in-Marsh, Gloucestershire GL56 9AW. Tel: 01386 700444

Greater Manchester

Heaton Hall – Heaton Park, Prestwich, Manchester, Greater Manchester M25 5SW. Tel: 0161 773 1231/ 0161 235 8888

Ordsall Hall Museum – Ordsall Lane, Salford, Greater Manchester M5 4WU. Tel: 0161 872 0251

Salford Museums & Art Gallery – Peel Park, Crescent, Salford, Greater Manchester M5 4WU. Tel: 0161 736 2649

Wythenshawe Hall – Wythenshawe Park, Northenden, Manchester, Greater Manchester M23 0AB. Tel: 0161 998 2331

Hampshire

Avington Park – Winchester, Hampshire SO21 1DB. Tel: 01962 779260

Beaulieu – John Montagu Building, Beaulieu, Hampshire SO42 7ZN. Tel: 01590 612345

Broadlands – Romsey, Hampshire SO51 9ZD. Tel: 01794 505010

256

HISTORIC HOUSES, CASTLES & GARDENS
Incorporating Museums & Galleries.
www.historichouses.co.uk

Gilbert White's House and The Oates Museum – Selborne, Hampshire GU34 3JH. Tel: 01420 511275

Greywell Hill House – Greywell, Hook, Hampshire RG29 1DG

Hall Farm – Bentworth, Alton, Hampshire GU34 5JU. Tel: 01420 564010

Mottisfont Abbey – Mottisfont, Nr Romsey, Hampshire SO51 0LP. Tel: 01794 340757

Pylewell Park – South Baddesley, Lymington, Hampshire SO41 5SJ. Tel: 01329 833130

The Vyne – The National Trust, Sherborne St John, Basingstoke, Hampshire RG24 9HL. Tel: 01256 881337

Uppark – South Harting, Petersfield, Hampshire GU31 5QR. Tel: 01730 825415

Herefordshire

Eastnor Castle – Eastnor, Ledbury, Herefordshire HR8 1RL. Tel: 01531 633160

Hertfordshire

Ashridge – Ringshall, Berkhamsted, Hertfordshire HP4 1NS. Tel: 01442 843491

Gorhambury – St. Albans, Hertfordshire AL3 6AH. Tel: 01727 855000

Hatfield House, Park & Gardens – Hatfield, Hertfordshire AL9 5NQ. Tel: 01707 287010

Isle of Wight

Deacons Nursery – Moor View, Godshill, Isle of Wight PO38 3HW. Tel: 01983 840750

Kent

Belmont House and Gardens – Belmont Park, Throwley, Nr Faversham, Kent ME13 0HH. Tel: 01795 890202

Cobham Hall – Cobham, Kent DA12 3BL. Tel: 01474 823371

Dickens House Museum – 2 Victoria Parade, Broadstairs, Kent CT10 1QS. Tel: 01843 863453

Finchcocks, Living Museum of Music – Goudhurst, Kent TN17 1HH. Tel: 01580 211702

Graham Clarke Up the Garden Studio – Green Lane, Boughton Monchelsea, Maidstone, Kent ME17 4LF. Tel: 01622 743938

Groombridge Place Gardens & Enchanted Forest – Groombridge, Tunbridge Wells, Kent TN3 9QG. Tel: 01892 861444

Hever Castle & Gardens – Edenbridge, Kent TN8 7NG. Tel: 01732 865224

Leeds Castle – Maidstone, Kent ME17 1PL. Tel: 01622 765400

Mount Ephraim Gardens – Hernhill, Nr Faversham, Kent ME13 9TX. Tel: 01227 751496

Penshurst Place & Gardens – Penshurst, Nr Tonbridge, Kent TN11 8DG. Tel: 01892 870307

Scotney Castle, Garden & Estate – Lamberhurst, Tunbridge Wells, Kent TN3 8JN. Tel: 01892 891081

Smallhythe Place – Smallhythe, Tenterden, Kent TN30 7NG. Tel: 01580 762334

The New College of Cobham – Cobhambury Road, Graves End, Kent DA12 3BG. Tel: 01474 814280

Lancashire

Stonyhurst College – Stonyhurst, Clitheroe, Lancashire BB7 9PZ. Tel: 01254 826345

Townhead House – Slaidburn, Via CLitheroe, Lancashire BBY 3AG

Leicestershire

Hazel Kaye's Garden & Nursery – 1700 Melton Rd, Rearsby, Leicester, Leicestershire LE7 4YR. Tel: 01664 424578

Stanford Hall – Stanford Park, Lutterworth, Leicestershire LE17 6DH. Tel: 01788 860250

Lincolnshire

Burghley House – Stamford, Lincolnshire PE9 3JY. Tel: 01780 752451

London

Burgh House – New End Square, Hampstead, London NW3 1LT. Tel: 020 7431 0144

Dulwich Picture Gallery – Gallery Road, London SE21 7AD. Tel: 020 8299 8711

Handel House Museum – 25 Brook Street, London W1K 4HB. Tel: 020 7495 1685

Imperial War Museum – Lambeth Road, London SE1 6HZ. Tel: 020 7416 5000

Kensington Palace State Apartments – Kensington, London W8 4PX. Tel: 0870 751 5176

Leighton House Museum – 12 Holland Park Road, London W14 8LZ. Tel: 020 7602 3316

National Portrait Gallery – St Martin's Place, London WC2H 0HE. Tel: 020 7306 0055

Pitshanger Manor House – Walpole Park, Mattock Lane, Ealing, London W5 5EQ. Tel: 020 8567 1227

Royal Institution Michael Faraday Museum – 21 Albemarle Street, London W1S 4BS. Tel: 020 7409 2992

Sir John Soane's Museum – 13 Lincoln's Inn Fields, London WC2A 3BP. Tel: 020 7405 2107

Somerset House – Strand, London WC2R 1LA. Tel: 020 7845 4600

St. John's Gate – St John's Lane, Clerkenwell, London EC1M 4DA. Tel: 020 7324 4070

The Fan Museum – 12 Crooms Hill, Greenwich, London SE10 8ER. Tel: 020 8305 1441

The Traveller's Club – 106 Pall Mall, London SW1Y 5EP. Tel: 020 7930 8688

Tower of London – Tower Hill, London EC3N 4AB. Tel: 0870 751 5177

Middlesex

Orleans House Gallery – Riverside, Twickenham, Middlesex TW1 3DJ. Tel: 020 8892 0221

Strawberry Hill House – St. Mary's University College, Strawberry Hill, Waldegrave Road, Twickenham, Middlesex TW1 4SX. Tel: 020 8270 4114

Syon Park – London Road, Brentford, Middlesex TW8 8JF. Tel: 020 8560 0882

Norfolk

Hoveton Hall Gardens – Hoveton, Wroxham, Norfolk NR12 8RJ. Tel: 01603 782798

Walsingham Abbey Grounds – c/o The Estate Office, Little Walsingham, Norfolk NR22 6BP. Tel: 01328 820259 / 820510

Wolterton and Mannington Estate – Mannington Hall, Norwich, Norfolk NR11 7BB. Tel: 01263 584175

North Yorkshire

Castle Howard – York, North Yorkshire YO6 7DA. Tel: 01653 648333

Duncombe Park – Helmsley, York, North Yorkshire YO62 5EB. Tel: 01439 770213

Hovingham Hall – Hovingham, York, North Yorkshire YO62 4LU. Tel: 01653 628771

Ripley Castle – Ripley Castle Estate, Harrogate, North Yorkshire HG3 3AY. Tel: 01423 770152

Sion Hill Hall – Kirby Wiske, Thirsk, North Yorkshire YO7 4EU. Tel: 01845 587206

The Forbidden Corner – The Tupgill Park Estate, Coverham, Middleham, North Yorkshire DL8 4TJ. Tel: 01969 640638

The Royal Horticultural Society Garden Harlow Carr – Crag Lane, Harrogate, North Yorkshire HG3 1QB. Tel: 01423 565418

Thorp Perrow Arboretum & The Falcons of Thorp Perrow – Bedale, North Yorkshire DL8 2PR. Tel: 01677 425323

Yorkshire Garden World – Main Road, West Haddlesey, Nr Selby, North Yorkshire YO8 8QA. Tel: 01757 228279

Northamptonshire

Althorp – Northampton, Northants NN7 4HQ. Tel: 01604 770107

Cottesbrooke Hall and Gardens – Cottesbrooke, Northampton, Northamptonshire NN6 8PF. Tel: 01604 505808

Haddonstone Show Garden – The Forge House, Church Lane, East Haddon, Northamptonshire NN6 8DB. Tel: 01604 770711

Kelmarsh Hall & Gardens – Kelmarsh, Northampton, Northamptonshire NN6 9LT. Tel: 01604 686543

Northumberland

Alnwick Castle – Alnwick, Northumberland NE66 1NQ. Tel: 01665 510777/ 511100

Chillingham Castle – Chillingham, Alnwick, Northumberland NE66 5NJ. Tel: 01668 215359

Chipchase Castle – Chipchase, Wark on Tyne, Hexham, Northumberland NE48 3NT. Tel: 01434 230203

Paxton House & Country Park – Berwick-upon-Tweed, Northumberland TD15 1SZ. Tel: 01289 386291

Seaton Delaval Hall – Seaton Sluice, Whitley Bay, Northumberland NE26 4QR. Tel: 0191 237 1493 / 0786

Oxfordshire

Ditchley Park – Enstone, Chipping Norton, Oxfordshire OX7 4ER. Tel: 01608 677346

Kingston Bagpuize House – Kingston Bagpuize, Abingdon, Oxfordshire OX13 5AX. Tel: 01865 820259

Mapledurham House – Mapledurham, Nr Reading, Oxfordshire RG4 7TR. Tel: 01189 723350

River & Rowing Museum – Mill Meadows, Henley-on-Thames, Oxfordshire RG9 1BF. Tel: 01491 415600

Stonor Park – Stonor, Henley-on-Thames, Oxfordshire RG9 6HF. Tel: 01491 638587

Sulgrave Manor – Manor Road, Sulgrave, Banbury, Oxfordshire OX17 2SD. Tel: 01295 760205

Historic Houses, Castles & Gardens

Incorporating Museums & Galleries.
www.historichouses.co.uk

Upton House – Nr Banbury, Oxon OX15 6HT.
Tel: 01295 670266

Wallingford Castle Gardens – Castle Street, Wallingford, Oxfordshire. Tel: 01491 835373

Shropshire

Hawkstone Park & Follies – Weston-under-Redcastle, Shrewsbury, Shropshire SY4 5UY. Tel: 01939 200 611

Hodnet Hall Gardens – Hodnet, Market Drayton, Shropshire TF9 3NN. Tel: 01630 685786

Hopton Court – Kidderminster, Shropshire DY14 0EF. Tel: 01299 270734

Royal Air force Museum – Cosford, Shifnal, Shropshire TF11 8UP. Tel: 01902 376200

Shipton Hall – Shipton, Much Wenlock, Shropshire TF13 6JZ. Tel: 01746 785225

Shrewsbury Castle & Shropshire Regimental Museum – Castle Street, Shrewsbury, Shropshire SY1 2AT. Tel: 01743 358516

Shrewsbury Museum & Art Gallery – Barker Street, Shrewsbury, Shropshire SY1 1QH. Tel: 01743 361196

The Dorothy Clive Garden – Willoughbridge, Market Drayton, Shropshire TF9 4EU. Tel: 01630 647237

Weston Park – Weston-under-Lizard, Nr Shifnal, Shropshire TF11 8LE. Tel: 01952 852100

Somerset

Barford Park – Enmore, Nr Bridgwater, Somerset TA5 1AG. Tel: 01278 671269

Great House Farm – Wells Road, Theale, Wedmore, Somerset BS28 4SJ. Tel: 01934 713133

Milton Lodge Gardens – Old Bristol Road, Wells, Somerset BA5 3AQ. Tel: 01749 672168

Museum of Costume & Assembly Rooms – Bennett Street, Bath, Somerset BA1 2QH. Tel: 01225 477789 / 477785

Orchard Wyndham – Williton, Taunton, Somerset TA4 4HH. Tel: 01984 632309

▼
Roman Baths & Pump Room – Abbey Church Yard, Bath, Somerset BA1 1LZ. **Tel: 01225 477785**

The American Museum in Britain – Claverton Manor, Bath, Somerset BA2 7BD. Tel: 01225 460503

Staffordshire

Ford Green Hall – Ford Green Road, Smallthorne, Stoke-on-Trent, Staffordshire ST6 1NG. Tel: 01782 233195

Sandon Hall – Sandon, Staffordshire ST18 0BZ. Tel: 01889 508004

Whitmore Hall – Whitmore, Newcastle-under-Lyme, Staffordshire ST5 5HW. Tel: 01782 680478

Suffolk

Ancient House – Clare, Suffolk CO10 8NY. Tel: 01628 825920

Otley Hall – Hall Lane, Otley, Ipswich, Suffolk IP6 9PA. Tel: 01473 890264

Shrubland Park Gardens – Shrubland Estate, Coddenham, Ipswich, Suffolk IP6 9QQ. Tel: 01473 830221

Surrey

Clandon Park – West Clandon, Guildford, Surrey GU4 7RQ. Tel: 01483 222482

Claremont House – Claremont Drive, Esher, Surrey KT10 9LY. Tel: 01372 467841

Goddards – Abinger Common, Dorking, Surrey RH5 6TH. Tel: 01628 825920

Great Fosters – Stroude Road, Egham, Surrey TW20 9UR. Tel: 01784 433822

Hampton Court Palace – East Molesey, Surrey KT8 9AU. Tel: 0870 751 5175

Hatchlands – East Clandon, Guildford, Surrey GU4 7RT. Tel: 01483 222482

Loseley Park – Estate Office, Guildford, Surrey GU3 1HS. Tel: 01483 304440

Merton Heritage Centre – The Canons, Madeira Road, Mitcham, Surrey CR4 4HD. Tel: 020 8640 9387

Painshill Landscape Garden – Portsmouth Road, Cobham, Surrey KT11 1JE. Tel: 01932 868113

The Royal Horticultural Society, Wisley Garden – Nr Woking, Surrey GU23 6QB. Tel: 01483 224234

Warwickshire

Arbury Hall – Nuneaton, Warwickshire CV10 7PT. Tel: 024 7638 2804

Ragley Hall – Alcester, Warwickshire B49 5NJ. Tel: 01789 762090

Shakespeare Houses – The Shakespeare Centre, Henley Street, Stratford-upon-Avon, Warwickshire CV37 6QW. Tel: 01789 204016

West Midlands

Barber Institute of Fine Arts – The University of Birmingham, Edgbaston, Birmingham, West Midlands B15 2TS. Tel 0121 414 7333

Castle Bromwich Hall Gardens – Chester Road, Castle Bromwich, Birmingham, West Midlands B36 9BT. Tel: 0121-749 4100

The Birmingham Botanical Gardens and Glasshouses – Westbourne Road, Edgbaston, Birmingham, West Midlands B15 3TR. Tel: 0121 454 1860

West Sussex

Borde Hill Garden – Balcombe Road, West Sussex RH16 1XP. Tel: 01444 450326

Chichester District Museum – 29 Little London, Chichester, West Sussex PO19 1PB. Tel: 01243 784683

Denmans Garden – Clock House, Denmans, Fontwell, West Sussex BN18 0SU. Tel: 01243 542808

Goodwood House – Goodwood, Chichester, West Sussex PO18 0PX. Tel: 01243 755000

High Beeches Gardens – High Beeches, Handcross, West Sussex RH17 6HQ. Tel: 01444 400589

Leonardslee - Lakes & Gardens – Lower Beeding, Horsham, West Sussex RH13 6PP. Tel: 01403 891212

Weald and Downland Open Air Museum – Singleton, Chichester, West Sussex PO21 4JU. Tel: 01243 811363

West Dean Gardens – West Dean, Chichester, West Sussex PO18 0QZ. Tel: 01243 818210

Worthing Museum & Art Gallery – Chapel Road, Worthing, West Sussex BN11 1HP. Tel: 01903 239999

West Yorkshire

Bramham Park – Estate Office, Bramham Park, Wetherby, West Yorkshire LS23 6ND. Tel: 01937 846000

Harewood House – The Harewood House Trust, Moorhouse. Harewood, Leeds, West Yorkshire LS17 9LQ. Tel: 0113 218 1010

Ledston Hall – Hall Lane, Ledstone, West Yorkshire WF10 2BB. Tel: 01423 523 423

Wiltshire

Charlton Park House – Charlton, Malmesbury, Wiltshire SN16 9DG. Tel: 01666 824389

Hamptworth Lodge – Landford, Salisbury, Wiltshire SP5 2EA. Tel: 01794 390215

▼
Longleat – Warminster, Wiltshire BA12 7NW.
Tel: 01985 844400

Salisbury Cathedral – Visitor Services, 33 The Close, Salisbury, Wiltshire SP1 2EJ. Tel: 01722 555120

Sheldon Manor – Nr Chippenham, Wiltshire SN14 0RG. Tel: 01249 653120

The Peto Garden At Iford Manor – Bradford-on-Avon, Wiltshire BA15 2BA. Tel: 01225 863146

Worcestershire

Hagley Hall – Hagley, Worcestershire DY9 9LG. Tel: 01562 882408

Harvington Hall – Harvington, Kidderminster, Worcester DY10 4LR. Tel: 01562 777846

Little Malvern Court – Nr Malvern, Worcestershire WR14 4JN. Tel: 01684 892988

Spetchley Park Gardens – Spetchley Park, Worcester, Worcestershire WR5 1RS. Tel: 01453 810303

Ireland

Co Antrim

Benvarden Gardens – Benvarden Dervolk, Co Antrim BT53 6NN. Tel: 028 2074 1331

Co Cork

Bantry House & Gardens – Bantry, Co Cork. Tel: + 353 2 750 047

Co Down

North Down Heritage Centre – Town Hall, Bangor, Co Down BT20 4BT. Tel: 028 9127 1200

Seaforde Gardens – Seaforde, Downpatrick, Co Down BT30 8PG. Tel: 028 4481 1225

Historic Houses, Castles & Gardens
Incorporating Museums & Galleries.

www.historichouses.co.uk

Co Kildare

Japanese Gardens & St Fiachra's Garden – Tully, Kildare Town, Co Kildare. Tel: +353 45 521617

Co Wicklow

Powerscourt Gardens & Waterfall – Powerscourt Estate, Enniskerry, Co Wicklow. Tel: +353 1 204 6000

Scotland

Aberdeenshire

Craigston Castle – Turriff, Aberdeenshire AB53 5PX. Tel: 01888 551228

Angus

Glamis Castle – Glamis, by Forfar, Angus DD8 1RJ. Tel: 01307 840393

Ayrshire

Auchinleck House – Ochiltree, Ayrshire. Tel: 01628 825920
Kelburn Castle and Country Centre – Kelburn, Fairlie (Nr Largs), Ayrshire KA29 0BE. Tel: 01475 568685

▼
Inveraray Castle – Cherry Park, Inveraray, Argyll PA32 8XE. Tel: 01499 302203
Maybole Castle – Maybole, Ayrshire KA19 7BX. Tel: 01655 883765
Sorn Castle – Sorn, Mauchline, Ayrshire KA5 6HR. Tel: 0141 942 6460

Dumfries

Drumlanrig Castle, Gardens and Country Park – Nr Thornhill, Dumfries DG3 4AQ. Tel: 01848 330248

East Lothian

Lennoxlove House – Haddington, East Lothian EH41 4NZ. Tel: 01620 823720

Edinburgh

Dalmeny House – South Queensferry, Edinburgh EH30 9TQ. Tel: 0131 331 1888

Fife

Callendar House – Callendar Park, Falkirk, Fife FK1 1YR. Tel: 01324 503770

Isle of Skye

Armadale Castle, Gardens & Museum of the Isles – Armadale, Sleat, Isle of Skye IV45 8RS. Tel: 01471 844305

Perthshire

Scone Palace – Scone, Perth, Perthshire PH2 6BD. Tel: 01738 552300

Scottish Borders

Bowhill House & Country Park – Bowhill, Selkirk, Scottish Borders TD7 5ET. Tel: 01750 22204
Traquair House – Innerleithen, Peebles EH44 6PW. Tel: 01896 830323

South Lanarkshire

New Lanark World Heritage Site – New Lanark Mills, South Lanarkshire ML11 9DB. Tel: 01555 661345

West Lothian

Hopetoun House – South Queensferry, West Lothian EH30 9SL. Tel: 0131 331 2451
Newliston – Kirkliston, West Lothian EH29 9EB. Tel: 0131 333 3231

Wales

Carmarthenshire

Aberglasney Gardens – Llangathen, Carmarthenshire SA32 8QH. Tel: 01558 668998

Conway

Bodnant Garden – Tal-y-Cafn, Nr Colwyn Bay, Conway LL28 5RE. Tel: 01492 650460

Flintshire

Golden Grove – Llanasa, Nr. Holywell, Flintshire CH8 9NA. Tel: 01745 854452

Gwynedd

Gwydir Castle – Llanrwst, Gwynedd LL26 0PN. Tel: 01492 641687

Monmouthshire

Llanvihangel Court – Llanvihangel Crucorney, Abergavenny, Monmouthshire NP7 8DH. Tel: 01873 890217
Penhow Castle – Penhow, Monmouthshire NP26 3AD. Tel: 01633 400800
Usk Castle – Usk, Monmouthshire NP15 1SD. Tel: 01291 672563

Newport

Fourteen Locks Canal Centre – High Cross, Newport NP10 9GN. Tel: 01633 894802
Newport Museum and Art Gallery – John Frost Square, Newport NP20 1PA. Tel: 01633 840064
Newport Transporter Bridge Visitor Centre – Usk Way, NewPort, South Wales NP20 2JT. Tel: 01633 250322
Tredegar House – Newport NP10 8YW. Tel: 01633 815880

Pembrokeshire

Carew Castle & Tidal Mill – Carew, Nr.Tenby, Pembrokeshire SA70 8SL. Tel: 01646 651782

Powys

The Judge's Lodging – Broad Street, Presteigne, Powys LD8 2AD. Tel: 01544 260650

South Glamorgan

Museum Of Welsh Life – St Fagans, Cardiff, South Glamorgan CF5 6XB. Tel: 029 2057 3500

Continental Europe

Belgium

Kasteel Ooidonk – Ooidonkdreef 9, B9800 Deinze. Tel: 0032 9 282 35 70

France

▼
Château de Chenonceau – 37150 Chenonceaux. Tel: +33 2 47 23 90 07
Chateau Royal D'Amboise – Chateau Royal, B.P. 271, 37403 Amboise. Tel: 00 33 2 47 57 00 98
Floral Park and Chateau of Martinvast – Domaine de Beaurepaire, 50690 Martinvast. Tel: +33 2 33 87 20 80

The Netherlands

Palace Het Loo National Museum – Koninklijk Park 1, 7315 JA Apeldoorn, Holland. Tel: +31 55 577 2400

Mini Listings Europe

Condé Nast Johansens are delighted to recommend over 320 properties across Europe & The Mediterranean.
Call 1-800-564-7518 or see the order forms on page 285 to order guides.

ANDORRA (PAS DE LA CASA)
Hotel Font d'Argent
C/ Bearn 20, 22, 24, Pas De La Casa, Andorra
Tel: +376 739 739
Fax: +376 739 800

AUSTRIA / KÄRNTEN (KLAGENFURT)
Hotel Palais Porcia
Neuer Platz 13, 9020 Klagenfurt, Austria
Tel: +43 463 51 15 90
Fax: +43 463 51 15 90 30

AUSTRIA / KÄRNTEN (PATERGASSEN)
Almdorf "Seinerzeit"
Fellacheralm, 9564 Patergassen, Austria
Tel: +43 4275 7201
Fax: +43 4275 7380

AUSTRIA / KÄRNTEN (VELDEN)
Seeschlössl Velden
Klagenfurter Strasse 34, 9220 Velden, Austria
Tel: +43 4274 2824
Fax: +43 4274 2824 44

AUSTRIA / NIEDERÖSTERREICH (DÜRNSTEIN)
Hotel Schloss Dürnstein
3601 Dürnstein, Austria
Tel: +43 2711 212
Fax: +43 2711 21230

AUSTRIA / SALZBURG (BAD GASTEIN)
Hotel & Spa Haus Hirt
An Der Kaiserpromenade 14, 5640 Bad Gastein, Austria
Tel: +43 64 34 27 97
Fax: +43 64 34 27 97 48

AUSTRIA / SALZBURG (BAD HOFGASTEIN)
Das Moser
Kaiser-Franz-Platz 2, 5630 Bad Hofgastein, Austria
Tel: +43 6432 6209
Fax: +43 6432 6209 88

AUSTRIA / SALZBURG (BAD HOFGASTEIN)
Grand Park Hotel Bad Hofgastein
Kurgartenstrasse 26, 5630 Bad Hofgastein, Austria
Tel: +43 6432 63560
Fax: +43 6432 8454

AUSTRIA / TIROL (IGLS)
Schlosshotel Igls
Viller Steig 2, 6080 Igls, Tirol, Austria
Tel: +43 512 37 72 17
Fax: +43 512 37 72 17 198

AUSTRIA / TIROL (IGLS)
Sporthotel Igls
Hilberstrasse 17, 6080 Igls, Tirol, Austria
Tel: +43 512 37 72 41
Fax: +43 512 37 86 79

AUSTRIA / VORARLBERG (LECH)
Sporthotel Kristiania
Omesberg 331, 6764 Lech Am Arlberg, Austria
Tel: +43 5583 25 610
Fax: +43 5583 3550

AUSTRIA / VORARLBERG (ZÜRS)
Thurnhers Alpenhof
6763 Zürs – Arlberg, Austria
Tel: +43 5583 2191
Fax: +43 5583 3330

AUSTRIA / WIEN (VIENNA)
Grand Hotel Wien
Kärntner Ring 9, 1010 Vienna, Austria
Tel: +43 1 515 80 0
Fax: +43 1 515 13 13

BELGIUM (ANTWERP)
Firean Hotel
Karel Oomsstraat 6, 2018 Antwerp, Belgium
Tel: +32 3 237 02 60
Fax: +32 3 238 11 68

BELGIUM (BRUGES)
Hotel Acacia
Korte Zilverstraat 3A, 8000 Bruges, Belgium
Tel: +32 50 34 44 11
Fax: +32 50 33 88 17

BELGIUM (BRUGES)
Hotel De Tuilerieën
Dyver 7, 8000 Bruges, Belgium
Tel: +32 50 34 36 91
Fax: +32 50 34 04 00

BELGIUM (BRUGES)
Hotel Montanus
Nieuwe Gentweg 78, 8000 Bruges, Belgium
Tel: +32 50 33 11 76
Fax: +32 50 34 09 38

BELGIUM (BRUGES)
Hotel Prinsenhof
Ontvangersstraat 9, 8000 Bruges, Belgium
Tel: +32 50 34 26 90
Fax: +32 50 34 23 21

BELGIUM (DE HAAN)
Romantik Manoir Carpe Diem
Prins Karellaan 12, 8420 De Haan, Belgium
Tel: +32 59 23 32 20
Fax: +32 59 23 33 96

BELGIUM (FLORENVILLE)
Hostellerie Le Prieuré de Conques
Rue De Conques 2, 6820 Florenville, Belgium
Tel: +32 61 41 14 17
Fax: +32 61 41 27 03

MINI LISTINGS EUROPE

Condé Nast Johansens are delighted to recommend over 320 properties across Europe & The Mediterranean.
Call 1-800-564-7518 or see the order forms on page 285 to order guides.

BELGIUM (KNOKKE~HEIST)
Romantik Hotel Manoir du Dragon
Albertlaan 73, 8300 Knokke~Heist, Belgium
Tel: +32 50 63 05 80
Fax: +32 50 63 05 90

BELGIUM (KORTRIJK)
Hotel Damier
Grote Markt 41, 8500 Kortrijk, Belgium
Tel: +32 56 22 15 47
Fax: +32 56 22 86 31

BELGIUM (MALMÉDY)
Hostellerie Trôs Marets
Route des Trôs Marets, 4960 Malmédy, Belgium
Tel: +32 80 33 79 17
Fax: +32 80 33 79 10

BELGIUM (MARCHE~EN~FAMENNE)
Château d'Hassonville
Route d'Hassonville 105, 6900 Marche~en~Famenne, Belgium
Tel: +32 84 31 10 25
Fax: +32 84 31 60 27

CYPRUS (LIMASSOL)
Le Meridien Limassol Spa & Resort
Po Box 56560, 3308 Limassol, Cyprus
Tel: +357 25 862 000
Fax: +357 25 634 222

CZECH REPUBLIC (PRAGUE)
Hotel Hoffmeister
Pod Bruskou 7, Klárov, 11800 Prague 1, Czech Republic
Tel: +420 2 51017 111
Fax: +420 2 51017 100

CZECH REPUBLIC (PRAGUE)
Romantik Hotel U Raka
Cerninska 10/93, 11800 Prague 1, Czech Republic.
Tel: +420 2205 111 00
Fax: +420 2333 580 41

CZECH REPUBLIC (PRAGUE)
Sieber Hotel & Apartments
Slezská 55, 130 00 Prague 3, Czech Republic
Tel: +420 2 24 25 00 25
Fax: +420 2 24 25 00 27

DENMARK (NYBORG)
Hotel Hesselet
Christianslundsvej 119, 5800 Nyborg, Denmark
Tel: +45 65 31 30 29
Fax: +45 65 31 29 58

ESTONIA (PÄRNU)
Villa Ammende
Mere Pst. 7, 80012 Pärnu, Estonia
Tel: +372 44 73888
Fax: +372 44 73887

FRANCE / ALSACE~LORRAINE (COLMAR)
Hostellerie Le Maréchal
4 Place Six Montagnes Noires, Petite Venise, 68000 Colmar, France
Tel: +33 3 89 41 60 32
Fax: +33 3 89 24 59 40

FRANCE / ALSACE~LORRAINE (COLMAR)
Hôtel Les Têtes
19 Rue de Têtes, 68000 Colmar, France
Tel: +33 3 89 24 43 43
Fax: +33 3 89 24 58 34

FRANCE / ALSACE~LORRAINE (COLMAR - ROUFFACH)
Château d'Isenbourg
68250 Rouffach, France
Tel: +33 3 89 78 58 50
Fax: +33 3 89 78 53 70

FRANCE / ALSACE~LORRAINE (GÉRARDMER – VOSGES)
Hostellerie Les Bas Rupts
88400 Gérardmer, Vosges, France
Tel: +33 3 29 63 09 25
Fax: +33 3 29 63 00 40

FRANCE / ALSACE~LORRAINE (MURBACH – BUHL)
Hostellerie St Barnabé
68530 Murbach – Buhl, France
Tel: +33 3 89 62 14 14
Fax: +33 3 89 62 14 15

FRANCE / ALSACE~LORRAINE (OBERNAI - OTTROTT)
A L'Ami Fritz
8 Rue Des Châteaux, 67530 Ottrott, France
Tel: +33 3 88 95 80 81
Fax: +33 3 88 95 84 85

FRANCE / ALSACE~LORRAINE (STRASBOURG – OSTWALD)
Château de L'Ile
4 Quai Heydt, 67540 Ostwald, France
Tel: +33 3 88 66 85 00
Fax: +33 3 88 66 85 49

FRANCE / ALSACE~LORRAINE (THIONVILLE)
L'Horizon
50 Route du Crève~Cœur, 57100 Thionville, France
Tel: +33 3 82 88 53 65
Fax: +33 3 82 34 55 84

FRANCE / AUVERGNE (SAINT~FLOUR)
Hostellerie Château de Varillettes
15100 Saint~Georges par Saint~Flour, France
Tel: +33 4 71 60 45 05
Fax: +33 4 71 60 34 27

FRANCE / BRITTANY (BILLIERS)
Domaine de Rochevilaine
Pointe de Pen Lan, 56190 Billiers, France
Tel: +33 2 97 41 61 61
Fax: +33 2 97 41 44 85

Mini Listings Europe

Condé Nast Johansens are delighted to recommend over 320 properties across Europe & The Mediterranean.
Call 1-800-564-7518 or see the order forms on page 285 to order guides.

FRANCE / BRITTANY (LA GOUESNIÈRE - SAINT~MALO)
Château de Bonaban
35350 La Gouesnière, France
Tel: +33 2 99 58 24 50
Fax: +33 2 99 58 28 41

FRANCE / BRITTANY (MISSILLAC)
Domaine de La Bretesche
44780 Missillac, France
Tel: +33 2 51 76 86 96
Fax: +33 2 40 66 99 47

FRANCE / BRITTANY (MOËLAN~SUR~MER)
Manoir de Kertalg
Route de Riec-Sur-Belon, 29350 Moelan~sur~Mer, France
Tel: +33 2 98 39 77 77
Fax: +33 2 98 39 72 07

FRANCE / BRITTANY (PLOERDÜT)
Château du Launay
56160 Ploerdüt, France
Tel: +33 2 97 39 46 32
Fax: +33 2 97 39 46 31

FRANCE / BRITTANY (RENNES)
LeCoq~Gadby
156 Rue d'Antrain, 35700 Rennes, France
Tel: +33 2 99 38 05 55
Fax: +33 2 99 38 53 40

FRANCE / BRITTANY (SAINT MALO – PLEVEN)
Manoir du Vaumadeuc
22130 Pleven, France
Tel: +33 2 96 84 46 17
Fax: +33 2 96 84 40 16

FRANCE / BRITTANY (SAINT MALO – SAINT BRIEUC)
Manoir de la Hazaie
22400 Planguenoual, France
Tel: +33 2 9632 7371
Fax: +33 2 9632 7972

FRANCE / BRITTANY (TREBEURDEN)
Ti Al Lannec
14 Allée de Mézo~Guen, BP 3, 22560 Trebeurden, France
Tel: +33 296 15 01 01
Fax: +33 2 96 23 62 14

FRANCE / BURGUNDY - FRANCHE~COMTÉ (AVALLON)
Château de Vault de Lugny
11 Rue du Château, 89200 Avallon, France
Tel: +33 3 86 34 07 86
Fax: +33 3 86 34 16 36

FRANCE / BURGUNDY- FRANCHE~COMTÉ (AVALLON)
Hostellerie de la Poste
13 Place Vauban, 89200 Avallon, France
Tel: +33 3 86 34 16 16
Fax: +33 3 86 34 19 19

FRANCE / BURGUNDY - FRANCHE ~COMTÉ (BEAUNE)
Ermitage de Corton
R.N. 74, 21200 Chorey~les~Beaune, France
Tel: +33 3 80 22 05 28
Fax: +33 3 80 24 64 51

FRANCE / BURGUNDY - FRANCHE~COMTÉ (POLIGNY – JURA)
Hostellerie des Monts de Vaux
Les Monts de Vaux, 39800 Poligny, France
Tel: +33 3 84 37 12 50
Fax: +33 3 84 37 09 07

FRANCE / BURGUNDY - FRANCHE~COMTÉ (VILLEFARGEAU – AUXERRE)
Le Petit Manoir des Bruyères
5 Allée de Charbuy~les~Bruyères, 89240 Villefargeau, France
Tel: +33 3 86 41 32 82
Fax: +33 3 86 41 28 57

FRANCE / BURGUNDY - FRANCHE~COMTÉ (VOUGEOT)
Château de Gilly
Gilly~lès~Citeaux, 21640 Vougeot, France
Tel: +33 3 80 62 89 98
Fax: +33 3 80 62 82 34

FRANCE / CHAMPAGNE - ARDENNES (ÉPERNAY)
Hostellerie La Briqueterie
4 Route de Sézanne, 51530 Vinay – Épernay, France
Tel: +33 3 26 59 99 99
Fax: +33 3 26 59 92 10

FRANCE / CHAMPAGNE - ARDENNES (TINQUEUX – REIMS)
L'Assiette Champenoise
40 Avenue Paul Vaillant Couturier, 51430 Tinqueux, France
Tel: +33 3 26 84 64 64
Fax: +33 3 26 04 15 69

FRANCE / CÔTE D'AZUR (CAGNES~SUR~MER)
Domaine Cocagne
Colline de La Route de Vence, 30, Chemin du Pain de Sucre, 08600 Cagnes~sur~Mer, France
Tel: +33 4 92 13 57 77
Fax: +33 4 92 13 57 89

FRANCE / CÔTE D'AZUR (CANNES)
Le Cavendish
11 Boulevard Carnot, 06400 Cannes, France
Tel: +33 4 97 06 26 00
Fax: +33 4 97 06 26 01

FRANCE / CÔTE D'AZUR (ÈZE VILLAGE)
Château Eza
Rue de La Pise, 06360 Èze Village, France
Tel: +33 4 93 41 12 24
Fax: +33 4 93 41 16 64

FRANCE / CÔTE D'AZUR LE RAYOL – CANADEL
Le Bailli de Suffren
Avenue des Américains – Goffe de Saint~Tropez, 83820 Le Rayol – Canadel, France
Tel: +33 4 98 04 47 00
Fax: +33 4 98 04 47 99

Mini Listings Europe

Condé Nast Johansens are delighted to recommend over 320 properties across Europe & The Mediterranean.
Call 1-800-564-7518 or see the order forms on page 285 to order guides.

FRANCE / CÔTE D'AZUR (MANDELIEU – CANNES)
Ermitage du Riou
Avenue Henri Clews, 06210 Mandelieu~La~Napoule, France
Tel: + 33 4 93 49 95 56
Fax: +33 4 92 97 69 05

FRANCE / CÔTE D'AZUR (MOUGINS)
Le Mas Candille
Boulevard Clément Rebuffel, 06250 Mougins, France
Tel: +33 4 92 28 43 43
Fax: +33 4 92 28 43 40

FRANCE / CÔTE D'AZUR (NICE)
Hôtel La Pérouse
11, Quai Rauba~Capeu, 06300 Nice, France
Tel: +33 4 93 62 34 63
Fax: +33 4 93 62 59 41

FRANCE / CÔTE D'AZUR (SAINT~TROPEZ - RAMATUELLE)
La Ferme d'Augustin
Plage de Tahiti, 83350 Ramatuelle, Nr Saint-Tropez, France
Tel: +33 4 94 55 97 00
Fax: +33 4 94 97 40 30

FRANCE / CÔTE D'AZUR (SAINT~PAUL~DE~VENCE)
Le Mas d'Artigny
Route de la Colle, 06570 Saint~Paul~de~Vence, France
Tel: +33 4 93 32 84 54
Fax: +33 4 93 32 95 36

FRANCE / CÔTE D'AZUR (SERRE~CHEVALIER)
L'Auberge du Choucas
05220 Monetier~Les~Bains, Serre~Chevalier, Hautes~Alpes, France
Tel: +33 4 92 24 42 73
Fax: +33 4 92 24 51 60

FRANCE / CÔTE D'AZUR (VENCE)
Relais Cantemerle
258 Chemin Cantemerle, 06140 Vence, France
Tel: +33 4 93 58 08 18
Fax: +33 4 93 58 32 89

FRANCE / LOIRE VALLEY (AMBOISE)
Château de Pray
Route de Chargé, 37400 Amboise, France
Tel: +33 2 47 57 23 67
Fax: +33 2 47 57 32 50

FRANCE / LOIRE VALLEY (AMBOISE)
Le Choiseul
36 Quai Charles Guinot, 37400 Amboise, France
Tel: +33 2 47 30 45 45
Fax: +33 2 47 30 46 10

FRANCE / LOIRE VALLEY (AMBOISE)
Le Manoir Les Minimes
34 Quai Charles Guinot, 37400 Amboise, France
Tel: +33 2 47 30 40 40
Fax: +33 2 47 30 40 77

FRANCE / LOIRE VALLEY (CHINON)
Château de Danzay
RD 749, 37420 Chinon, France
Tel: +33 2 47 58 46 86
Fax: +33 2 47 58 84 35

FRANCE / LOIRE VALLEY (CHISSAY~EN~TOURRAINE)
Hostellerie Château de Chissay
41400 Chissay~en~Touraine, France
Tel: +33 2 54 32 32 01
Fax: +33 2 54 32 43 80

FRANCE / LOIRE VALLEY (LANGEAIS)
Château de Rochecotte
Saint~Patrice, 37130 Langeais, France
Tel: +33 2 47 96 16 16
Fax: +33 2 47 96 90 59

FRANCE / LOIRE VALLEY (SAUMUR - CHENEHUTTE ~ LES ~ TUFFEAUX)
Le Prieuré
49350 Chênehutte~Les~Tuffeaux, France
Tel: +33 2 41 67 90 14
Fax: +33 2 41 67 92 24

FRANCE / LOIRE VALLEY (TOURS - LUYNES)
Domaine de Beauvois
Le Pont Clouet, Route de Clere~les~Pins, 37230 Luynes, France
Tel: +33 2 47 55 50 11
Fax: +33 2 47 55 59 62

FRANCE / LOIRE VALLEY (TOURS - MONTBAZON)
Château d'Artigny
37250 Montbazon, France
Tel: +33 2 47 34 30 30
Fax: +33 2 47 34 30 39

FRANCE / LOIRE VALLEY (TOURS - MONTBAZON)
Domaine de La Tortinière
Route de Ballan~Miré, 37250 Montbazon, France
Tel: +33 2 47 34 35 00
Fax: +33 2 47 65 95 70

FRANCE / MIDI~PYRÉNÉES (CORDES~SUR~CIEL)
Le Grand Ecuyer
Haute de la Cité, 81170 Cordes~Sur~Ciel, France
Tel: +33 5 63 53 79 50
Fax: +33 5 63 53 79 51

FRANCE / NORMANDY (BAGNOLES DE L'ORNE)
Bois Joli
12, Avenue Philippe du Rozier, 61140 Bagnoles de L'Orne, France
Tel: +33 2 33 37 92 77
Fax: +33 2 33 37 07 56

FRANCE / NORMANDY (BREUIL~EN~BESSIN)
Château de Goville
14330 Breuil~en~Bessin, France
Tel: +33 2 31 22 19 28
Fax: +33 2 31 22 68 74

Mini Listings Europe

Condé Nast Johansens are delighted to recommend over 320 properties across Europe & The Mediterranean.
Call 1-800-564-7518 or see the order forms on page 285 to order guides.

FRANCE / NORMANDY (ETRETAT)
Le Donjon
Chemin de Saint Clair, 76790 Etretat, France
Tel: +33 2 35 27 08 23
Fax: +33 2 35 29 92 24

FRANCE / NORTH - PICARDY (VERVINS)
La Tour du Roy
02140 Vervins, France
Tel: +33 3 23 98 00 11
Fax: +33 3 23 98 00 72

FRANCE / NORMANDY (HONFLEUR – CRICQUEBOEUF)
Manoir de la Poterie
Chemin Paul Ruel, 14113 Cricqueboeuf, France
Tel: +33 2 31 88 10 40
Fax: +33 2 31 88 10 90

FRANCE / PARIS (CHAMPS~ELYSÉES)
La Trémoille
14 Rue de La Trémoille, 75008 Paris, France
Tel: +33 1 56 52 14 00
Fax: +33 1 40 70 01 08

FRANCE / NORMANDY (PACY~SUR~EURE)
Hostellerie Château de Brécourt
Douains, 27120 Pacy~sur~Eure, France
Tel: +33 2 32 52 40 50
Fax: +33 2 32 52 69 65

FRANCE / PARIS (CHAMPS~ELYSÉES)
Hôtel Plaza Athénée
25 Avenue Montaigne, 75008 Paris, France
Tel: +33 1 53 67 66 65
Fax: +33 1 53 67 66 66

FRANCE / NORTH - PICARDY (ABBEVILLE – ST. RIQUIER)
Abbatis Villa Hôtel Jean De Bruges
18, Place de L'Eglise, 80135 St. Riquier, France
Tel: +33 3 22 28 30 30
Fax: +33 3 22 28 00 69

FRANCE / PARIS (CHAMPS~ELYSÉES)
Hôtel San Regis
12 Rue Jean Goujon, 75008 Paris, France
Tel: +33 1 44 95 16 16
Fax: +33 1 45 61 05 48

FRANCE / NORTH - PICARDY (BETHUNE - GOSNAY)
La Chartreuse du Val St Esprit
62199 Gosnay, France
Tel: +33 3 21 62 80 00
Fax: +33 3 21 62 42 50

FRANCE / PARIS (CHAMPS~ELYSÉES)
Résidence Alma Marceau**
5 Rue Jean Giraudoux, 75016 Paris, France
Tel: +33 1 53 57 67 89
Fax: +33 1 40 70 06 70

FRANCE / NORTH - PICARDY (CALAIS - RECQUES~SUR~HEM)
Château de Cocove
62890 Recques~sur~Hem, France
Tel: +33 3 21 82 68 29
Fax: +33 3 21 82 72 59

FRANCE / PARIS (ÉTOILE – PORTE MAILLOT)
L'Hôtel Pergolèse
3 Rue Pergolèse, 75116 Paris, France
Tel: +33 1 53 64 04 04
Fax: +33 1 53 64 04 40

FRANCE / NORTH - PICARDY
(ELINCOURT~SAINTE~MARGUERITE)
Château de Bellinglise
60157 Elincourt~Sainte~Marguerite, France
Tel: +33 3 44 96 00 33
Fax: +33 3 44 96 03 00

FRANCE / PARIS (ÉTOILE – PORTE MAILLOT)
La Villa Maillot
143 Avenue de Malakoff, 75116 Paris, France
Tel: +33 1 53 64 52 52
Fax: +33 1 45 00 60 61

FRANCE / NORTH - PICARDY (ERMENONVILLE)
Hostellerie Château d'Ermenonville
60950 Ermenonville, France
Tel: +33 3 44 54 00 26
Fax: +33 3 44 54 01 00

FRANCE / PARIS (INVALIDES)
Hôtel Le Tourville
16 Avenue de Tourville, 75007 Paris, France
Tel: +33 1 47 05 62 62
Fax: +33 1 47 05 43 90

FRANCE / NORTH - PICARDY (FÈRE~EN~TARDENOIS)
Château de Fère
02130 Fère~en~Tardenois, France
Tel: + 33 3 23 82 21 13
Fax: +33 3 23 82 37 81

FRANCE / PARIS (JARDIN DU LUXEMBOURG)
Le Sainte~Beuve
9 Rue Sainte~Beuve, 75006 Paris, France
Tel: +33 1 45 48 20 07
Fax: +33 1 45 48 67 52

FRANCE / NORTH - PICARDY (LILLE)
Carlton Hotel
Rue de Paris, 59000 Lille, France
Tel: +33 3 20 13 33 13
Fax: +33 3 20 51 48 17

FRANCE / PARIS (MADELEINE)
Hôtel de L'Arcade
9 Rue de L'Arcade, 75008 Paris, France
Tel: +33 1 53 30 60 00
Fax: +33 1 40 07 03 07

Mini Listings Europe

Condé Nast Johansens are delighted to recommend over 320 properties across Europe & The Mediterranean.
Call 1-800-564-7518 or see the order forms on page 285 to order guides.

FRANCE / PARIS (MADELEINE)
Hôtel Le Lavoisier
21 Rue Lavoisier, 75008 Paris, France
Tel: +33 1 53 30 06 06
Fax: +33 1 53 30 23 00

FRANCE / PARIS (OPÉRA – MONMATRE)
Hôtel Lamartine
39 Rue Lamartine, 75009 Paris, France
Tel: +33 1 48 78 78 58
Fax: +33 1 48 74 65 15

FRANCE / PARIS (PANTHÉON)
Hôtel des Grands Hommes
17 Place du Panthéon, 75005 Paris, France
Tel: +33 1 46 34 19 60
Fax: +33 1 43 26 67 32

FRANCE / PARIS (PANTHÉON)
Hôtel du Panthéon
19 Place du Panthéon, 75005 Paris, France
Tel: +33 1 43 54 32 95
Fax: +33 1 43 26 64 65

FRANCE / PARIS (SAINT~GERMAIN)
ArtusHotel
34 Rue de Buci, 75006 Paris, France
Tel: +33 1 43 29 07 20
Fax: +33 1 43 29 67 44

FRANCE / PARIS (SAINT~ GERMAIN)
Hôtel Le Saint~Grégoire
43 Rue de L'Abbé Grégoire, 75006 Paris, France
Tel: 33 1 45 48 23 23
Fax: +33 1 45 48 33 95

FRANCE / PARIS (SAINT~GERMAIN)
Hôtel Pont Royal
7 Rue de Montalembert, 75007 Paris, France
Tel: +33 1 42 84 70 00
Fax: +33 1 42 84 71 00

FRANCE / PARIS (SAINT~GERMAIN)
L' Hôtel
13, Rue des Beaux Arts, 75006 Paris, France
Tel: +33 1 44 41 99 00
Fax: +33 1 43 25 64 81

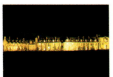

FRANCE / PARIS REGION (CERNAY-LA-VILLE)
Hostellerie Abbaye des Vaux de Cernay
78720 Cernay~La~Ville, France
Tel: +33 1 34 85 23 00
Fax: +33 1 34 85 11 60

FRANCE / PARIS REGION (ST. SYMPHORIEN~LE~CHÂTEAU)
Château d'Esclimont
28700 St. Symphorien~Le~Château, France
Tel: +33 2 37 31 15 15
Fax: +33 2 37 31 57 91

FRANCE / PARIS REGION (GRESSY~EN~FRANCE – CHANTILLY)
Le Manoir de Gressy
77410 Gressy~en~France, Roissy Cdg, Nr Paris, France
Tel: +33 1 60 26 68 00
Fax: +33 1 60 26 45 46

FRANCE / PARIS REGION (VILLE D'AVRAY)
Les Étangs de Corot
53 Rue de Versailles, 92410 Ville d'Avray, France
Tel: +33 1 41 15 37 00
Fax: +33 1 41 15 37 99

FRANCE / PARIS REGION (YERRES – ORLY)
Hostellerie Château du Maréchal de Saxe
Domaine de La Grange, 91330 Yerres, France
Tel: +33 1 69 48 78 53
Fax: +33 1 69 83 84 91

FRANCE / POITOU~CHARENTES (CHÂTEAUBERNARD)
Château de L'Yeuse
65 Rue de Belleville, Quartier de L'Ecassier, 16100 Châteaubernard, France
Tel: +33 5 45 36 82 60
Fax: +33 5 45 35 06 32

FRANCE / POITOU~CHARENTES (POITIERS – MIGNALOUX)
Manoir de Beauvoir Golf & Hôtel
635 Route de Beauvoir, 86550 Mignaloux – Beauvoir, France
Tel: +33 5 49 55 47 47
Fax: +33 5 49 55 31 95

FRANCE / POITOU~CHARENTES (POITIERS – SAINT~MAIXENT~L'ECOLE)
Logis St. Martin
Chemin de Pissot, 79400 Saint~Maixent~L'Ecole, France
Tel: +33 549 0558 68
Fax: +33 549 7619 93

FRANCE / PROVENCE (AIX~EN~PROVENCE)
Le Pigonnet
5 Avenue du Pigonnet, 13090 Aix~en~Provence, France
Tel: +33 4 42 59 02 90
Fax: +33 4 42 59 47 77

FRANCE / PROVENCE (GRIGNAN)
Le Clair de la Plume
Place du Mail, 26230 Grignan, France
Tel: +33 4 75 91 81 30
Fax: +33 4 75 91 81 31

FRANCE / PROVENCE (GRIGNAN)
Manoir de la Roseraie
Route de Valréas, 26230 Grignan, France
Tel: +33 4 75 46 58 15
Fax: +33 4 75 46 91 55

FRANCE / PROVENCE (LES~BAUX~DE~PROVENCE)
Mas de l'Oulivie
13520 Les~Baux~de~Provence, France
Tel: +33 4 90 54 35 78
Fax: +33 4 90 54 44 31

Mini Listings Europe

Condé Nast Johansens are delighted to recommend over 320 properties across Europe & The Mediterranean.
Call 1-800-564-7518 or see the order forms on page 285 to order guides.

FRANCE / PROVENCE (LES SAINTES~MARIES~DE~LA~MER)
Mas de La Fouque
Route du Petit Rhône, 13460 Les
Saintes~Maries~de~La~Mer, France
Tel: +33 4 90 97 81 02
Fax: +33 4 90 97 96 84

FRANCE / PROVENCE (SAINT~RÉMY~DE~PROVENCE)
Château des Alpilles
Route Départementale 31, Ancienne Route du Grès, 13210
Saint~Rémy~de~Provence, France
Tel: +33 4 90 92 03 33
Fax: +33 4 90 92 45 17

FRANCE / PROVENCE (UZÈS)
Château d'Arpaillargues
Hôtel Marie D'Agoult, 30700 Uzès, France
Tel: +33 4 66 22 14 48
Fax: +33 4 66 22 56 10

FRANCE / RHÔNE~ALPES (CHAMBERY – COISE~SAINT~JEAN)
Château de La Tour du Puits
73800 Coise~Saint~Jean, France
Tel: +33 4 79 28 88 00
Fax: +33 4 79 28 88 01

FRANCE / RHÔNE~ALPES (COURCHEVEL 1850)
Hôtel Annapurna
73120 Courchevel (1850), France
Tel: +33 4 79 08 04 60
Fax: +33 4 79 08 15 31

FRANCE / RHÔNE~ALPES (COURCHEVEL 1850)
Le Kilimandjaro
Route de L'Altiport, 73121 Courchevel 1850 Cedex, France
Tel: +33 4 79 01 18 74
Fax: +33 4 79 08 31 72

FRANCE / RHÔNE~ALPES (DIVONNE~LES~BAINS)
Château de Divonne
01220 Divonne~Les~Bains, France
Tel: +33 4 50 20 00 32
Fax: +33 4 50 20 03 73

FRANCE / RHÔNE~ALPES (DIVONNE~LES~BAINS)
Le Domaine de Divonne Golf & Spa Resort
Avenue des Thermes, 01220 Divonne-Les-Bains, France
Tel: +33 4 50 40 34 34
Fax: +33 4 50 40 34 24

FRANCE / RHÔNE~ALPES (LES GÊTS)
Chalet Hôtel La Marmotte
61 Rue du Chêne, 74260 Les Gêts, France
Tel: + 33 4 50 75 80 33
Fax: +33 4 50 75 83 26

FRANCE / RHÔNE~ALPES (LYON)
La Tour Rose
22 Rue du Boeuf, 69005 Lyon, France
Tel: +33 4 78 92 69 10
Fax: +33 4 78 42 26 02

FRANCE / RHÔNE~ALPES (SCIEZ~SUR~LÉMAN)
Château de Coudrée
Domaine de Coudrée, Bonnatrait, 74140 Sciez~sur~Léman,
France
Tel: +33 4 50 72 62 33
Fax: +33 4 50 72 57 28

FRANCE / SOUTH WEST (BIARRITZ)
Hôtel du Palais
Avenue de L'Impératrice, 64200 Biarritz, France
Tel: +33 5 59 41 64 00
Fax: +33 5 59 41 67 99

FRANCE / SOUTH WEST (LE BUISSON~DE~CADOUIN)
Le Manoir de Bellerive
Route de Siorac, 24480 Le-Buisson~De~Cadouin, France
Tel: +33 5 53 22 16 16
Fax: +33 5 53 22 09 05

FRANCE / SOUTH WEST (SAINT~JEAN~DE~LUZ)
Hotel Lehen Tokia
Chemin Achotarreta, 64500 Ciboure, Saint~Jean~De~Luz,
France
Tel: +33 5 59 47 18 16
Fax: +33 5 59 47 38 04

FRANCE / SOUTH WEST (SAINTE~RADEGONDE –
SAINT~EMILION)
Château de Sanse
33350 Sainte~Radegonde, France
Tel: +33 5 57 56 41 10
Fax: +33 5 57 56 41 29

FRANCE / WESTERN LOIRE (CHAMPIGNÉ)
Château des Briottières
49330 Champigné, France
Tel: +33 2 41 42 00 02
Fax: +33 2 41 42 01 55

FRANCE / WESTERN LOIRE (NANTES – LES SORINIÈRES)
Hostellerie Abbaye de Villeneuve
44480 Nantes – Les Sorinières, France
Tel: +33 2 40 04 40 25
Fax: +33 2 40 31 28 45

FRANCE / WESTERN LOIRE (NOIRMOUTIER)
Hostellerie du Général d'Elbée
Place du Château, 85330 Noirmoutier~en~L'Isle, France
Tel: +33 2 51 39 10 29
Fax: +33 2 51 33 08 23

GERMANY (DÜSSELDORF – WASSENBERG)
Hotel Burg Wassenberg ****
Auf Dem Burgberg 17, 41849 Wassenberg, Germany
Tel: +49 2432 9490
Fax: +49 2432 949100

GERMANY (OBERWESEL – RHEIN)
Burghotel auf Schönburg
55430 Oberwesel – Rhein, Germany
Tel: +49 67 44 93 930
Fax: +49 67 44 16 13

MINI LISTINGS EUROPE

Condé Nast Johansens are delighted to recommend over 320 properties across Europe & The Mediterranean.
Call 1-800-564-7518 or see the order forms on page 285 to order guides.

GERMANY (ROTHENBURG OB DER TAUBER)
Hotel Eisenhut
Herrngasse 3-7, 91541 Rothenburg Ob Der Tauber, Germany
Tel: +49 9861 7050
Fax: +49 9861 70545

GREAT BRITAIN & IRELAND / ENGLAND (AMBERLEY)
Amberley Castle
Amberley, Nr Arundel, West Sussex BN18 9ND, England
Tel: +44 1798 831 992
Fax: +44 1798 831 998

GREAT BRITAIN & IRELAND / ENGLAND (BAMBURGH)
Waren House Hotel
Waren Mill, Bamburgh, Northumberland NE70 7EE, England
Tel: +44 1668 214581
Fax: +44 1668 214484

GREAT BRITAIN & IRELAND (DERBY - NOTTINGHAM)
Risley Hall Country House Hotel
Derby Road, Risley, Derbyshire DE72 3SS, England
Tel: +44 115 939 9000
Fax: +44 115 939 7766

GREAT BRITAIN & IRELAND / ENGLAND (LONDON)
Beaufort House
45 Beaufort Gardens, Knightsbridge, London SW3 1PN, England
Tel: +44 20 7584 2600
Fax: +4 20 7584 6532

GREAT BRITAIN & IRELAND / ENGLAND (LONDON)
Draycott House Apartments
10 Draycott Avenue, Chelsea, London SW3 3AA, England
Tel: +44 20 7584 4659
Fax: +44 20 7225 3694

GREAT BRITAIN & IRELAND / ENGLAND (LONDON)
Kensington House Hotel
15-16 Prince Of Wales Terrace, Kensington, London W8 5PQ, England
Tel: +44 20 7937 2345
Fax: +44 20 7368 6700

GREAT BRITAIN & IRELAND / ENGLAND (LONDON)
Number Eleven Cadogan Gardens
11 Cadogan Gardens, Sloane Square, Knightsbridge, London SW3 2RJ
Tel: +44 20 7730 7000
Fax: +44 20 7730 5217

GREAT BRITAIN & IRELAND / ENGLAND (LONDON)
Number Sixteen
16 Sumner Place, London SW7 3EG, England
Tel: +44 20 7589 5232
Fax: +44 20 7584 8615

GREAT BRITAIN & IRELAND / ENGLAND (LONDON)
Pembridge Court Hotel
34 Pembridge Gardens, London W2 4DX, England
Tel: +44 20 7229 9977
Fax: +44 20 7727 4982

GREAT BRITAIN & IRELAND / ENGLAND (LONDON)
The Academy, The Bloomsbury Town House
21 Gower Street, London WC1E 6HG, England
Tel: +44 20 7631 4115
Fax: +44 20 7636 3442

GREAT BRITAIN & IRELAND / ENGLAND (LONDON)
The Beaufort
33 Beaufort Gardens, Knightsbridge, London SW3 1PP, England
Tel: +44 20 7584 5252
Fax: +44 20 7589 2834

GREAT BRITAIN & IRELAND / ENGLAND (LONDON)
The Colonnade, The Little Venice Town House
2 Warrington Crescent, London W9 1ER, England
Tel: +44 20 7286 1052
Fax: +44 20 7286 1057

GREAT BRITAIN & IRELAND / ENGLAND (LONDON)
The Cranley
10–12 Bina Gardens, South Kensington, London SW5 0LA, England
Tel: +44 20 7373 0123
Fax: +44 20 7373 9497

GREAT BRITAIN & IRELAND / ENGLAND (LONDON)
The Dorchester
Park Lane, Mayfair, London W1A 2HJ, England
Tel: +44 20 7629 8888
Fax: +44 20 7409 0114

GREAT BRITAIN & IRELAND / ENGLAND (LONDON)
The Halkin
5 Halkin Street, Belgravia, London SW1X 7DJ, England
Tel: +44 20 7333 1000
Fax: +44 20 7333 1100

GREAT BRITAIN & IRELAND / ENGLAND (LONDON)
The Leonard
15 Seymour Street, London W1H 7JW, England
Tel: +44 20 7935 2010
Fax: +44 20 7935 6700

GREAT BRITAIN & IRELAND / ENGLAND (LONDON)
The Milestone Hotel and Apartments
1 Kensington Court, London, W8 5Dl, England
Tel: +44 20 7917 1000
Fax: +44 20 7917 1010

GREAT BRITAIN & IRELAND / ENGLAND (LONDON)
Twenty Nevern Square
20 Nevern Square, London SW5 9PD, England
Tel: +44 20 7565 9555
Fax: +44 20 7565 9444

GREAT BRITAIN & IRELAND / ENGLAND (LYNTON)
Hewitt's - Villa Spaldi
North Walk, Lynton, Devon EX35 6HJ, England
Tel: +44 1598 752 293
Fax: +44 1598 752 489

Mini Listings Europe

Condé Nast Johansens are delighted to recommend over 320 properties across Europe & The Mediterranean.
Call 1-800-564-7518 or see the order forms on page 285 to order guides.

GREAT BRITAIN & IRELAND / ENGLAND (MELTON MOWBRAY)
Stapleford Park Hotel, Spa, Golf & Sporting Estate
Nr Melton Mowbray, Leicestershire LE14 2EF, England
Tel: +44 1572 787 522
Fax: +44 1572 787 651

GREECE (ATHENS)
Hotel Pentelikon
66 Diligianni Street, 14562 Athens, Greece
Tel: +30 10 62 30 650-6
Fax: +30 10 80 19 223

GREECE (CRETE)
St Nicolas Bay Hotel
72100 Agios Nikolaos, Crete, Greece
Tel: +30 2841 025041/2/3
Fax: +30 2841 024556

GREECE (CRETE)
The Peninsula at Porto Elounda de luxe Resort
72053 Elounda, Crete, Greece
Tel: +30 84 10 41 903
Fax: +30 84 10 41 889

GREECE (PAROS)
Astir of Paros
Kolymbithres, Naoussa, 84401 Paro, Greece
Tel: +30 284 51976
Fax: +30 284 51985

ITALY / CAMPANIA (POSITANO)
Hotel Villa Franca
Viale Pasitea 318, 84017 Positano (SA), Italy
Tel: +39 089 875655
Fax: +39 089 875735

ITALY / CAMPANIA (POSITANO)
Hotel Poseidon
Via Pasitea 148, 84017 Positano (Salerno), Italy
Tel: +39 089 811111
Fax: +39 089 875833

ITALY / CAMPANIA (RAVELLO)
Hotel Villa Maria
Via S.Chiara 2, 84010 Ravello (SA), Italy
Tel: +39 089 857255
Fax: +39 089 857071

ITALY / CAMPANIA (SAN. AGATA SUI DUE GOLFI)
Oasi Olimpia Relais
Via Deserto 26, San Agata sui due Golfi, 80064 Hassa Lubrense (NA), Italy
Tel: +39 081 8080560
Fax: +39 081 8085214

ITALY / CAMPANIA (SORRENTO)
Grand Hotel Cocumella
Via Cocumella 7, 80065 Sant'Agnello, Sorrento, Italy
Tel: +39 081 878 2933
Fax: +39 081 878 3712

ITALY / CAMPANIA (SORRENTO)
Grand Hotel Excelsior Vittoria
Piazza Tasso 34, 80067 Sorrento (Naples), Italy
Tel: +39 081 807 1044
Fax: +39 081 877 1206

ITALY / EMILIA ROMAGNA (BAGNO DI ROMAGNA TERME)
Hotel Tosco Romagnolo
Piazza Dante Alighieri 2, 47021 Bagno di Romagna Terme, Italy
Tel: +39 0543 911260
Fax: +39 0543 911014

ITALY / EMILIA ROMAGNA (BOLOGNA)
Grand Hotel Baglioni
Via Indipendenza 8, 40121 Bologna, Italy
Tel: +39 051 225445
Fax: +39 051 234840

ITALY / EMILIA ROMAGNA (BRISIGHELLA)
Relais Torre Pratesi
Via Cavina 11, 48013 Brisighella, Italy
Tel: +39 0546 84545
Fax: +39 0546 84558

ITALY / EMILIA ROMAGNA (FERRARA)
Ripagrande Hotel
Via Ripagrande 21, 44100 Ferrara, Italy
Tel: +39 0532 765250
Fax: +39 0532 764377

ITALY / EMILIA ROMAGNA (RICCIONE)
Hotel des Nations
Lungomare Costituzione 2, 47838 Riccione (Rn), Italy
Tel: +39 0541 647878
Fax: +39 0541 645154

ITALY / LAZIO (PALO LAZIALE – ROME)
La Posta Vecchia
Loc. Palo Laziale, 00055 Ladispoli, Rome, Italy
Tel: +39 0699 49501
Fax: +39 0699 49507

ITALY / LAZIO (ROME)
Hotel Aventino
Via San. Domenico 10, 00153 Rome, Italy
Tel: +39 06 5745 174
Fax: +39 06 5783 604

ITALY / LAZIO (ROME)
Hotel Farnese
Via Alessandro Farnese 30 (Angolo Viale Giulio Cesare), 00192 Rome, Italy
Tel: +39 06 321 25 53/4
Fax: +39 06 321 51 29

ITALY / LAZIO (ROME)
Hotel Giulio Cesare
Via degli Scipioni 287, 00192 Rome, Italy
Tel: +39 06 321 0751
Fax: +39 06 321 1736

Mini Listings Europe

Condé Nast Johansens are delighted to recommend over 320 properties across Europe & The Mediterranean.
Call 1-800-564-7518 or see the order forms on page 285 to order guides.

ITALY / LIGURIA (FINALE LIGURE)
Hotel Punta Est
Via Aurelia 1, 17024 Finale Ligure, Italy
Tel: +39 019 600611/2
Fax: +39 019 600611

ITALY / LIGURIA (SESTRI - LEVANTE)
Hotel Vis à Vis
Via della Chiusa 28, 16039 Sestri Levante, (GE), Italy
Tel: +39 0185 42661/480801
Fax: +39 0185 480853

ITALY / LOMBARDY (ERBUSCO - FRANCIACORTA)
L'Albereta
Via Vittorio Emanuele 11, 25030 Erbusco (Bs), Italy
Tel: +39 030 7760 550
Fax: +39 030 7760 573

ITALY / LOMBARDY (MANTOVA)
Albergo San Lorenzo
Piazza Concordia 14, 46100 Mantova, Italy
Tel: +39 0376 220500
Fax: +39 0376 327194

ITALY / PIEMONTE (CUNEO)
Lovera Palace Hotel
Via Roma, 37, 12100 Cuneo, Italy
Tel: +39 0171 690 420
Fax: +39 0171 603 435

ITALY / PIEMONTE (STRESA – LAKE MAGGIORE)
Hotel Villa Aminta
Via Sempione Nord 123, 28838 Stresa (VB), Italy
Tel: +39 0323 933 818
Fax: +39 0323 933 955

ITALY / PIEMONTE (TORINO)
Hotel Victoria
Via Nino Costa 4, 10123 Torino, Italy
Tel: +39 011 56 11909
Fax: +39 011 56 11806

ITALY / PUGLIA (SAVELLETRI DI FASANO)
Masseria San Domenico
Litoranea 379, 72010 Savelletri di Fasano (Brindisi) Italy
Tel: +39 080 482 7990
Fax: +39 080 482 7978

ITALY / SICILY (ETNA)
Hotel Villa Paradiso dell'Etna
Via Per Viagrande 37, 95037 San Giovanni La Punta, Italy
Tel: +39 095 7512409
Fax: +39 095 7413861

ITALY / SICILY (GIARDINI NAXOS)
Hellenia Yachting Hotel
Via Jannuzzo 41, 98035 Giardini Naxos (Me), Italy
Tel: +39 (0)942 51737
Fax: +39 (0)942 54310

ITALY / SICILY (TAORMINA RIVIERA – MARINA D'AGRO)
Hotel Baia Taormina
Statale Dello Ionio 39, 98030 Marina D'Agro (Me), Italy
Tel: +39 0942 756292
Fax: +39 0942 756603

ITALY / TRENTINO - ALTO ADIGE (MADONNA DI CAMPIGLIO)
Hotel Lorenzetti
Via Dolomiti Di Brenta 119, 38084 Madonna Di Campiglio (Tn) Italy
Tel: +39 0465 44 14 04
Fax: +39 0465 44 06 88

ITALY / TRENTINO - ALTO ADIGE (MARLING – MERAN)
Romantik Hotel Oberwirt
St Felixweg 2, 39020 Marling – Meran, Italy
Tel: +39 0473 44 71 11
Fax: +39 0473 44 71 30

ITALY / TRENTINO - ALTO ADIGE (MERAN)
Park Hotel Mignon
Via Grabmayr 5, 39012 Meran, Italy
Tel: +39 0473 230353
Fax: +39 0473 230644

ITALY / TRENTINO – ALTO ADIGE (NOVA LEVANTE)
Posthotel Weisses Rössl
Via Carezza 30, 39056 Nova Levante (Bz), Dolomites, Italy
Tel: +39 0471 613113
Fax: +39 0471 613390

ITALY / TRENTINO - ALTO ADIGE (SAN CASSIANO)
Hotel & Spa Rosa Alpina
Strada Micura De Rue 20, 39030 San Cassiano (BZ) Italy.
Tel: +39 0471 841500
Fax: +39 0471 841377

ITALY / TUSCANY (ASCIANO - SIENA)
CasaBianca
Loc. Casabianca Asciano, Asciano, Italy
Tel: +39 0577 704362
Fax: +39 0577 704622

ITALY / TUSCANY (CASTIGLION FLORENTINO)
Relais San Pietro in Polvano
Località Polvano, 52043 Castiglion Fiorentino (AR), Italy
Tel: +39 0575 650100
Fax: +39 0575 650255

ITALY / TUSCANY (COLLE VAL D'ELSA - SIENA)
Relais Della Rovere
Via Piemonte 10, Loc. Badia, 53034 Colle Val D'Elsa (SI), Italy
Tel: +39 0577 924696
Fax: +39 0577 924489

ITALY / TUSCANY (ELBA ISLAND - CAPOLIVERI)
Grand Hotel Elba International
Baia della Fontanella, Isola D'Elba, 57031 Capoliveri (LI), Italy
Tel: +39 0565 946111
Fax: +39 0565 946662

Mini Listings Europe

Condé Nast Johansens are delighted to recommend over 320 properties across Europe & The Mediterranean.
Call 1-800-564-7518 or see the order forms on page 285 to order guides.

ITALY / TUSCANY (FLORENCE)
Hotel J and J
Via di Mezzo 20, 50121 Florence, Italy
Tel: +39 055 263121
Fax: +39 055 240282

ITALY / TUSCANY (FLORENCE)
Villa Montartino
Via Gherardo Silvani 151, 50125 Florence, Italy
Tel: +39 055 223520
Fax: +39 055 223495

ITALY / TUSCANY (LIDO DI CAMAIORE)
Hotel Villa Ariston
Viale C. Colombo 355, 55043 Lido Di Camaiore – Lucca, Italy
Tel: +39 0584 610633
Fax: +39 0584 610631

ITALY / TUSCANY (MONTERIGGIONI – SIENA)
Hotel Monteriggioni
Via 1 Maggio 4, 53035 Monteriggioni, Italy
Tel: +39 0577 305009
Fax: +39 0577 305011

ITALY / TUSCANY (MONTERIGGIONI – STROVE)
Castel Pietraio
Strada Di Strove 33, 53035 Monteriggioni, Italy
Tel: +39 0577 300020
Fax: +39 0577 300977

ITALY / TUSCANY (PIEVESCOLA)
Hotel Relais La Suvera
53030 Pievescola – Siena, Italy
Tel: +39 0577 960300
Fax: +39 0577 960220

ITALY / TUSCANY (PORTO ERCOLE)
Il Pellicano
58018 Porto Ercole (Gr), Tuscany, Italy
Tel: +39 0564 858111
Fax: +39 0564 833418

ITALY / TUSCANY (PORTO SANTO STEFANO – ARGENTARIO)
Hotel Torre di Cala Piccola
Porto Santo Stefano, 58019 Argentario, Italy
Tel: +39 0564 825111
Fax: +39 0564 825235

ITALY / TUSCANY (PUNTA ALA)
Hotel Cala del Porto
Via Del Pozzo, 58040 Punta Ana, Italy
Tel: +39 0564 922455
Fax: +39 0564 920716

ITALY / TUSCANY (RADDA IN CHIANTI)
Palazzo Leopoldo
Via Roma 33, 53017 Radda In Chianti, Italy
Tel: +39 0577 735605
Fax: +39 0577 738031

ITALY / TUSCANY (SIENA)
Hotel Certosa Di Maggiano
Starda Di Certosa 82, 53100 Siena, Italy
Tel: +39 0577 288180
Fax: +39 0577 288189

ITALY / UMBRIA (ASSISI)
Romantik Hotel Le Silve di Armenzano
06081 Loc. Armenzano, Assisi (PG), Italy
Tel: +39 075 801 9000
Fax: +39 075 801 9005

ITALY / UMBRIA (COLLE SAN PAOLO - PERUGIA)
Romantik Hotel Villa di Monte Solare
Via Montali 7, 06070 Colle San Paolo - Panicale (PG), Italy
Tel: +39 075 832376
Fax: +39 075 8355818

ITALY / UMBRIA (GUBBIO)
Castello di Petroia
Località Petroia, 06020 Gubbio (PG), Italy
Tel: +39 075 92 02 87 / 92 01 09
Fax: +39 075 92 01 08

ITALY / UMBRIA (OSCANO - PERUGIA)
Castello Dell'Oscano Residenza D'Epoca
Localita Cenerente, 06134 Perugia, Italy
Tel: +39 075 584371
Fax: +39 075 630666

ITALY / UMBRIA (PIAZZANO - CORTONA)
Villa di Piazzano
Localita Piazzano, 06069 Tuoro Sul Trasimeno (PG), Italy
Tel: +39 075 826226
Fax: +39 075 826336

ITALY / UMBRIA (SPOLETO)
Villa Milani - Residenza d'Epoca
Loc. Colle Attivoli 4, 06049 Spoleto, Italy
Tel: +39 0743 225056
Fax: +39 0743 49824

ITALY / UMBRIA (TODI)
Hotel Bramante
Via Orvietana 48, 06059 Todi (PG), Italy
Tel: +39 075 8348381/2/3
Fax: +39 075 8948074

ITALY / VENETIA (BASSANO DEL GRAPPA)
Hotel Ca' Sette
Via Cunizza Da Romano 4, 36061 Bassano Del Grappa, Italy
Tel: +39 0424 383350
Fax: +39 0424 393287

ITALY / VENETIA (LIDO DI JESOLO)
Park Hotel Brasilia
Via Levantina, 30017 Lido Di Jesolo, Italy
Tel: +39 0421 380851
Fax: +39 0421 92244

MINI LISTINGS EUROPE

Condé Nast Johansens are delighted to recommend over 320 properties across Europe & The Mediterranean.
Call 1-800-564-7518 or see the order forms on page 285 to order guides.

ITALY / VENETIA (MOGLIANO – VENETO)
Hotel Villa Condulmer
Via Preganziol 1, 31020 Mogliano Veneto, Italy
Tel: +39 041 5972 700
Fax: +39 041 5972 777

ITALY / VENETIA (NEGRAR – VERONA)
Relais La Magioca
Via Moron 3, 37024 Negrar (Verona), Italy
Tel: +39 045 600 0167
Fax: +39 045 600 0840

ITALY / VENETIA (SARCEDO - VICENZA)
Casa Belmonte Relais
Via Belmonte 2, 36030 Sarcedo, Italy
Tel: +39 0445 884833
Fax: +39 0445884 134

ITALY / VENETIA (VENICE)
Hotel Giorgione
Ss. Apostoli 4587, 30131 Venice, Italy
Tel: +39 041 522 5810
Fax: +39 041 523 9092

ITALY / VENETIA (VENICE – LIDO)
Albergo Quattro Fontane
30126 Lido Di Venezia, venice, Italy
Tel: +39 041 526 0227
Fax: +39 041 526 0726

LUXEMBOURG (REMICH)
Hotel Saint~Nicolas
31 Esplanade, 5533 Remich, Luxembourg
Tel: +352 2666 3
Fax: +352 2666 3666

MONACO (MONTE~CARLO)
Monte~Carlo Beach Hotel
Avenue Princesse Grace, 06190 Roquebrune – Cap~Martin, France
Tel: +377 92 16 25 25
Fax: +377 92 16 26 26

THE NETHERLANDS (AMSTERDAM)
Ambassade Hotel
Herengracht 341, 1016 Az Amsterdam, The Netherlands
Tel: +31 20 5550222
Fax: +31 20 5550277

THE NETHERLANDS (AMSTERDAM)
Blakes
Keizersgracht 384, 1016 GB Amsterdam, The netherlands
Tel: +31 20 530 20 10
Fax: +31 20 530 20 30

THE NETHERLANDS (AMSTERDAM)
Seven One Seven
Prinsengracht 717, 1017 Jw Amsterdam, The Netherlands
Tel: +31 20 42 70 717
Fax: +31 20 42 30 717

THE NETHERLANDS (LATTROP)
Hotel de Holtweijde
Spiekweg 7, 7635 Lattrop, The Netherlands
Tel: +31 541 229 234
Fax: +31 541 22 94 45

THE NETHERLANDS (MAASTRICHT)
Château St Gerlach
Joseph Corneli Allée 1, 6301 KK Valkenburg A/D Geul, Maastricht, The Netherlands
Tel: +43 608 88 88
Fax: +43 604 28 83

THE NETHERLANDS (OOTMARSUM)
Hotel de Wiemsel
Winhofflaan 2, 7631 Hx Ootmarsum, The Netherlands
Tel: +31 541 292 155
Fax: +31 541 293 295

NORWAY (OPPDAL – DOVREFJELL)
Kongsvold Fjeldstue
Dovrefjell, 7340 Oppdal, Norway
Tel: +47 72 40 43 40
Fax: +47 72 40 43 41

NORWAY (OSLO)
Hotel Bastion
Skippergaten 7, 0152 Oslo, Norway
Tel: +47 22 47 77 00
Fax: +47 22 33 11 80

NORWAY (SOLVORN)
Walaker Hotell
6879 Solvorn, Sogn, Norway
Tel: +47 576 82080
Fax: +47 576 82081

NORWAY (VOSS)
Fleischers Hotel
5700 Voss, Norway
Tel: +47 56 52 05 00
Fax: +47 56 52 05 01

PORTUGAL / ALENTEJO (REDONDO)
Convento de São Paulo
Aldeia Da Serra, 7170 –120 Redondo, Portugal
Tel: +351 266 989160
Fax: +351 266 999104

PORTUGAL / ALGARVE (LAGOS)
Romantik Hotel Vivenda Miranda
Porto De Mós, 8600 Lagos, Portugal
Tel: +351 282 763222
Fax: +351 282 760342

PORTUGAL / LISBON & TAGUS VALLEY (LISBON)
Solar do Castelo
Rua das Cozinhas 2, 1100–181 Lisbon, Portugal
Tel: +351 218 870 909
Fax: +351 218 870 907

Mini Listings Europe

Condé Nast Johansens are delighted to recommend over 320 properties across Europe & The Mediterranean.
Call 1-800-564-7518 or see the order forms on page 285 to order guides.

PORTUGAL / LISBON & TAGUS VALLEY (SINTRA)
Tivoli Hotel Palácio de Seteais
Rua Barbosa de Bocage, 10, Seteais, 2710 Sintra, Portugal
Tel: +351 219 233 200
Fax: +351 219 234 277

PORTUGAL / MADEIRA (FUNCHAL)
Quinta da Bela Vista
Caminho do Avista Navios 4, 9000 Funchal, Madeira, Portugal
Tel: +351 291 706400
Fax: +351 291 706411

PORTUGAL / MADEIRA (FUNCHAL)
Quinta das Vistas Palacio Gardens
Caminho de Santa Antonio 52-A, 9000-187 Funchal, Madeira, Portugal
Tel: +351 291 750 007
Fax: +351 291 750 017

PORTUGAL / MADEIRA (FUNCHAL)
Quinta do Estreito
Rua José Joaquim da Costa, Estreito de Câmara De Lobos, 9325–034 Madeira, Portugal
Tel: +351 291 910530
Fax: +351 291 910549

PORTUGAL / MADEIRA (FUNCHAL)
Quinta do Monte
Caminho do Monte 192, 9050-288 Funchal, Madeira, Portugal
Tel: +351 291 780 100
Fax: +351 291 780 110

PORTUGAL / MADEIRA (FUNCHAL)
Quinta Perestrello
Rua do Dr. Pita 3, 9000-089 Funchal, Madeira, Portugal
Tel: +351 291 706700
Fax: +351 291 706706

PORTUGAL / OPORTO & NORTHERN PORTUGAL (PINHÃO)
Vintage House Hotel
Lugar da Ponte, 5085-034 Pinhão, Portugal
Tel: +351 22 371 999 / 375 4633
Fax: +351 22 370 5407

SPAIN / ANDALUCÍA (ANTEQUERA)
Hotel Antequera Golf
Sta Catalina S/N, 29200 Antequera, Spain
Tel: +34 95 27 04 531
Fax: +34 95 28 45 232

SPAIN / ANDALUCÍA (ARCOS DE LA FRONTERA)
Hacienda El Santiscal
Avda. El Santiscal 129 (Lago De Arcos), 11630 Arcos de La Frontera, Spain
Tel: +34 956 70 83 13
Fax: +34 956 70 82 68

SPAIN / ANDALUCÍA (BENAHAVIS – MARBELLA)
Amanhavis Hotel
Calle del Pilar 3, 29679 Benahavis, Málaga, Spain
Tel: +34 952 85 60 26
Fax: +34 952 85 61 51

SPAIN / ANDALUCIA (DOÑANA NATIONAL PARK)
El Cortijo de Los Mimbrales
Ctra del Rocio - Matalascañas, Km 30, 21750 Almonte (Huelva), Spain
Tel: +34 959 44 22 37
Fax: +34 959 44 24 43

SPAIN / ANDALUCÍA (GRANADA)
Hotel La Bobadilla
Finca La Bobadilla, Apto. 144, 18300 Loja, Granada, Spain
Tel: +34 958 32 18 61
Fax: +34 958 32 18 10

SPAIN / ANDALUCÍA (JEREZ DE LA FRONTERA)
Hotel Villa Jerez
Avda. de La Cruz Roja 7, 11407 Jerez de La Frontera, Spain
Tel: +34 956 15 31 00
Fax: +34 956 30 43 00

SPAIN / ANDALUCÌA (MÁLAGA)
Hotel La Casona de la Ciudad ★★★★
C/Marqués de Salvatierra 5, 29400 Ronda, Málaga, Spain
Tel: +34 952 87 95 95/96
Fax: +34 952 16 10 95

SPAIN / ANDALUCÍA (MÁLAGA)
Hotel La Fuente de La Higuera
Partido de Los Frontones, 29400 Ronda, Málaga, Spain
Tel: +34 95 2 11 43 55
Fax: +34 95 2 11 43 56

SPAIN / ANDALUCÍA (MÁLAGA)
La Posada del Torcal
29230 Villanueva de La Concepción, Málaga, Spain
Tel: +34 952 03 11 77
Fax: +34 952 03 10 06

SPAIN / ANDALUCÍA (MÁLAGA)
El Molino de Santillán
Ctra. de Macharaviaya, Km 3, 29730 Rincón de La Victoria, Málaga, Spain
Tel: +34 952 40 09 49
Fax: +34 952 40 09 50

SPAIN / ANDALUCÍA (MARBELLA – ESTEPONA)
Las Dunas Beach Hotel & Spa
La Boladilla Baja, Crta. de Cádiz Km 163.5, 29689 Marbella – Estepona (Málaga), Spain
Tel: +34 952 79 43 45
Fax: +34 952 79 48 25

SPAIN / ANDALUCÍA (MIJAS~COSTA)
Hotel Byblos Andaluz
Mijas Golf, 29650 Mijas~Costa, Málaga, Spain
Tel: +34 952 47 30 50
Fax: +34 952 58 63 27

SPAIN / ANDALUCÍA (SEVILLA)
Cortijo El Esparragal
Ctra. de Merida, KM 795, 41860 Gerena (Sevilla), Spain
Tel: +34 955 78 27 02
Fax: +34 955 78 27 83

Mini Listings Europe

Condé Nast Johansens are delighted to recommend over 320 properties across Europe & The Mediterranean.
Call 1-800-564-7518 or see the order forms on page 285 to order guides.

SPAIN / ANDALUCÍA (SEVILLA)
Hacienda Benazuza El Bulli Hotel
41800 Sanlúcar La Mayor, Sevilla, Spain
Tel: +34 955 70 33 44
Fax: +34 955 70 34 10

SPAIN / ANDALUCÍA (SEVILLA)
Hotel Cortijo Águila Real
Ctra. Guillena–Burguillos Km 4, 41210 Guillena, Sevilla, Spain
Tel: +34 955 78 50 06
Fax: +34 955 78 43 30

SPAIN / ANDALUCÍA (SEVILLA)
Hotel Hacienda La Boticaria
Ctra. Alcalá - Utrera Km.2, 41500 Alcalá de Guadaira, Sevilla, Spain
Tel: +34 955 69 88 20
Fax: +34 955 99 00 95

SPAIN / ANDALUCÍA (SEVILLA)
Palacio Marqués de la Gomera
C/ San Pedro 20, 41640 Osuna, Sevilla, Spain
Tel: +34 95 4 81 22 23
Fax: +34 95 4 81 02 00

SPAIN / ANDALUCÍA (SEVILLA)
Palacio de San Benito
c/San Benito S/N, 41370 Cazalla de La Sierra, Sevilla, Spain
Tel: +34 954 88 33 36
Fax: +34 954 88 31 62

SPAIN / ANDALUCÍA (SOTOGRANDE)
Almenara Golf Hotel & Spa
Avenida Almenara, 11310 Sotogrande, Spain
Tel: + 34 956 58 20 00
Fax: +34 956 58 20 01

SPAIN / ARAGÓN (TERUEL)
La Parada del Compte
Antigua Estación de Ferrocarril, 44597 Torre del Compte, Teruel, Spain
Tel: +34 978 76 90 72
Fax: +34 978 76 90 74

SPAIN / ASTURIAS (VILLAMAYOR)
Palacio de Cutre
La Goleta S/N Villamayor, 33583 Infiesto, Asturias, Spain
Tel: +34 985 70 80 72
Fax: +34 985 70 80 19

SPAIN / BALEARIC ISLANDS (IBIZA)
Cas Gasi
Apdo. Correos 117, 07814 Santa Gertrudis, Ibiza, Balearic Islands.
Tel: +34 971 19 71 73
Fax: +34 971 19 71 73

SPAIN / BALEARIC ISLANDS (MALLORCA)
Ca's Xorc
Carretera de Deía, Km 56,1 07100 Sóller, Mallorca, Balearic Islands
Tel: +34 971 63 82 80
Fax: +34 971 63 29 49

SPAIN / BALEARIC ISLANDS (MALLORCA)
Can Furiós Petit Hotel
Cami Vell Binibona 11, Binibona, 07314 Caimari, Mallorca, balearic islands
Tel: +34 971 51 57 51
Fax: +34 971 87 53 66

SPAIN / BALEARIC ISLANDS (MALLORCA)
Hotel Monnaber Nou
Possessió Monnaber Nou, 07310 Campanet, Mallorca, Balearic Islands
Tel: +34 971 87 71 76
Fax: +34 971 87 71 27

SPAIN / BALEARIC ISLANDS (MALLORCA)
Hotel Vistamar de Valldemossa
Ctra Valldemossa, Andratx Km. 2, 07170 Valldemossa, Mallorca, Balearic Islands
Tel: +34 971 61 23 00
Fax: +34 971 61 25 83

SPAIN / BALEARIC ISLANDS (MALLORCA)
Read's
Ca'N Moragues, 07320 Santa María, Mallorca, Balearic Islands
Tel: +34 971 14 02 62
Fax: +34 971 14 07 62

SPAIN / BALEARIC ISLANDS (MALLORCA)
Sa Posada d'Aumallia
Camino Son Prohens 1027, 07200 Felanitx, Mallorca, Balearic Islands
Tel: +34 971 58 26 57
Fax: +34 971 58 32 69

SPAIN / BALEARIC ISLANDS (MALLORCA)
Scott's
Plaza de La Iglesia 12, 07350 Binissalem, Mallorca, Balearic Islands
Tel: +34 971 87 01 00
Fax: +34 971 87 02 67

SPAIN / CANARY ISLANDS (FUERTEVENTURA)
Elba Palace Golf Hotel
Urb. Fuerteventura Golf Club, Crta. de Jandia, Km 11, 35610 Antigua, Fuerteventura, Canary Islands
Tel: +34 928 16 39 22
Fax: +34 928 16 39 23

SPAIN / CANARY ISLANDS (GRAN CANARIA)
Gran Hotel Costa Meloneras
C/Mar Mediterráneo 1, 35100 Maspalomas, Gran Canaria, Canary Islands, Spain
Tel: +34 928 12 81 00
Fax: +34 928 12 81 22

SPAIN / CANARY ISLANDS (LANZAROTE)
Finca de Las Salinas
C/ La Cuesta 17, 35570 Yaiza, Lanzarote, Canary Islands
Tel: +34 928 83 03 25
Fax: +34 928 83 03 29

SPAIN / CANARY ISLANDS (LANZAROTE)
Gran Meliá Volcán
Urb. Castillo del Aguila, Playa Blanco, Lanzarote, Canary Islands
Tel: +34 928 51 91 85
Fax: +34 928 51 91 32

Mini Listings Europe

Condé Nast Johansens are delighted to recommend over 320 properties across Europe & The Mediterranean.
Call 1-800-564-7518 or see the order forms on page 285 to order guides.

SPAIN / CANARY ISLANDS (TENERIFE)
Gran Hotel Bahía del Duque Resort
38660 Adeje, Costa Adeje, Tenerife South, Canary Islands
Tel: +34 922 74 69 33/34
Fax: +34 922 74 69 25

SPAIN / CANARY ISLANDS (TENERIFE)
Hotel Botánico *****GL
Avda. Richard J. Yeoward, Urb. Botánico, 38400 Puerto de La Cruz, Tenerife, Canary Islands
Tel: +34 922 38 14 00
Fax: +34 922 38 39 93

SPAIN / CANARY ISLANDS (TENERIFE)
Hotel Jardín Tropical
Calle Gran Bretaña, 38670 Costa Adeje, Tenerife, Canary Islands
Tel: +34 922 74 60 00
Fax: +34 922 74 60 60

SPAIN / CANTABRIA (VILLACARRIEDO)
Palacio de Soñanes
Bomo Quintanal 1, Villacarriedo, Cantabria, Spain
Tel: +34 942 59 06 00
Fax: +34 942 59 06 14

SPAIN / CASTILLA~LA MANCHA (ALMAGRO)
La Casa del Rector
c/Pedro Oviedo 8, 13270 Almagro, Ciudad Real, Spain
Tel: +34 926 26 12 59
Fax: +34 926 26 12 60

SPAIN / CASTILLA Y LEÓN (ÁVILA)
El Milano Real
C/ Toleo S/N, Hoyos del Espino, 05634 Ávila, Spain
Tel: +34 920 349 108
Fax: +34 920 349 156

SPAIN / CASTILLA Y LEÓN (SALAMANCA)
Hotel Rector
Rector Esperabé 10–Apartado 399, 37008 Salamanca, Spain
Tel: +34 923 21 84 82
Fax: +34 923 21 40 08

SPAIN / CASTILLA Y LEÓN (SEGOVIA)
Caserío de Lobones
Valverde del Majano, 40140 Segovia, Spain
Tel: +34 921 12 84 08
Fax: +34 921 12 83 44

SPAIN / CATALUÑA (BARCELONA)
Hotel Claris
Pau Claris 150, 08009 Barcelona, Spain
Tel: +34 934 87 62 62
Fax: +34 932 15 79 70

SPAIN / CATALUÑA (BARCELONA)
Hotel Colón
Avenida de La Catedral 7, 08002 Barcelona, Spain
Tel: +34 933 01 14 04
Fax: +34 933 17 29 15

SPAIN / CATALUÑA (BARCELONA)
The Gallery
Rossellón 249, 08008 Barcelona, Spain
Tel: +34 934 15 99 11
Fax: +34 934 15 91 84

SPAIN / CATALUÑA (COSTA BRAVA)
Hotel Rigat Park
Playa de Fenals, 17310 Lloret de Mar, Costa Brava, Spain
Tel: +34 972 36 52 00
Fax: +34 972 37 04 11

SPAIN / CATALUÑA (GERONA)
Hotel Golf Peralada
C/Rocaberti S/N, 17491 Gerona, Spain
Tel: +34 972 53 88 30
Fax: +34 972 53 88 07

SPAIN / CATALUÑA (GERONA)
Mas Falgarona
Avinyonet de Puigventos, 17742 Gerona, Spain
Tel: +34 972 54 66 28
Fax: +34 972 54 70 71

SPAIN / CATALUÑA (SITGES)
Hotel Estela Barcelona
Avda. Port d'Aiguadolç S/N, 08870 Sitges (Barcelona), Spain
Tel: +34 938 11 45 45
Fax: +34 938 11 45 46

SPAIN / CATALUÑA (TARRAGONA)
Hotel Termes Montbrió Resort, Spa & Park
Carrer Nou 38, 43340 Montbrió del Camp (Tarragona), Spain
Tel: +34 977 81 40 00
Fax: +34 977 82 69 69

SPAIN / CATALUÑA (VILADRAU - GERONA)
Xalet La Coromina
Carretera de Vic S/N, 17406 Viladrau, Spain
Tel: +34 938 84 92 64
Fax: +34 938 84 81 60

SPAIN / MADRID (MADRID)
Antiguo Convento
C/ de Las Monjas, S/N Boadilla del Monte, 28660 Madrid, Spain.
Tel: + 34 91 632 22 20
Fax: +34 91 633 15 12

SPAIN / MADRID (MADRID)
Hotel Villa Real
Plaza de Las Cortes 10, 28014 Madrid, Spain
Tel: +34 914 20 37 67
Fax: +34 914 20 25 47

SPAIN / MURCIA (CARTAGENA - LA MANGA)
Hyatt Regency La Manga
Los Belones, Cartagena, 30385 Murcia, Spain
Tel: +34 968 33 12 34
Fax: +34 968 33 12 35

Mini Listings Europe

Condé Nast Johansens are delighted to recommend over 320 properties across Europe & The Mediterranean.
Call 1-800-564-7518 or see the order forms on page 285 to order guides.

SPAIN / VALENCIA (DÉNIA)
Hotel Buena Vista
Partida Tossalet 82, La Xara, 03709 Dénia, Spain
Tel: +34 965 78 79 95
Fax: +34 966 42 71 70

SPAIN / VALENCIA (XÀTIVA)
Hotel Mont Sant
Subida Al Castillo, s/n Xàtiva, 46800 Valencia, Spain
Tel: +34 962 27 50 81
Fax: +34 962 28 19 05

SWEDEN (BORGHOLM)
Halltorps Gästgiveri
38792 Borgholm, Sweden
Tel: +46 485 85000
Fax: +46 485 85001

SWEDEN (HESTRA – SMÅLAND)
Hestravikens Wärdshus
Hestra, 33027 Småland, Sweden
Tel: +46 370 33 68 00
Fax: +46 370 33 62 90

SWEDEN (LAGAN)
Romantik Hotel Toftaholm Herrgård
Toftaholm Pa, 34014 Lagan, Sweden
Tel: +46 370 440 55
Fax: +46 370 440 45

SWEDEN (MALMO - GLENARP)
Häckerberga Manor
24013 Genarp, Sweden
Tel: +46 40 48 04 40
Fax: +46 40 48 04 02

SWEDEN (TÄLLBERG)
Romantik Hotel Åkerblads
79370 Tällberg, Sweden
Tel: +46 247 50800
Fax: +46 247 50652

SWITZERLAND (CHÂTEAU D'OEX)
Hostellerie Bon Accueil
1837 Château d'Oex, Switzerland
Tel: +41 26 924 6320
Fax: +41 26 924 5126

SWITZERLAND (GSTAAD)
Le Grand Chalet
Neueretstrasse, 3780 Gstaad, Switzerland
Tel: +41 33 748 7676
Fax: +41 33 748 7677

SWITZERLAND (KANDERSTEG)
Royal Park *** Hotel**
3718 Kandersteg, Bernese Oberland, Switzerland
Tel: +41 33 675 88 88
Fax: +41 33 675 88 80

TURKEY (ANTALYA)
Marina Residence & Restaurant
Mermerli Sokak No. 15, Kaleici, 07100 Antalya, Turkey
Tel: +90 242 247 5490
Fax: +90 242 241 1765

TURKEY (ANTALYA)
Outdoor Centre Resort
Gift Gesmeier Mevkii, Beldibi, Antalya, Turkey
Tel: +90 242 824 9666
Fax: +90 242 824 9393

TURKEY (ANTALYA)
Renaissance Antalya Resort
PO Box 654, 07004 Beldibi - Kemer, Antalya, Turkey
Tel: +90 242 824 84 31
Fax: +90 242 824 84 30

TURKEY (ANTALYA)
Talya Hotel
Fevzi Çakmak Caddesi No. 30, 07100 Antalya, Turkey
Tel: +90 242 248 6800
Fax: +90 242 241 5400

TURKEY (ANTALYA – KALEICI)
Tekeli Konaklari
Dizdar Hasan Sokak, Kaleici, Antalya, Turkey
Tel: +90 242 244 54 65
Fax: +90 242 242 67 14

TURKEY (ANTALYA)
Tuvana Residence
Tuzcular Mahallesi, Karanlik Sokak 7, 07100 Kaleiçi - Antalya,Turkey
Tel: +90 242 247 60 15
Fax: +90 242 241 19 81

TURKEY (BODRUM)
Divan Palmira Hotel
Kelesharim Cad 6, 48483 Türkbükü – Bodrum, Turkey
Tel: +90 252 377 5601
Fax: +90 252 377 5952

TURKEY (BODRUM)
L'Ambience Hotel - Bodrum
Eski ÇeSme Meukii, Gümbet Kavsagi, 48400 Bodrum - Mugla, Turkey
Tel: +90 252 313 83 30
Fax: +90 252 313 82 00

TURKEY (GÖREME – CAPPADOCIA)
CCS - Cappadocia Cave Suites
Gafelli Mahallesi, Cevizler Sokak, 05180 Göreme – Nevsehir, Turkey
Tel: +90 384 271 2800
Fax: +90 384 271 27 99

TURKEY (KALKAN)
Hotel Villa Mahal
P.K. 4 Kalkan, 07960 Antalya, Turkey
Tel: +90 242 844 32 68
Fax: +90 242 844 21 22

Mini Listings Europe

Condé Nast Johansens are delighted to recommend over 320 properties across Europe & The Mediterranean.
Call 1-800-564-7518 or see the order forms on page 285 to order guides.

TURKEY (UGHISAR - CAPPADOCIA)
Museum Hotel
Tekelli Mahallesi 1, Urghisar - Nevsehir
Tel: +90 384 219 22 20
Fax: +90 384 219 24 44

TURKEY / NORTHERN CYPRUS (GIRNE)
Hotel Bellapais Gardens
Crusader Road, Bellapais, Girne, Cyprus
Tel: +90 392 815 60 66
Fax: +90 392 815 76 67

TURKEY (ÜRGÜP - CAPPADOCIA)
Ürgüp Evi
Esbelli Mahallesi 54, 5400 Ürgüp-Nevsehir, Turkey
Tel: +90 384 341 3173
Fax: +90 384 341 6269

TURKEY / NORTHERN CYPRUS (GIRNE)
The Hideaway Club
Karaman Road, Edremit, Girne, Northen Cyprus
Tel: +90 392 822 2620
Fax: +90 392 822 3133

Condé Nast Johansens Guides
Recommending only the finest hotels in the world

As well as this guide Condé Nast Johansens also publishes the following titles:

Recommended Hotels Great Britain & Ireland

440 unique and luxurious hotels, town houses, castles and manor houses chosen for their superior standards and individual character

Recommended Country Houses, Small Hotels & Inns, Great Britain & Ireland

280 smaller more rural properties, ideal for short breaks or more intimate stays

Recommended Hotels, Europe & the Mediterranean

320 continental gems featuring châteaux, resorts and Charming countryside hotels

Recommended Venues for Business Meetings, Conferences and Events, Great Britain & Europe

230 venues that cater specifically for a business audience

Also available, Worldwide Listings Pocket Guide, featuring all of Johansens recommendations, ideal when travelling light
When you purchase two guides or more we will be pleased to offer you a reduction in the cost.
The complete set of Condé Nast Johansens guides may be purchased as 'The Chairman's Collection'.

To order guides please complete the order form on page 285 or call FREEPHONE 1-800-564-7518

Index by Property

Bermuda

Ariel Sands	Devonshire	196
Cambridge Beaches	Somerset	200
Fourways Inn	Paget	198
Newstead Hotel	Paget	199
The Reefs	Southampton	201

Rosedon Hotel	Hamilton	197
Surf Side Beach Club	Warwick	202

The Caribbean

Anse Chastanet	St Lucia	230
Avila Beach Hotel	Curaçao	214
Blue Lagoon Villas	Jamaica	218
Blue Waters	Antigua	206
Camelot Inn - A Boutique Hotel	St. Vincent	233
Coral Reef Club	Barbados	211
Curtain Bluff	Antigua	207
Frangipani Beach Club	Anguilla	204
Galley Bay	Antigua	208
The Golden Lemon	St Kitts	226
Grand Lido Sans Souci	Jamaica	219
Grand View Beach Hotel	St. Vincent	234
Half Moon Golf, Tennis & Beach Club	Jamaica	220
The Hermitage	Nevis	223
The inn at English Harbour	Antigua	209
Mago Estate Hotel	St Lucia	231
Mocking Bird Hill	Jamaica	221
Montpelier Plantation Inn	Nevis	224
Nisbet Plantation Beach Club	Nevis	225
Ottley's Plantation Inn	St Kitts	227
Palm Island	St Vincent & The Grenadines	235
Point Grace	Turks & Caicos Islands	237
Rawlins Plantation Inn	St Kitts	228
The Sandpiper	Barbados	212
The Sands at Grace Bay	Turks & Caicos	238
Spice Island Beach Resort	Grenada	216

Mexico

Casa Natalia	Baja California	190
Hotel Villa Del Sol	Zihuatanejo	194
La Casa De Los Sueños	Isla Mujeres	192
Maroma	Riviera Maya	193
Villas Tacul	Cancun	191

The Pacific

Aggie Grey's Hotel	Samoa - Apia	249
Blue Lagoon Cruises	Fiji Islands - Lautoka	241
Namale	Fiji Islands - Savu Savu	242
Nukubati Island	Fiji Islands - Labasa	240
Toberua Island Resort	Fiji Islands - Toberua Island	244
Turtle Island	Fiji Islands - Yasawa Islands	245
Vomo Island	Fiji Islands - Vomo Islands	245
The Wakaya Club	Fiji Islands - Suva	243
Yasawa Island Resort	Fiji Islands - Yasawa Island	247

The United States of America

1811 House	Vermont - Manchester Village	114
200 South Street Inn	Virginia - Charlottesville	178
A Cambridge House	Massachusetts - boston	88
The Adolphus	Texas - Dallas	173
Albergo Allegria	New York - Northern Catskill Mountains	134
Anchuca Historic Mansion & Inn	Mississippi - Vicksburg	68
The Annapolis Inn	Maryland - Annapolis	60
Antrim 1844	Maryland - Taneytown	61
The Atlantic Inn	Rhode Island - Block Island	106
Augustus T Zevely Inn	North Carolina - Winston Salem	157
Ballantyne Resort	North Carolina - Charlotte	144
Balsam Mountain Inn	North Carolina - Balsam	139
The Bed & Breakfast Inn At La Jolla	California - La Jolla	20
Bishop's Lodge	New Santa Fe	124
Blackberry Farm	Tennessee - Walland	170
Blackberry Inn	Maine - Camden	80
Boardwalk Plaza Hotel	Delaware - Rehoboth Beach	41
The Boulders Inn	Connecticut - New Preston	77
The Brewster Inn	New York - Cazenovia	128
Bryant Park Hotel	New York - New York City	132
Caliente Tropics Resort	California - Palm Springs	24
Camden Maine Stay	Maine - Camden	81
Canyon Villa Inn	Arizona - Sedona	12
Captain Lindsey House	Maine - Rockland	87
The Captain Lord Mansion	Maine - Kennebunkport	84
The Captain's House Inn	Massachusetts - Cape Cod	91
Carter House	California - Eureka	18
Casitas at El Monte	New Taos	125
Castle Marne	Colorado - Denver	35
The Cedars Inn	North Carolina - Beaufort	140
The Charles Street Inn	Massachusetts - Boston	89
Chase Park Plaza Hotel	Missouri - St Louis	71
Chesterfield Inn	New Hampshire - Chesterfield	103
Chetola Resort	North Carolina - Blowing Rock	141
Claddagh Inn	North Carolina - Hendersonville	149
The Cliff House at Pikes Peak	Colorado - Manitou Springs	37
Cliffside Inn	Rhode Island - Newport	107
Clifton - The Country Inn & Estate	Virginia - Charlottesville	179
Copper Beech Inn	Connecticut - Ivoryton	74
Deerfield Inn	Massachusetts - Deerfield	94
Doryman's Inn	California - Newport Beach	22
The Duff Green Mansion	Mississippi - Vicksburg	69
Dunleith Plantation	Mississippi - Natchez	66

277

Index by Property

Property	Location	Page
The Eliza Thompson House	Georgia - Savannah	51
Fairview Inn	Mississippi - Jackson	65
Fisher Island	Florida - Miami Beach	46
Four Columns Inn	Vermont - Newfane	116
Fox Creek Inn	Vermont - Chittenden	111
The Francis Malbone House	Rhode Island - Newport	108
Frederick House	Virginia - Staunton	184
Geneva On The Lake	New York - Geneva	130
The George Washington University Inn	Maryland - Wasington D.C.	62
The Georgian Hotel	California - Santa Monica	31
Gerstle Park Inn	California - San Francisco Bay Area	28
Gideon Ridge	North Carolina - Blowing Rock	142
Gingerbread Mansion Inn	California - Ferndale	19
The Goodstone Inn & Estate	Virginia - Middleburg	182
Granite Steps	Georgia - Savannah	52
Green Oaks	Mississippi - Biloxi	64
Greenville Inn	Maine - Moosehead Lake	85
The Harbor Light Inn	Massachusetts - Marblehead	96
Hartstone Inn	Maine - Camden	82
Havana River Walk Inn	Texas - San Antonio	175
Henderson Village	Georgia - Perry	50
Historic Jacob Hill Inn	Rhode Island - Providence	110
Hob Knob Inn	Massachusetts - Martha's Vineyard	97
Hotel Escalante	Florida - Naples	47
Hotel Maison De Ville	Louisiana - New Orleans	58
Hotel St Francis	New Santa Fe	123
The Inn Above Onion Creek	Texas - Kyle	174
The Inn at Beaver Creek	Colorado - Beaver Creek	34
Inn at Half - Mile Farm	North Carolina - Highlands	150
The Inn at Mystic	Connecticut - Mystic	75
The Inn At Shadow Lawn	Rhode Island - Newport	109
The Inn at Thorn Hill	New Hampshire - Jackson	105
The Inn At Weston	Vermont - Weston	119
The Inn on La Loma Plaza	New Taos	126
Innisfree Victorian Inn and Garden House	North Carolina - Glenville	148
The Jackson House Inn	Vermont - Woodstock	120
Kiepersol Estates	Texas - Tyler	176
The Kitano New York	New York - New York City	133
L'Auberge De Sedona	Arizona - Sedona	13
L'Auberge Provençale	Virginia - White Post	185
L'Horizon	California - Palm Springs	25
La Bastide	South Carolina - Travelers Rest	167
Legacy of Williamsburg Inn	Virginia - Williamsburg	186
The Lenox Hotel	Massachusetts - Boston	90
Litchfield Plantation	South Carolina - Pawleys Island	166
The Lodge At Moosehead Lake	Maine - Greenville	83
The Lords Proprietors' Inn	North Carolina - Edenton	147
The Manor on Golden Pond	New Hampshire - Holderness	104
Mill Valley Inn	California - Mill Valley	21
Millstone Inn	North Carolina - Cashiers	143
Monmouth Plantation	Mississippi - Natchez	67
Morehead Manor Bed & Breakfast	North Carolina - Durham	146
The Mountain Road Resort At Stowe	Vermont - Stowe	117
Mountain Top Inn & Resort	Vermont - Chittenden	112
Nagle Warren Mansion	Wyoming - Cheyenne	188
The Newcastle Inn	Maine - NeWCastle	86
Nob Hill Lambourne	California - San Francisco	27
The Old Mystic Inn	Connecticut - Old Mystic	78
The Park	North Carolina - Charlotte	145
Pine Crest Inn	North Carolina - Tryon	154
The Pineapple Inn	Massachusetts - Nantucket	100
The President's Quarters	Georgia - Savannah	53
Prince Michel Restaurant & Suites	Virginia - Culpeper	181
Prospect Hill Plantation Inn	Virginia - Charlottesville	180
Rabbit Hill Inn	Vermont - Lower Waterford	113
Rittenhouse Square European Boutique Hotel	Pennsylvania - Philadelphia	161
Rosemary & Lookaway Inn	South Carolina - Aiken	164
Roycroft Inn	New York - East Aurora	129
Saratoga Arms	New York - Saratoga Springs	135
Seacrest Manor	Massachusetts - Rockport	102
Shadow Mountain Resort & Club	California - Palm Desert	23
The Siena Hotel	North Carolina - Raleigh - Durham	152
Simonton Court Historic Inn & Cottages	Florida - Key West	45
Snowbird Mountain Lodge	North Carolina - Robbinsville	153
Sonnenalp Resort of Vail	Colorado - Vail	39
The Stanley Hotel	Colorado - Estes Park	36
Stonecroft Country Inn	Connecticut - Mystic	76
The Sundy House Resort	Florida - Delray Beach	44
The Sutton Place Hotel	Illinois - Chicago	55
The Swag Country Inn	North Carolina - Waynesville	155
Tanque Verde Ranch	Arizona - Tucson	14
Theodosia's Bed & Breakfast	North Carolina - Bald Head Island	138
The Thomas Bond House	Pennsylvania - Philidelphia	162
Thorncroft Inn	Massachusetts - Martha's Vineyard	98
Union Street Inn	Massachusetts - Nantucket	101
Upham Hotel	California - Santa Barbara	30
Vendue Inn	South Carolina - Charleston	165
The Verandas	North Carolina - Wilmington	156
The Victorian Inn	Massachusetts - Martha's Vineyard	99
The Village Country Inn	Vermont - Manchester Village	115
Vista Verde Guest Ranch	Colorado - Steamboat Springs	38
Waters Edge Hotel	California - Tiburon	32
Weasku Inn	Oregon - Grants Pass	159
Wedgewood Inn	Massachusetts - Cape Cod	92
West Lane Inn & The Inn at Ridgefield	Connecticut - Ridgefield	79
The Whalewalk Inn	Massachusetts - Cape Cod	93
Wheatleigh	Massachusetts - Lenox	95
The White Doe Inn & Whispering Bay	North Carolina - Manteo	151
White Stallion Ranch	Arizona - Tucson	15
Whitestone Country Inn	Tennessee - Kingston	169
William Henry Miller Inn	New York - Ithaca	131
Willow Grove Inn	Virginia - Orange	183
The Willows	California - Palm Springs	26
Windham Hill Inn	Vermont - West Townshend	118
Woodstock Inn & Resort	Vermont - Woodstock	121
Woolley's Petite Suites	California - Santa Ana	29
The Wright Inn & Carriage House	North Carolina - Asheville	137
Ye Kendall Inn	Texas - Boerne	172

Madewood Plantation House — Louisiana - Napoleanville — 57

INDEX BY LOCATION

Bermuda

Devonshire	Ariel Sands	196
Hamilton	Rosedon Hotel	197
Paget	Fourways Inn	198
Paget	Newstead Hotel	199
Somerset	Cambridge Beaches	200
Southampton	The Reefs	201
Warwick	Surf Side Beach Club	202

The Caribbean

Anguilla	Frangipani Beach Club	204
Antigua	Blue Waters	206
Antigua	Curtain Bluff	207
Antigua	Galley Bay	208
Antigua	The inn at English Harbour	209
Barbados	Coral Reef Club	211
Barbados	The Sandpiper	212
Curaçao	Avila Beach Hotel	214
Grenada	Spice Island Beach Resort	216
Jamaica	Blue Lagoon Villas	218
Jamaica	Grand Lido Sans Souci	219
Jamaica	Half Moon Golf, Tennis & Beach Club	220
Jamaica	Mocking Bird Hill	221
Nevis	The Hermitage	223
Nevis	Montpelier Plantation Inn	224
Nevis	Nisbet Plantation Beach Club	225
St Kitts	The Golden Lemon	226
St Kitts	Ottley's Plantation Inn	227
St Kitts	Rawlins Plantation Inn	228
St Lucia	Anse Chastanet	230
St Lucia	Mago Estate Hotel	231
St. Vincent	Camelot Inn - A Boutique Hotel	233
St. Vincent	Grand View Beach Hotel	234
St Vincent & The Grenadines	Palm Island	235
Turks & Caicos	The Sands at Grace Bay	238
Turks & Caicos Islands	Point Grace	237

The Pacific

Apia	Aggie Grey's Hotel	249
Labasa	Nukubati Island	240
Lautoka	Blue Lagoon Cruises	241
Savu Savu	Namale	242
Suva	The Wakaya Club	243
Toberua Island	Toberua Island Resort	244
Vomo Islands	Vomo Island	245
Yasawa Island	Yasawa Island Resort	247
Yasawa Islands	Turtle Island	246

Mexico

Baja California	Casa Natalia	190
Cancun	Villas Tacul	191
Isla Mujeres	La Casa De Los Sueños	192
Riviera Maya	Maroma	193
Zihuatanejo	Hotel Villa Del Sol	194

The United States of America

Aiken	Rosemary & Lookaway Inn	164
Annapolis	The Annapolis Inn	50
Asheville	The Wright Inn & Carriage House	137
Bald Head Island	Theodosia's Bed & Breakfast	138
Balsam	Balsam Mountain Inn	139
Beaufort	The Cedars Inn	140
Beaver Creek	The Inn at Beaver Creek	34
Biloxi	Green Oaks	64
Block Island	The Atlantic Inn	106
Blowing Rock	Chetola Resort	141
Blowing Rock	Gideon Ridge	142
Boerne	Ye Kendall Inn	172
boston	A Cambridge House	88
Boston	The Charles Street Inn	89
Boston	The Lenox Hotel	90
Camden	Blackberry Inn	80
Camden	Camden Maine Stay	81
Camden	Hartstone Inn	82
Cape Cod	The Captain's House Inn	91
Cape Cod	Wedgewood Inn	92
Cape Cod	The Whalewalk Inn	93
Cashiers	Millstone Inn	143
Cazenovia	The Brewster Inn	128
Charleston	Vendue Inn	165
Charlotte	Ballantyne Resort	144
Charlotte	The Park	145
Charlottesville	200 South Street Inn	178
Charlottesville	Clifton - The Country Inn & Estate	179
Charlottesville	Prospect Hill Plantation Inn	180
Chesterfield	Chesterfield Inn	103
Cheyenne	Nagle Warren Mansion	188
Chicago	The Sutton Place Hotel	55
Chittenden	Fox Creek Inn	111
Chittenden	Mountain Top Inn & Resort	112
Culpeper	Prince Michel Restaurant & Suites	181
Dallas	The Adolphus	173
Deerfield	Deerfield Inn	94
Delray Beach	The Sundy House Resort	44
Denver	Castle Marne	35
Durham	Morehead Manor Bed & Breakfast	146
East Aurora	Roycroft Inn	129
Edenton	The Lords Proprietors' Inn	147
Estes Park	The Stanley Hotel	36
Eureka	Carter House	18
Ferndale	Gingerbread Mansion Inn	19
Geneva	Geneva On The Lake	130

279

Index by Location

Location	Inn	Page
Glenville	Innisfree Victorian Inn and Garden House	148
Grants Pass	Weasku Inn	159
Greenville	The Lodge At Moosehead Lake	83
Hendersonville	Claddagh Inn	149
Highlands	Inn at Half - Mile Farm	150
Holderness	The Manor on Golden Pond	104
Ithaca	William Henry Miller Inn	131
Ivoryton	Copper Beech Inn	74
Jackson	Fairview Inn	65
Jackson	The Inn at Thorn Hill	105
Kennebunkport	The Captain Lord Mansion	84
Key West	Simonton Court Historic Inn & Cottages	45
Kingston	Whitestone Country Inn	169
Kyle	The Inn Above Onion Creek	174
La Jolla	The Bed & Breakfast Inn At La Jolla	20
Lenox	Wheatleigh	95

Location	Inn	Page
Lower Waterford	Rabbit Hill Inn	113
Manchester Village	1811 House	114
Manchester Village	The Village Country Inn	115
Manitou Springs	The Cliff House at Pikes Peak	37
Manteo	The White Doe Inn & Whispering Bay	151
Marblehead	The Harbor Light Inn	96
Martha's Vineyard	Hob Knob Inn	97
Martha's Vineyard	Thorncroft Inn	98
Martha's Vineyard	The Victorian Inn	99
Miami Beach	Fisher Island	46
Middleburg	The Goodstone Inn & Estate	182
Mill Valley	Mill Valley Inn	21
Moosehead Lake	Greenville Inn	85
Mystic	The Inn at Mystic	75
Mystic	Stonecroft Country Inn	76
Nantucket	The Pineapple Inn	100
Nantucket	Union Street Inn	101
Naples	Hotel Escalante	47
Napoleanville	Madewood Plantation House	57
Natchez	Dunleith Plantation	66
Natchez	Monmouth Plantation	67
New Orleans	Hotel Maison De Ville	58
New Preston	The Boulders Inn	77
New York City	Bryant Park Hotel	132
New York City	The Kitano New York	133
NeWCastle	The Newcastle Inn	86
Newfane	Four Columns Inn	116
Newport	Cliffside Inn	107
Newport	The Francis Malbone House	108
Newport	The Inn At Shadow Lawn	109
Newport Beach	Doryman's Inn	22
Northern Catskill Mountains	Albergo Allegria	134
Old Mystic	The Old Mystic Inn	78
Orange	Willow Grove Inn	183
Palm Desert	Shadow Mountain Resort & Club	23
Palm Springs	Caliente Tropics Resort	24
Palm Springs	L'Horizon	25
Palm Springs	The Willows	26
Pawleys Island	Litchfield Plantation	166
Perry	Henderson Village	50
Philadelphia	Rittenhouse Square European Boutique Hotel	161
Philidelphia	The Thomas Bond House	162
Providence	Historic Jacob Hill Inn	110
Raleigh - Durham	The Siena Hotel	152
Rehoboth Beach	Boardwalk Plaza Hotel	41
Ridgefield	West Lane Inn & The Inn at Ridgefield	79
Robbinsville	Snowbird Mountain Lodge	153
Rockland	Captain Lindsey House	87
Rockport	Seacrest Manor	102
San Antonio	Havana River Walk Inn	175
San Francisco	Nob Hill Lambourne	27
San Francisco Bay Area	Gerstle Park Inn	28
Santa Ana	Woolley's Petite Suites	29
Santa Barbara	Upham Hotel	30
Santa Fe	Bishop's Lodge	124
Santa Fe	Hotel St Francis	123
Santa Monica	The Georgian Hotel	31
Saratoga Springs	Saratoga Arms	135
Savannah	The Eliza Thompson House	51
Savannah	Granite Steps	52
Savannah	The President's Quarters	53
Sedona	Canyon Villa Inn	12
Sedona	L'Auberge De Sedona	13
St Louis	Chase Park Plaza Hotel	71
Staunton	Frederick House	184
Steamboat Springs	Vista Verde Guest Ranch	38
Stowe	The Mountain Road Resort At Stowe	117
Taneytown	Antrim 1844	61
Taos	Casitas at El Monte	125
Taos	The Inn on La Loma Plaza	126
Tiburon	Waters Edge Hotel	32
Travelers Rest	La Bastide	167
Tryon	Pine Crest Inn	154
Tucson	Tanque Verde Ranch	14
Tucson	White Stallion Ranch	15
Tyler	Kiepersol Estates	176
Vail	Sonnenalp Resort of Vail	39
Vicksburg	Anchuca Historic Mansion & Inn	68
Vicksburg	The Duff Green Mansion	69
Walland	Blackberry Farm	170
Wasington D.C.	The George Washington University Inn	62
Waynesville	The Swag Country Inn	155
West Townshend	Windham Hill Inn	118
Weston	The Inn At Weston	119
White Post	L'Auberge Provençale	185
Williamsburg	Legacy of Williamsburg Inn	186
Wilmington	The Verandas	156
Winston Salem	Augustus T Zevely Inn	157
Woodstock	The Jackson House Inn	120
Woodstock	Woodstock Inn & Resort	121

Index by Activity

≈ Hotels with heated indoor swimming pool

Bermuda

Cambridge Beaches ....Somerset 200

Caribbean

Mago Estate Hotel ....St Lucia 231

The United State of America

L'Auberge De Sedona ....Arizona 13
Tanque Verde Ranch.................Arizona 14
L'Horizon ....California 25
The Stanley Hotel ....Colorado 36
Boardwalk Plaza Hotel ....Delaware 41
Bishop's Lodge ....New Mexico 124

Ballantyne Resort ....North Carolina 144
Chetola Resort ....North Carolina 141
The Park ....North Carolina 145
The Mountain Road
   Resort At Stowe ....Vermont 117
Woodstock Inn & Resort ....Vermont 121

≈ Outdoor pool

Bermuda

Cambridge Beaches ....Somerset 200
Fourways Inn ....Paget 198
Newstead Hotel........................Paget 199
Rosedon Hotel ....Hamilton 197
Surf Side Beach Club ....Warwick 202

Caribbean

Frangipani Beach Club..............Anguilla 204
Blue Waters ....Antigua................206
Curtain Bluff ....Antigua................207
Galley Bay................................Antigua................208
The inn at English Harbour ....Antigua................209
Coral Reef Club ....Barbados 211
The Sandpiper ....Barbados 212

Spice Island Beach Resort........Grenada 216
Blue Lagoon Villas ....Jamaica...............218
Grand Lido Sans Souci ....Jamaica...............219
Half Moon Golf,
   Tennis & Beach Club ....Jamaica...............220
Mocking Bird Hill ....Jamaica...............221
The Hermitage..........................Nevis 223
Montpelier Plantation Inn ....Nevis 224
Nisbet Plantation Beach Club ...Nevis 225
The Golden Lemon ....St Kitts 226

Ottley's Plantation Inn ....St Kitts 227
Rawlins Plantation Inn ....St Kitts 228
Mago Estate Hotel ....St Lucia 231
Palm Island ....St Vincent 235
Camelot Inn - A Boutique Hotel.St. Vincent 233
Grand View Beach Hotel ....St. Vincent 234
The Sands at Grace Bay ....Turks & Caicos 238
Point Grace ....Turks & Caicos 237

Mexico

Casa Natalia..............................Baja California 190
Hotel Villa Del Sol ....Zihuatanejo 194
La Casa De Los Sueños............Isla Mujeres.........192
Maroma.....................................Riviera Maya 193
Villas Tacul ....Cancun 191

The Pacific

Blue Lagoon Cruises ....Fiji Islands 241
Namale ....Fiji Islands 242
Toberua Island Resort...............Fiji Islands 244
Vomo Island ....Fiji Islands 245
The Wakaya Club ....Fiji Islands 243
Yasawa Island Resort ....Fiji Islands 247
Aggie Grey's Hotel ....Samoa 249

The United State of America

Canyon Villa Inn ....Arizona 12
L'Auberge De Sedona ....Arizona 13
Tanque Verde Ranch.................Arizona 14
White Stallion Ranch.................Arizona 15
Caliente Tropics Resort ....California 24
L'Horizon ....California 25
Shadow Mountain Resort & Club .....California 23
The Willows ....California 26
Woolley's Petite Suites ....California 29
The Inn at Beaver Creek...........Colorado..............34
Sonnenalp Resort of Vail ....Colorado..............39
The Inn at Mystic......................Connecticut 75
Fisher Island ....Florida 46

Hotel Escalante ....Florida 47
Simonton Court
   Historic Inn & Cottages ....Florida 45
The Sundy House Resort ....Florida 44
Henderson Village ....Georgia 50
Hotel Maison De Ville ....Louisiana 58
Antrim 1844 ....Maryland 61
The Captain's House Inn ....Massachusetts 91
The Harbor Light Inn.................Massachusetts 96
Wheatleigh ....Massachusetts 95
Anchuca Historic Mansion & Inn ......Mississippi ...68
The Duff Green Mansion ....Mississippi 69
Dunleith Plantation ....Mississippi 66
Chase Park Plaza Hotel.............Missouri 71
The Inn at Thorn Hill ....New Hampshire ..105
The Manor on Golden Pond .....New Hampshire ..104
Bishop's Lodge ....New Mexico 124
Geneva On The Lake................New York 130
Inn at Half - Mile Farm ....North Carolina.....150
The Park ....North Carolina.....145
Litchfield Plantation ....South Carolina 166
Blackberry Farm ....Tennessee 170
The Inn Above Onion Creek ....Texas 174
Four Columns Inn......................Vermont 116
The Mountain Road
   Resort At Stowe ....Vermont 117
Mountain Top Inn & Resort ......Vermont 112
The Village Country Inn ....Vermont 115
Windham Hill Inn ....Vermont 118
Woodstock Inn & Resort ....Vermont 121
Clifton - The Country
   Inn & Estate ....Virginia 179
The Goodstone Inn & Estate ....Virginia 182
L'Auberge Provençale ....Virginia 185
Prospect Hill Plantation Inn .....Virginia 180

☘ Horse riding nearby

Bermuda

Fourways Inn ....Paget 198
Newstead Hotel........................Paget 199
Rosedon Hotel ....Hamilton 197
Surf Side Beach Club ....Warwick 202

The Caribbean

Frangipani Beach Club..............Anguilla 204
The inn at English Harbour ....Antigua................209
Half Moon Golf,
   Tennis & Beach Club ....Jamaica...............220
The Hermitage..........................Nevis 223
Montpelier Plantation Inn ....Nevis 224
Ottley's Plantation Inn ....St Kitts 227
Camelot Inn - A Boutique Hotel.St. Vincent 233
Grand View Beach Hotel ....St. Vincent 234
The Sands at Grace Bay ....Turks & Caicos 238

Mexico

Hotel Villa Del Sol ....Zihuatanejo 194
La Casa De Los Sueños............Isla Mujeres.........192
Maroma.....................................Riviera Maya 193

231

Index by Activity

The Pacific

Namale	Fiji Islands	242
Turtle Island	Fiji Islands	246

The United States of America

Canyon Villa Inn	Arizona	12
Tanque Verde Ranch	Arizona	14

White Stallion Ranch	Arizona	15
The Bed & Breakfast Inn At La Jolla	California	20
Carter House	California	18
The Georgian Hotel	California	31
Shadow Mountain Resort & Club	California	23
Castle Marne	Colorado	35
The Cliff House at Pikes Peak	Colorado	37
The Inn at Beaver Creek	Colorado	34
The Stanley Hotel	Colorado	36
Vista Verde Guest Ranch	Colorado	38
Copper Beech Inn	Connecticut	74
West Lane Inn & The Inn at Ridgefield	Connecticut	79
Fisher Island	Florida	46
Granite Steps	Georgia	52
Henderson Village	Georgia	50
Camden Maine Stay	Maine	81
Greenville Inn	Maine	85
The Lodge At Moosehead Lake	Maine	83
Antrim 1844	Maryland	61
The Captain's House Inn	Massachusetts	91
Wedgewood Inn	Massachusetts	92
The Whalewalk Inn	Massachusetts	93
Wheatleigh	Massachusetts	95
Bishop's Lodge	New Mexico	124
Casitas at El Monte	New Mexico	125
Hotel St Francis	New Mexico	123
The Inn on La Loma Plaza	New Mexico	126
Albergo Allegria	New York	134
The Brewster Inn	New York	128
Geneva On The Lake	New York	130
Balsam Mountain Inn	North Carolina	139
Chetola Resort	North Carolina	141
Inn at Half - Mile Farm	North Carolina	150
Pine Crest Inn	North Carolina	154
Snowbird Mountain Lodge	North Carolina	153
The Swag Country Inn	North Carolina	155
The Atlantic Inn	Rhode Island	106
Historic Jacob Hill Inn	Rhode Island	110
The Inn At Shadow Lawn	Rhode Island	109
La Bastide	South Carolina	167
Litchfield Plantation	South Carolina	166
Blackberry Farm	Tennessee	170
Whitestone Country Inn	Tennessee	169
Ye Kendall Inn	Texas	172
1811 House	Vermont	114
Four Columns Inn	Vermont	116
Fox Creek Inn	Vermont	111
The Inn At Weston	Vermont	119
The Mountain Road Resort At Stowe	Vermont	117
Mountain Top Inn & Resort	Vermont	112
The Village Country Inn	Vermont	115
Windham Hill Inn	Vermont	118
Woodstock Inn & Resort	Vermont	121
200 South Street Inn	Virginia	178
Clifton - The Country Inn & Estate	Virginia	179
Frederick House	Virginia	184
The Goodstone Inn & Estate	Virginia	182
L'Auberge Provençale	Virginia	185
Legacy of Williamsburg Inn	Virginia	186
Prince Michel Restaurant & Suites	Virginia	181
Willow Grove Inn	Virginia	183
Nagle Warren Mansion	Wyoming	188

Skiing nearby

The United States of America

Caliente Tropics Resort	California	24
The Inn at Beaver Creek	Colorado	34
Sonnenalp Resort of Vail	Colorado	39

Vista Verde Guest Ranch	Colorado	38
Blackberry Inn	Maine	80
Camden Maine Stay	Maine	81
Captain Lindsey House	Maine	87
Greenville Inn	Maine	85
The Lodge At Moosehead Lake	Maine	83
The Inn at Thorn Hill	New Hampshire	105
The Manor on Golden Pond	New Hampshire	104
Bishop's Lodge	New Mexico	124
Casitas at El Monte	New Mexico	125
Hotel St Francis	New Mexico	123
The Inn on La Loma Plaza	New Mexico	126
Albergo Allegria	New York	134
The Brewster Inn	New York	128
Geneva On The Lake	New York	130
Roycroft Inn	New York	129
William Henry Miller Inn	New York	131
Balsam Mountain Inn	North Carolina	139
Chetola Resort	North Carolina	141
Four Columns Inn	Vermont	116
Fox Creek Inn	Vermont	111
The Inn At Weston	Vermont	119
The Mountain Road Resort At Stowe	Vermont	117
Mountain Top Inn & Resort	Vermont	112
Rabbit Hill Inn	Vermont	113
The Village Country Inn	Vermont	115
Windham Hill Inn	Vermont	118
Woodstock Inn & Resort	Vermont	121
200 South Street Inn	Virginia	178
Frederick House	Virginia	184
Prince Michel Restaurant & Suites	Virginia	181

Golf course on-site

The Caribbean

Half Moon Golf, Tennis & Beach Club	Jamaica	220

The United States of America

Shadow Mountain Resort & Club	California	23
Ballantyne Resort	North Carolina	144

Tennis on-site

Bermuda

Ariel Sands	Devonshire	196
Cambridge Beaches	Somerset	200
Newstead Hotel	Paget	199
The Reefs	Southampton	201
Surf Side Beach Club	Warwick	202

The Caribbean

Frangipani Beach Club	Anguilla	204
Blue Waters	Antigua	206
Curtain Bluff	Antigua	207
Galley Bay	Antigua	208
The inn at English Harbour	Antigua	209

Index by Activity

Coral Reef Club	Barbados	211
Avila Beach Hotel	Curaçao	214
Spice Island Beach Resort	Grenada	216
Grand Lido Sans Souci	Jamaica	219
Half Moon Golf, Tennis & Beach Club	Jamaica	220
The Hermitage	Nevis	223
Montpelier Plantation Inn	Nevis	224
Nisbet Plantation Beach Club	Nevis	225
The Golden Lemon	St Kitts	226
Ottley's Plantation Inn	St Kitts	227
Rawlins Plantation Inn	St Kitts	228
Anse Chastanet	St Lucia	230
Palm Island	St Vincent	235
Grand View Beach Hotel	St. Vincent	234
The Sands at Grace Bay	Turks & Caicos	238

Mexico

| Hotel Villa Del Sol | Zihuatanejo | 194 |
| Villas Tacul | Cancun | 191 |

The Pacific

Namale	Fiji Islands	242
Nukubati Island	Fiji Islands	240
Vomo Island	Fiji Islands	245
Yasawa Island Resort	Fiji Islands	247

The United States of America

Tanque Verde Ranch	Arizona	14
White Stallion Ranch	Arizona	15
The Bed & Breakfast Inn At La Jolla	California	20
Caliente Tropics Resort	California	24

Shadow Mountain Resort & Club	California	23
Sonnenalp Resort of Vail	Colorado	39
The Stanley Hotel	Colorado	36
The Inn at Mystic	Connecticut	75
Fisher Island	Florida	46
Antrim 1844	Maryland	61
Wheatleigh	Massachusetts	95
The Manor on Golden Pond	New Hampshire	104
Chetola Resort	North Carolina	141
The Atlantic Inn	Rhode Island	106
La Bastide	South Carolina	167
Litchfield Plantation	South Carolina	166
Blackberry Farm	Tennessee	170
Whitestone Country Inn	Tennessee	169
The Mountain Road Resort At Stowe	Vermont	117
Mountain Top Inn & Resort	Vermont	112

Windham Hill Inn	Vermont	118
Clifton - The Country Inn & Estate	Virginia	179
Legacy of Williamsburg Inn	Virginia	186

SPA Spa/health/fitness facilities

Bermuda

| Ariel Sands | Devonshire | 196 |
| Cambridge Beaches | Somerset | 200 |

The Caribbean

| Spice Island Beach Resort | Grenada | 216 |
| Grand Lido Sans Souci | Jamaica | 219 |

Mexico

| Maroma | Mexico | 193 |

The United States of America

| Nob Hill Lambourne | California | 27 |

▼
Bishop's Lodge .... New Mexico 124
Ballantyne Resort .... North Carolina 144

M¹⁰⁰ Conference facilities for 100 delegates or more

The Caribbean

Avila Beach Hotel	Curaçao	214
Grand Lido Sans Souci	Jamaica	219
Half Moon Golf, Tennis & Beach Club	Jamaica	220

The Pacific

| Blue Lagoon Cruises | Fiji Islands | 241 |

The United States of America

| Tanque Verde Ranch | Arizona | 14 |
| Caliente Tropics Resort | California | 24 |

Shadow Mountain Resort & Club	California	23
The Cliff House at Pikes Peak	Colorado	37
The Inn at Beaver Creek	Colorado	34
Sonnenalp Resort of Vail	Colorado	39
The Stanley Hotel	Colorado	36
Fisher Island	Florida	46
The Sutton Place Hotel	Illinois	55
Antrim 1844	Maryland	61
The Lenox Hotel	Massachusetts	90
Anchuca Historic Mansion & Inn	Mississippi	68
The Duff Green Mansion	Mississippi	69
Dunleith Plantation	Mississippi	66
Fairview Inn	Mississippi	65
Green Oaks	Mississippi	64
Monmouth Plantation	Mississippi	67
Chase Park Plaza Hotel	Missouri	71
Bishop's Lodge	New Mexico	124
The Kitano New York	New York	133
Roycroft Inn	New York	129
Ballantyne Resort	North Carolina	144
Balsam Mountain Inn	North Carolina	139
Chetola Resort	North Carolina	141
The Park	North Carolina	145
The Siena Hotel	North Carolina	152
Whitestone Country Inn	Tennessee	169
The Adolphus	Texas	173
Kiepersol Estates	Texas	176
Mountain Top Inn & Resort	Vermont	112
Woodstock Inn & Resort	Vermont	121
Prince Michel Restaurant & Suites	Virginia	181
Willow Grove Inn	Virginia	183

The Caribbean

Avila Beach Hotel	Curaçao	214
Grand Lido Sans Souci	Jamaica	219
Half Moon Golf, Tennis & Beach Club	Jamaica	220

The Pacific

| Blue Lagoon Cruises | Fiji Islands | 241 |

DINE members
(Distinctive Inns of New England)

The United States of America

The Boulders Inn	Connecticut	77
Camden Maine Stay	Maine	81
The Newcastle Inn	Maine	86
The Captain's House Inn	Massachusetts	91
Deerfield Inn	Massachusetts	94
Chesterfield Inn	New Hampshire	103
The Manor on Golden Pond	New Hampshire	104
The Inn at Thorn Hill	New Hampshire	105
Cliffside Inn	Rhode Island	107
Rabbit Hill Inn	Vermont	113
The Village Country Inn	Vermont	115
Windham Hill Inn	Vermont	118

283

Home cinema from two speakers

The *New* Bose 3·2·1 digital home entertainment system

The critics approved: "Even though I knew the midrange and high frequency sound were emanating from only two speakers at the front of the room, it sure didn't sound that way – I know I heard swords clanking where surround speakers should have been." – Sound & Vision (US)

Bass module not shown

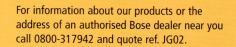
For information about our products or the address of an authorised Bose dealer near you call 0800-317942 and quote ref. JG02.

Hear it! Believe it! Ask for a demonstration.

Better sound through research®
www.bose.co.uk

ORDER FORM
Choose from our wide range of titles below

Order 2 guides get $8 off • Order 3 guides get $15 off • Order 4 guides get $30 off
Order the Chairman's Collection worth $150 for just $110

Simply complete the form below, total the cost and then deduct the appropriate discount. State your preferred method of payment and mail to Condé Nast Johansens, 100 Newfield Avenue, Edison, NJ 08837.

ALTERNATIVELY YOU CAN ORDER IMMEDIATELY, CALL TOLL FREE 1-800-564-7518, please quote ref: D010

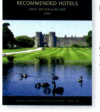

440 Recommendations
I wish to order
QUANTITY
copy/ies priced at $29.95 each.
Total cost

$

282 Recommendations
I wish to order
QUANTITY
copy/ies priced at $26.95 each.
Total cost

$

324 Recommendations
I wish to order
QUANTITY
copy/ies priced at $26.95 each.
Total cost
$

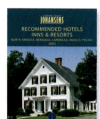

199 Recommendations
I wish to order
QUANTITY
copy/ies priced at $18.95 each.
Total cost
$

230 Recommendations
(published Feb 2003)
I wish to order
QUANTITY
copy/ies priced at $35.00 each.
Total cost

$

Pocket Guide
1250 Recommendations
I wish to order
QUANTITY
copy/ies priced at $15.95 each.
Total cost

$

Johansens Gold Blocked Slip Case priced at $8 each

Johansens Luxury Luggage Tag priced at $23 each

To order these items please fill in the appropriate section below

The Chairman's Collection
Order the complete collection of
Condé Nast Johansens Recommended Guides for only **$110**
PLUS FREE Luxury Luggage Tag worth $23
PLUS FREE Slip Case worth $8

The Chairman's Collection contains all six titles pictured above. The Recommended Venues guide will be dispatched separately on publication in February 2003.

Now please complete your order and payment details

	tick	
I have ordered 2 titles - $8 off		−$8.00
I have ordered 3 titles - $15 off		−$15.00
I have ordered 4 titles - $30 off		−$30.00
Total cost of books ordered minus discount (excluding the Chairman's Collection)		$
Luxury Luggage Tag at $23 Quantity and total cost:		$
Johansens Gold Blocked SLIP CASE at $8 Quantity and total cost:		$
I wish to order the **Chairman's Collection** at $110 Quantity and total cost:		$
Packing & delivery: (all US orders) add $6.00 per guide or Chairman's Collection add $25.00		$
GRAND TOTAL		$

I have chosen my Condé Nast Johansens Guides and (please tick)
I enclose a cheque payable to Condé Nast Johansens ☐
Please debit my credit/charge card account ☐

☐ MasterCard ☐ Visa ☐ Switch (Issue Number) ____

Card Holders Name (Mr/Mrs/Miss)

Address

Postcode

Telephone

E-mail

Card No.   Exp Date

Signature

NOW send to
Condé Nast Johansens, 100 Newfield Avenue, Edison, NJ 08837

The details provided may be used to keep you informed of future products and special offers provided by Condé Nast Johansens and other carefully selected third parties. If you do not wish to recieve such information please tick this box ☐.
(Your phone number will only be used to ensure the fast and safe delivery of your order).

GUEST SURVEY REPORT
Evaluate your stay in a Condé Nast Johansens Recommendation

Dear Guest,

Following your stay in a Condé Nast Johansens recommendation, please spare a moment to complete this Guest Survey Report. This is an important source of information for Johansens, to maintain the highest standards for our recommendations and to support the work of our team of inspectors.

It is also the prime source of nominations for Condé Nast Johansens Awards for Excellence, which are made annually to those properties worldwide that represent the finest standards and best value for money in luxury, independent travel.

Thank you for your time and I hope that when choosing future accommodation Condé Nast Johansens will be your guide.

Yours faithfully,

Tim Sinclair
Sales & Marketing Director, Condé Nast Johansens

p.s. Guest Survey Reports may also be completed online at www.johansens.com

1. Your details

Your name:

Your address:

Postcode:

Telephone:

E-mail:

2. Hotel details

Name of hotel:

Location:

Date of visit:

3. Your rating of the hotel

Please tick one box in each category below (as applicable)

	Excellent	Good	Disappointing	Poor
Bedrooms	○	○	○	○
Public Rooms	○	○	○	○
Food/Restaurant	○	○	○	○
Service	○	○	○	○
Welcome/Friendliness	○	○	○	○
Value For Money	○	○	○	○

4. Any other comments

If you wish to make additional comments, please write separately to the Publisher, Condé Nast Johansens Ltd, 6-8 Old Bond Street, London W1S 4PH

Please return completed form to Condé Nast Johansens, 19/21 Chapel Road, london SE27 0TP, Great Britain.
Alternatively send by fax to +44 20 8766 6096

ORDER FORM
Choose from our wide range of titles below

Order 2 guides get $8 off • Order 3 guides get $15 off • Order 4 guides get $30 off

Order the Chairman's Collection worth $150 for just $110

Simply complete the form below, total the cost and then deduct the appropriate discount. State your preferred method of payment and mail to Condé Nast Johansens, 100 Newfield Avenue, Edison, NJ 08837.

ALTERNATIVELY YOU CAN ORDER IMMEDIATELY, CALL TOLL FREE 1-800-564-7518, please quote ref: D010

440 Recommendations
I wish to order
QUANTITY
copy/ies priced at $29.95 each.
Total cost
$

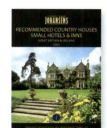

282 Recommendations
I wish to order
QUANTITY
copy/ies priced at $26.95 each.
Total cost
$

324 Recommendations
I wish to order
QUANTITY
copy/ies priced at $26.95 each.
Total cost
$

199 Recommendations
I wish to order
QUANTITY
copy/ies priced at $18.95 each.
Total cost
$

230 Recommendations (published Feb 2003)
I wish to order
QUANTITY
copy/ies priced at $35.00 each.
Total cost
$

Pocket Guide
1250 Recommendations
I wish to order
QUANTITY
copy/ies priced at $15.95 each.
Total cost
$

Johansens Gold Blocked Slip Case priced at $8 each

Johansens Luxury Luggage Tag priced at $23 each

To order these items please fill in the appropriate section below

The Chairman's Collection
Order the complete collection of
Condé Nast Johansens Recommended Guides for only **$110**
PLUS FREE Luxury Luggage Tag worth $23
PLUS FREE Slip Case worth $8
The Chairman's Collection contains all six titles pictured above. The Recommended Venues guide will be dispatched separately on publication in February 2003.

Now please complete your order and payment details

tick
I have ordered 2 titles - $8 off	−$8.00
I have ordered 3 titles - $15 off	−$15.00
I have ordered 4 titles - $30 off	−$30.00
Total cost of books ordered minus discount (excluding the Chairman's Collection)	$
Luxury Luggage Tag at $23 Quantity and total cost:	$
Johansens Gold Blocked SLIP CASE at $8 Quantity and total cost:	$
I wish to order the **Chairman's Collection** at $110 Quantity and total cost:	$
Packing & delivery: (all US orders) add $6.00 per guide or Chairman's Collection add $25.00	$
GRAND TOTAL	$

I have chosen my Condé Nast Johansens Guides and (please tick)
I enclose a cheque payable to Condé Nast Johansens ☐
Please debit my credit/charge card account ☐

☐ MasterCard ☐ Visa ☐ Switch (Issue Number)

Card Holders Name (Mr/Mrs/Miss)

Address

Postcode

Telephone

E-mail

Card No. Exp Date

Signature

NOW send to
Condé Nast Johansens, 100 Newfield Avenue, Edison, NJ 08837

The details provided may be used to keep you informed of future products and special offers provided by Condé Nast Johansens and other carefully selected third parties. If you do not wish to recieve such information please tick this box ☐.
(Your phone number will only be used to ensure the fast and safe delivery of your order)

GUEST SURVEY REPORT

Evaluate your stay in a Condé Nast Johansens Recommendation

Dear Guest,

Following your stay in a Condé Nast Johansens recommendation, please spare a moment to complete this Guest Survey Report. This is an important source of information for Johansens, to maintain the highest standards for our recommendations and to support the work of our team of inspectors.

It is also the prime source of nominations for Condé Nast Johansens Awards for Excellence, which are made annually to those properties worldwide that represent the finest standards and best value for money in luxury, independent travel.

Thank you for your time and I hope that when choosing future accommodation Condé Nast Johansens will be your guide.

Yours faithfully,

Tim Sinclair
Sales & Marketing Director, Condé Nast Johansens

p.s. Guest Survey Reports may also be completed online at www.johansens.com

1. Your details

Your name:

Your address:

Postcode:

Telephone:

E-mail:

2. Hotel details

Name of hotel:

Location:

Date of visit:

3. Your rating of the hotel

Please tick one box in each category below (as applicable)

	Excellent	Good	Disappointing	Poor
Bedrooms	○	○	○	○
Public Rooms	○	○	○	○
Food/Restaurant	○	○	○	○
Service	○	○	○	○
Welcome/Friendliness	○	○	○	○
Value For Money	○	○	○	○

4. Any other comments

If you wish to make additional comments, please write separately to the Publisher, Condé Nast Johansens Ltd, 6-8 Old Bond Street, London W1S 4PH

Please return completed form to Condé Nast Johansens, 19/21 Chapel Road, london SE27 0TP, Great Britain.
Alternatively send by fax to +44 20 8766 6096